W9-BLE-396

WINNERS

WINNERS

How Good Baseball Teams
Become Great Ones
(and It's Not the Way You Think)

DAYN PERRY

WILEY

John Wiley & Sons, Inc.

Published by John Wiley & Sons, Inc., Hoboken, New Jersey
Published simultaneously in Canada

Design and composition by Navta Associates, Inc.

For general information about our other products and services, please contact our Customer Care Department within the United States at (800) 762-2974, outside the United States at (317) 572-3993 or fax (317) 572-4002.

Wiley also publishes its books in a variety of electronic formats. Some content that appears in print may not be available in electronic books. For more information about Wiley products, visit our web site at www.wiley.com.

Library of Congress Cataloging-in-Publication Data:

Perry, Dayn, date.
  Winners : how good baseball teams become great ones (and it's not the way you think) / Dayn Perry.
    p. cm.
  Includes bibliographical references and index.
  ISBN-13: 978-0-471-72174-1 (cloth)
  ISBN-10: 0-471-72174-3 (cloth)
  1. Baseball–United States–Miscellanea. I. Title.
 GV873.P415   2006
796.357'06–dc22

2005015111

Printed in the United States of America

10 9 8 7 6 5 4 3 2 1

For my Mother and Father

Contents

Introduction

Your team is a loser.

They're not irredeemably awful—they have a handful of elite performers, and there are worse clubs. But your team isn't within hailing distance of the truly great teams of the day. They're graced with the odd All-Star and what seems to be a spare menagerie of haphazardly identified prospects, but your team's high command does a poor job of filling out the roster and navigating the club through the treacherous shoals of the late season. They either mindlessly adhere to the tactical approaches of the past or, on occasion, fecklessly ape the strategy du jour. They misread the markets, judge hitters with flawed metrics, and fail to covet repeatable skills in pitchers. So they lose. And they lose.

You may have picked up this book because you'd like to be a better fan, a better unpaid organizational watchdog. You'd like to know what your team can learn from the winners of the recent past. You'd like to know what they've got that your team doesn't.

The book in your hands attempts to answer the following queries: How do baseball teams win? More specifically, what things are important? What do they tend to excel at? What do they tend to ignore? In essence: How'd they do that?

To cobble together answers to these questions, I've examined each team to make the postseason between 1980 and 2003, with the 1981 and 1994 seasons excluded. I'm excluding those years because they culminated like no two other seasons in baseball. In 1981, a players' strike forced the season to be truncated to a total of just more than 100 games per team. Because MLB decided to determine the playoff pool based on first-half and second-half division winners—a patently silly decision—teams such as the Cardinals and the Reds, who had the two best records in the NL that season, were left out despite meriting inclusion. So to include playoff teams from the '81 season in my research would be to pollute the sample with teams that weren't *really* playoff teams. As for the 1994 season, labor troubles once again fouled up the process, except this time no playoffs at all occurred. However, even with those two seasons left out of the calculus, 124 playoff teams remain, and it's those teams and what they did to be successful, to reach the wilder shores of October, that drive this book.

As for the 1980 cutoff date, I think it's more instructive to keep the focus on recent history. Even so, since 1980 the vicissitudes of the game have allowed us to see an array of organizational styles and tactical approaches employed by great teams. That affords us a look at the strains of greatness that have persisted over the past quarter century or so, despite broad and frequent changes to the playing environment.

To divine what's important and what's not important to winning teams, I've used statistics of all sorts. First, know this: I'm a former humanities major who for many years had math skills that could be charitably characterized as tutor-worthy. So I'm not going to sail over anyone's head with all things quantitative. From time to time I'll wield some scary-sounding metrics, but they'll be explained, and along the way I'll also explain why they're superior to the baseball stats you're used to seeing. If you like, think of these statistics as an ideological counterweight to the stuff that's on the backs of baseball cards. But moreover think of them as tools that help tell the stories of these great teams.

Speaking of statistics and those who like to monkey around with them, there's been a recent percolating controversy over whether it's better to run a baseball team with reliance on traditional scouting methods or with a statistics-driven approach. This debate is as big a waste of time as your average Yanni album. Developing a prevailing organizational strategy isn't some Boolean "either-or" dilemma; it's using all the resources at your disposal, be they scouting reports or

Excel files. There's no reason why your favorite team can't use both to its distinct advantage. No, the debate exists mostly because of the scant few haughty bomb-throwers on each side.

The vast majority of the analytical community has long since disabused itself of the Panglossian notion that anything that matters in baseball can be quantified. Most of us don't believe that for a second (although our missionary hardiness in advocating what we *do* believe carries with it a certain reputation). In fact, although it's beyond my ken to measure such intangibles, I do believe that things such as team chemistry and leadership not only exist but also are brought to bear in the standings.

All that said, the arguments and positions staked out in the pages ahead are framed by the numbers. Almost all of these numbers will be adjusted to correct for the effects of a player's home park and league. This is necessary because, unlike football fields or basketball courts, there's only a glancing uniformity to baseball parks. Fence distances and heights, altitudes, hitting visuals, foul territories, weather patterns, etc., all vary greatly from park to park. The upshot is that because of these meaningful differences among playing environments, some parks help the hitter, some parks help the pitcher, and some parks play essentially neutral. If we're to gain useful knowledge from the numbers, we must correct for what's called "park effects"—or how a park influences statistics. Additionally, I'll adjust for the league in almost all the numbers you'll find. This is done because eras, like parks, exert substantial influence over the game on the field. Mostly this phenomenon is owing to rule changes, particularly with regard to how umpires call the strike zone. To cite one example that draws on both elements, a run scored in Dodger Stadium in 1968 means much more than one scored in Coors Field in 1998. Numbers *must* be adjusted to reflect that fundamental tenet of serious analysis.

At its core, however, this book is about great teams and the players who make them great. The numbers will be here, but so will the stories of the flesh-and-blood folks who generate those numbers. I'll examine in great depth the roles and guises that come to mind when you ruminate on this game—the slugger, the ace, the closer, the glove man, the speed merchant, the setup man, the doe-eyed youngster, the salt-cured veteran, the money player—all toward learning what's really the stuff of winning baseball. This is the story of how great baseball teams got that way.

CHAPTER 1

The Slugger

(or, Why Power Rules)

In 1985 you couldn't hit in Dodger Stadium. Just couldn't be done. Singles? Sure. Doubles, triples, homers? Forget it. The foul territory was vast, which meant tepid pop-outs by the bushel. The hitting visuals—the shadows, the hue of the outfield walls in the Los Angeles sun—were brutal, and rumors had persisted since the days of Sandy Koufax that the groundskeepers at Chavez Ravine would illegally heighten the mound when an especially potent offense paid a visit. It just wasn't the place for a hitter. Unless you were Pedro Guerrero.

That season, Guerrero spent time at first base, third base, and the outfield corners, but despite being yanked about the diamond, he put together the best season of what was to be a 15-year career. Guerrero, although playing in one of the toughest environments for hitters in the league, paced the National League in on-base (OBP) and slugging percentage (SLG) and finished second to Willie McGee of the Cardinals for the batting title. At one point during the season, Guerrero reached base in fourteen consecutive plate appearances. He also tied a major league record (held by Babe Ruth, Roger Maris, and Bob Johnson) by hitting 15 homers in the month of June, and his tally of 33 home runs for the season tied the Los Angeles Dodger record set by Steve Garvey in 1977. Away from Dodger Stadium, Guerrero slugged .665, almost

300 points higher than the National League average that season. What Guerrero did was cobble together one of the great power seasons of all time.

The Indians originally signed Guerrero in 1973 out of the Dominican Republic as a 17-year-old, slightly built shortstop. However, following Guerrero's first season as a pro—one in which he managed to hit only two home runs the entire year for the farm club at Sarasota—the Indians, in a stunningly ill-considered deal, traded him to the Dodgers for pitcher Bruce Ellingsen, who would log a grand total of 42 major league innings in his career. Guerrero, meanwhile, began heaping a multitude of abuses upon opposing pitchers. He broke into the majors as a replacement at second base for the injured Davey Lopes, and Guerrero started hitting almost immediately. In '81 he slugged .762 in the World Series and rang up five RBI in the decisive sixth game. He and third baseman Ron Cey shared Series MVP honors.

The following season, Guerrero became the first player in Dodger history to hit 30 home runs and steal 20 bases in the same season. The next year, he turned the trick once again. If not for Guerrero's maddening penchant for injury, he'd have likely put together a Hall of Fame career. In '77 he missed most of the Triple-A season with a broken ankle. In '80 he injured his knee in one of his famously violent slides (he didn't so much slide as heave himself in the general direction of the bag) and missed the final two months of the season (it was after that injury that manager Tommy Lasorda retrenched Guerrero's base stealing). In '84 it was an ailing shoulder. In '85 it was a sprained wrist, and in '86 it was a ruptured tendon in his knee. Guerrero came back potently in 1987, slugging .539, walking 74 times, and posting the highest batting average by a Dodger since Tommy Davis in 1962. For his efforts the UPI bestowed upon him the Comeback Player of the Year Award. However, Guerrero once again landed on the DL in '88, this time with a pinched nerve, and the Dodgers sent him to St. Louis for lefty John Tudor. Guerrero, it turned out, had another season in him. In 1989, for an otherwise inconsequential Cardinals team, he batted .300, led the NL in doubles with 42, and posted the league's sixth-best OBP. Yet another shoulder injury limited him to 43 games in 1992, and he opted for retirement after the season. He left the game with a career batting line of .300 AVG/.370 OBP/.480 SLG, and 215 home runs.

In retirement, Guerrero met with trouble. On September 29, 1999, he and longtime friend Adan Cruz met with three men at a Miami restaurant to arrange a $200,000 cocaine deal. Unbeknownst to Guerrero, the three men he and Cruz liased with were two informants and one undercover DEA agent. Prosecutors would later argue that Guerrero agreed to guarantee payment for the shipment. One of the informants, who was wearing a wire, told Guerrero that he would deliver "15 little animals" to Cruz and that Guerrero would ensure that Cruz delivered the money. "If he doesn't show up," Guerrero allegedly replied, "I'll take care of that."

The following day, the informant called Guerrero, told him the cocaine was ready, and said, "You're on the hook if he [Cruz] doesn't pay."

"Fine, fine, okay," said Guerrero. "No problem."

The next day, agents delivered the faux coke to Cruz and arrested him at a grocery store near Guerrero's house. Later that same day, Guerrero and another accomplice were arrested. Guerrero soon posted his $100,000 bond.

While out on bail, he met with further controversy. In October, acquitted (wink, wink) murderer and former NFL star O. J. Simpson phoned police in South Florida and told them his girlfriend 26-year-old Christie Prody (who presumably had never performed even a cursory, fact-finding Google search on her new boyfriend) was in the midst of a two-day cocaine bender with Guerrero. "We have a problem here," Simpson told the 911 operator. "I'm trying to get a girl to go to rehab. . . . She's been doing drugs for two days with Pedro Guerrero, who just got arrested for cocaine, and I'm trying to get her to leave her house and go into rehab right now."

Police responded to Prody's house but found only Simpson, who told them Prody had left. Simpson also told police that he and Prody had suffered a "verbal dispute" before she departed. The cops, in what's surely one of the most hollow gestures in the history of recorded time, gave Simpson a brochure on domestic violence and then left. Simpson would later deny telling police that Prody had been on a coke binge with Guerrero. Instead, Simpson claimed he had been trying to get help for one of Prody's friends who went by the name "Pinky."

With the Simpson-Prody flap behind him, Guerrero was ready for his trial on drug conspiracy charges. Guerrero's attorney, Milton Hirsch, mustered a surprising defense by arguing that his client had been an unwitting dupe in the whole thing. The crux of Hirsch's case was that Guerrero was, in essence, a man-child lacking the faculties to participate meaningfully in such an affair. "He never really understood that he was being asked to involve himself in a drug deal," Hirsch told the jury.

According to the defense, Guerrero's IQ was a mere 70. Some psychometric specialists say that those testing at an IQ level between 60 and 75 would have significant difficulty in being educated beyond a sixth-to-eighth-grade range. Hirsch said that Guerrero had little functional ability in the real world. To wit, he couldn't write a check or make his own bed, and he subsisted off a modest allowance given to him by his wife. True or not, after four hours of deliberation, the jury acquitted Guerrero.

Still, for all of Guerrero's foibles, missteps, and frailties, we as fans, in what's perhaps a frailty of our own, prefer to remember him only as Pedro Guerrero the hitter. And he *was* that.

From the beginning, that's what baseball has been about—the hitter. When the game was in its nascent stages, the pitcher served as little more than an obsequious valet to the batter. Indeed, during various points in the 19th century, pitchers were limited by rules that forced them to throw underhanded; keep both feet in contact with the ground; maintain straightened elbows throughout their delivery; keep their hands below their hips at the point of release; and, for a time, throw pitches according to the specific instructions of the batter (seriously). Of course, by now baseball is drastically different, but in its genesis, it was a game for hitters.

Without getting all Jungian on you, there's probably something about wielding a cudgel that taps into our atavistic, hunter-gatherer notions of lumbering through the forest primeval and overbludgeoning something hairy and dangerous so our hominid family can have dinner that night. Or maybe it's just cool to knock the insides out of stuff. Whatever the underlying reasons, I'd argue that the hitter and his accoutrements sit atop the baseball iconography. Then again . . .

One of baseball's bits of convention that's excruciatingly parroted by fans and media alike is that pitching and defense ultimately hold sway over offense. The observation is likely rooted in the faulty notion that good pitching and sound defense demand lofty levels of intelligence and execution, whereas teams reliant upon run scoring prowess are cut from the "see ball, hit ball" cloth. This is especially true, we're told, in times of critical mass. Pitching-and-defense teams are more acclimated to the nip-and-tuck environs of the 3–2, 2–0, 1–0 games that seem to flourish when the bunting hangs in October.

Laying aside the extending generalizations, conventional wisdom is mostly correct in this instance. Given the cultural prominence of the hitter—both as an idea and as an individual—it might be surprising to learn that the 124 teams I've studied for this book tend to be more successful at run prevention than run scoring. The imbalance isn't overwhelming, but it's there. Great teams, at least within the confines of recent history, are more often more adept at keeping runs off the board than putting them up.

If the game of baseball is reducible to a single fundament, it's the run—both the run scored and the run allowed. It's this principle that informs many of our best analytical tools. In fact, by plugging runs scored and runs allowed into any of the various Pythagorean-inspired theorems (more on these later), we can predict a team's success in the following season better than we can using that team's won-lost record in the previous year. By extension, runs scored and runs allowed are the best ways to judge offense and defense (and by defense we mean pitching and fielding) on the team level.

It's runs analysis that leads to the conclusion that our pool of 124 playoff teams depended more on good pitching and fielding than hitting to win games. By comparing these teams' park-adjusted runs scored and runs allowed totals and comparing them to their respective league averages, we make some interesting findings:

- Playoff teams since 1980, on average, ranked 3.85 in their respective league in runs allowed and 4.18 in runs scored.
- These teams outperformed league average runs allowed marks by 8.2 percent and runs scored by 7.4 percent.
- Fifteen teams made the postseason despite below-league-average park-adjusted runs-allowed totals, and 17 teams passed playoff muster despite below-average adjusted-runs-scored totals.

It's certainly not a staggering margin, but it is apparent that the teams analyzed were better on the run-prevention side of the ledger than on the run-scoring side. As the data above show, on average these teams ranked higher in runs allowed than in runs scored, they bettered the league averages by a wider margin in runs allowed, and more teams made the playoffs despite suboptimal offensive attacks than with suboptimal pitching and fielding.

So is the hitter as important as we've always believed? In a word, yes. Run prevention may be slightly more crucial to great teams than run scoring is, but examining the "division of labor" of these two elements reveals the prevailing vitality of the hitter. Run prevention is the dual responsibility of the pitcher and the defense behind him. Precisely divvying up who's responsible for exactly how much is a bit of a fool's errand, but we can make some assumptions. Most of the onus is on the pitcher, but a substantial percentage of run prevention falls to the defense. As for run scoring, it's achieved at two places—at the plate and on the bases. While good base running is certainly helpful, it withers in comparison to the contributions of the batter. The upshot is that the hitter, in rough and broad terms, adds more to his team than does the pitcher, the fielder, or the base runner. Of course, value varies widely on an individual basis, but the general truth holds that the batter is the most important player on the diamond. This brings us to the matter of what the hitter does.

Many of those who approach baseball from a traditional mind-set place a great deal of value on clutch performances—those players who, time and again, seem to perform at a high level during critical junctures. Unlike many analysts of my stripe, I happen to believe in the existence of clutch hitters. However, I think it's quite difficult to wield "clutchness" in your favor. That's because by the time we have a meaningful enough data sample to adequately identify clutch hitters, those hitters are usually within hailing distance of retirement. There may be those who can divine clutch hitters in the callow stages, but I've never met them. And that's part of the problem with trying to build a team around this notion. Additionally, the way many fans, analysts, and executives have come to identify clutch performers in particular and hitters in general is profoundly flawed.

Time was when analysts and executives alike used only the hoariest and most familiar of offensive measures—for example, batting average (AVG) and RBI—to evaluate the performance of a hitter. Thanks to pioneers such as Allan Roth (Branch Rickey's trusted statistician) and Bill James, whose early writings served as a "tent revival" of sorts, not only do we know what traditional offensive statistics matter most, but also this knowledge has gained surprising traction over the years. Still, innovation often requires us to break some china, and the downright seditious notion that RBI and batting average were manifestly and greatly inferior to less familiar metrics such as on-base percentage

(OBP) and slugging percentage (SLG) was met with much resistance over the years. By now, however, if someone within the game is relying on the former two at the neglect of the latter two, he or she is either willfully ignorant or baselessly contrary.

That isn't to say that those traditional statistics are completely useless; they're just far less utile than other measures found on almost every stat line. To your rank-and-file fan, understanding some of your more advanced statistics is harder than unscrambling an egg, but we're not talking about those. We're talking about gleaning genuine wisdom about a hitter's performance by using commonplace measures such as OBP, SLG, and plate appearances. While those highfalutin stats (the ones whose acronyms sound like German obscenities) most assuredly have their place—I use them quite often in this very book—you can often approximate the conclusions they provide without needing product documentation to get there.

This leads us to why batting average and RBI—and runs scored, while we're at it—are so overrated and misapplied. There are, broadly speaking, two subsets of standard offensive statistics: counting stats and rate stats. Counting stats are—prepare for stunning lucidity—stats that count things. For example, five triples, 30 homers, 110 RBI, 90 runs scored. Rate stats are percentages: a .300 average, a .400 OBP, a slugging percentage of .500, etc. Both have their uses, and both have their weaknesses. Counting stats are highly dependent upon playing time and, in some cases, lineup slotting and the overall quality of the offense. In the right lineup and during an offensive era, it's perfectly possible to rack up 100 RBI, which is one of the more misleading benchmarks in sports, and still be a generally lousy hitter. If you tell me a hitter has exactly 100 RBI over a full season and revealed nothing else, I could safely surmise he wasn't the worst player in the annals of the game. But that's about it. Any offensive statistic is prone to the foibles of home park and era, but counting stats such as RBI are even more context-dependent and can be greatly influenced by a panoply of factors that have almost nothing to do with a hitter's true abilities.

For instance, Ruben Sierra earned cachet as a "good RBI man"—one of baseball's most revered mythical beasts and the kind of thing that beguiles more than a few mainstream observers—because in the late '80s and early '90s he'd back his ass into a 100-RBI season every other year or so. Still, despite his putting together an 18-year (and counting) major league career, there are only about three seasons in which I'd have wanted him as a regular on my team. In fact, in 1993 Sierra put together what I believe is the worst 100-RBI season ever. That season he tallied 101 ribbies, but in the process he posted a putrid OBP of .288 and a patently inadequate slugging percentage of .390. Account for the fact that he was a corner outfielder and thus had a greater offensive onus (and account for the fact that he often played right field like a prop comic), and those numbers look even worse. What helped Sierra to ring up all those RBI was that for more than half the season he batted a couple of spots behind Rickey Henderson and his .469 OBP. I don't care how many runs you're driving in, if you're making outs in more than 72 percent of your plate appearances, you're a cipher. Cipher, thy name is '93 Ruben Sierra.

Come to think of it, if we carry conventional wisdom to its logical margins, it should be easier to hit a grand slam and rack up four RBI (because the pitcher supposedly has no latitude to nibble with the bases loaded and must give the batter the much-dreaded "something to hit") than it is to launch a solo shot. I'm not saying that's the case, but according to doctrinal thinking it *should be* the case.

All of this isn't to suggest that RBI are utterly useless; as with any deeply flawed metric, it's evocative at the margins, but only at the margins. For example, it's still rather hard to total, say, 140 RBI and somehow suck. On the other hand, it's entirely conceivable that a player with 115 RBI had a much better season than someone with 130 RBI.

The shortfalls of batting average are of a different rubric. The problem with rate stats in general is that they don't provide any indication of playing time. To cite an extreme example, you can see a hitter's average of .333 and not know whether he went 1 for 3 on the season or, for instance, 196 for 588, as Will Clark did in 1989. Unless you have some vague handle on the number of plate appearances involved, rate stats aren't useful. However, batting average has further weaknesses. Batting average tells you how often a hitter reached base via a hit. It doesn't tell what kind of hits those were, and it gives no indication of how often he reached base by other means. Those are vital pieces of information that can't be discerned from batting average alone. Batting average (in the presence of some indicator of playing time) is more useful than RBI, but it's still suboptimal.

The more informative rate stats—the ones that fill the voids left by batting average—are OBP and SLG. These tell you how often a hitter reached base and how much power he hit for. If you subtract batting average from SLG, you're left with isolated SLG, or ISO. ISO is a good indicator of how much "raw" power a hitter has, and it communicates that by removing his singles from the calculus. Knowing the basic rate stats—AVG, OBP, and SLG—in the presence of plate appearances and making at least cursory adjustments for park, league, and era, you can soundly evaluate a player's offensive contributions. And from those numbers, you can determine ISO, which provides you with another perspective on a hitter's level of power. As rate stats go, it's become received wisdom in the analytical community that OBP is the most important, closely followed by SLG. However, this simply isn't the case.

Certainly, SLG has its flaws. Most notably, it operates under the assumption that a home run is as valuable as four singles, which it plainly isn't (roughly speaking, four singles are worth two runs, while a home run is worth a little less than 1.5 runs). However, among widely available and familiar rate statistics, it actually fares better than the recently lionized OBP.

Here's how the four rate stats—AVG, OBP, SLG, and ISO—correlate with run scoring over the years, with the numbers closest to 1.0 indicating superior correlation:

Years	AVG	OBP	SLG	ISO
1871–1900	.888	.892	.901	.764
1901–1925	.846	.878	.861	.717
1926–1950	.834	.898	.914	.817
1951–1975	.774	.841	.897	.784
1976–2000	.752	.811	.868	.728
1871–2003	.828	.866	.890	.762

Some musings on these data:

- For our purposes, the 1976–2000 period is the most germane one. Over that span, SLG is more closely associated with scoring runs, and it's not a particularly close call.

- Observe the steep downward trend undergone by AVG. The 1871–2003 numbers don't do justice to just how less important AVG is when compared to OBP and SLG.

- There don't seem to be any discernible trends in how ISO relates to run scoring.

- Through much of the deadball era, OBP was more important than SLG; however, as run-scoring levels increased, SLG became the more vital measure. That's especially the case in the contemporary period.

- SLG is the only rate stat ever to have a correlation with run scoring of .900 or higher.

- All four rate stats have declined in terms of correlation from the 1951–1975 period to the current one.

- Despite the "OBP is life" movement spurred along, in part, by *Moneyball* and the success of the Oakland A's in recent seasons, hitting for power is more important than getting on base. However, both SLG and OBP are substantially more important than AVG.

Knowing this, let's take these commonplace yet useful tools and apply them to the teams we're studying, with an eye toward figuring out what makes these offenses go. When we think in terms of "power hitters" what comes to mind is that middle-of-the-lineup force of nature who hits for, novelty of novelties, power. As discussed above, two familiar and roughly efficient ways to evaluate power production are SLG and ISO. However, if we're to wring any meaningful conclusions from the numbers, we need to park-adjust them. This will be the first of many times you'll see numbers adjusted for playing environment. The concept of "park effects," or how a home ballpark exerts its influence over the events of a ball game, has gained belated credence among mainstream fans and media in recent years. Part of this is owing to the fact Coors Field, which had provided us with an offensive environment unmatched in the history of the sport, came online within the past decade and called attention to just how drastically parks and environments can alter the game on the field. (For instance, in 1995, the first year of Coors Field, the Rockies and their opponents hit 241 homers in Denver and only 119 in other parks.) Parks do this in a variety of ways. In some it's fence distance, fence height, or amount of foul territory; in some it's weather and altitude; in others it's less conspicuous traits, such as mound quality and hitting visuals; and in most it's some combination of all of these things. Whatever the reasons for these phenomena, discussions of park effects too often are wrongly limited to how a park disturbs the scoring of runs. For instance, Dodger Stadium and Shea Stadium both, generally speaking, suppress the scoring of runs. However, they do it in different ways. Dodger is actually an average park for home runs, but it drastically reduces the number of doubles and triples. Shea, in contrast, is especially unaccommodating toward home run hitters.

As such, we need to analyze park effects on the component level (unless, of course, we're specifically concerned with runs scored). That means analyzing how parks alter the means to runs (i.e., SLG, AVG, OBP, left-handed batters, right-handed batters, strikeouts, etc.) and not just the runs themselves. So in this chapter, when I say that sets of numbers are park-adjusted, it means they're adjusted for that individual statistic and not just runs scored. Thanks to gracious and cherished resources such as David Smith and Retrosheet.org, this kind of necessary anal retention is a breeze.

As we ponder the slugger, it's worth asking which of these four measures—AVG, OBP, SLG, and ISO—is most closely associated with winning teams in the contemporary era. To do this, let's first look at how our 124 teams fare in terms of the park-adjusted percentage of the league average for each of these metrics:

Statistic	Adjusted Percentage of League Average
Batting average	100.6
On-base percentage	101.1
Slugging percentage	101.8
Isolated slugging percentage	104.6

These numbers reflect how much our sample of teams exceeded the park-adjusted league averages for AVG, OBP, SLG, and ISO. As you can see, these teams excel at ISO, SLG, OBP, and AVG, in that order. Now let's look at what percentage of our teams finished above the park-adjusted league average:

Statistic	Percentage of Teams Better Than League Average
Batting average	54.0
On-base percentage	58.9
Slugging percentage	61.3
Isolated slugging percentage	65.3

The order of importance is the same. These results speak to the vital nature of power production for winning teams (ISO, oddly enough, appears to be more important than SLG) and also to the overrated nature of batting average. It's also worth pointing out once again that the recent obsession with OBP is not quite justified, at least in comparison to the others. So when we think of the slugger and what makes offenses thunder in recent years, it's power that should be foremost in our analysis.

Among the teams I've studied, here are the top ten individual SLGs relative to the league average and adjusted for each player's home park:

Ranking	Player	Adjusted Percentage of League SLG
1.	Barry Bonds, '02 Giants	207.6
2.	Barry Bonds, '03 Giants	176.5
3.	Mike Schmidt, '80 Phillies	166.8
4.	George Brett, '80 Royals	166.4
5.	Pedro Guerrero, '85 Dodgers	166.0
6.	Darryl Strawberry, '88 Mets	162.8
6.	Barry Bonds, '92 Pirates	162.8
8.	Albert Belle, '95 Indians	160.2
9.	Rickey Henderson, '90 A's	158.2
10.	Jason Giambi, '01 A's	157.2

And here's the list—again relative to league and adjusted for park—for ISO:

Ranking	Player	Adjusted Percentage of League ISO
1.	Barry Bonds, '02 Giants	317.2
2.	Mike Schmidt, '80 Phillies	293.9
3.	Reggie Jackson, '80 Yankees	291.6
4.	Kevin Mitchell, '87 Giants	287.4
5.	Barry Bonds, '03 Giants	272.3
6.	Darryl Strawberry, '88 Mets	272.2

7.	Barry Bonds, '92 Giants	257.8
8.	George Brett, '80 Royals	255.1
9.	Pedro Guerrero, '85 Dodgers	246.7
10.	Albert Belle, '95 Indians	235.7
10.	Jose Canseco, '90 A's	235.7

Not surprisingly, many of the same names are on both lists. Several Barry Bonds iterations, Mike Schmidt and George Brett from the unheralded 1980 season, and Darryl Strawberry and Albert Belle all rank in the top ten for SLG and ISO. And, of course, there's Guerrero, lurking behind the potted palm of history.

As for Bonds, we're almost out of ways to rhapsodize about what he's done in recent seasons, but observe that his '92 season, long before he perhaps began indulging in performance-enhancing pharmacology or, I dunno, eating live howler monkeys to increase his hormone intake (read: cheating), still holds up as one of the best power seasons of recent history. In 2002, however, he was something else altogether. I once wrote a column for *Baseball Prospectus* that attempted to show what Bonds's numbers from his mind-blowing 2001–2004 epoch would look like if he were a pitcher. I did this by manipulating traditional pitching statistics so they'd yield the same Value Over Replacement Player/Pitcher (VORP)* figures that Bonds had produced as a hitter in these seasons. The results were stupidly sublime. If Bonds had, for instance, equaled his 2002 VORP of 147.4 as a pitcher, he would've worked 260 innings (innings totals were tied to the league-leading figure) and posted an ERA of exactly 1.00. As I said, stupidly sublime.

I'll leave it to historians to decide whether his place in the baseball pantheon has been compromised (hint: it has) by his use of this or that substance or his refusal to round the bases with head bowed like a

---

*VORP is a *Baseball Prospectus* invention that measures, in the currency of runs, a player's level of production relative to a hypothetical, widely available, and cheaply gotten "replacement" talent—the waiver claim, the B-list prospect, the minor league veteran, the bench player—who could be summoned in an emergency. The baseline that's established by the replacement player is always lower than the league average at that particular position, the logic being that the league-mean player is superior to players who are imminently available to teams in need of emergency filler talent.

penitent. That's beyond the concerns of this book. Still, wherever Bonds winds up along the daisy chain of history, his accomplishments will probably have the whiff of fraudulence about them.

What you might also notice about the above lists is that they comprise players who, one and all, played one of the four corner positions. On one level, this isn't surprising, since we expect those positions to produce the gaudiest power numbers. After all, left fielders usually aren't in the lineup for their artifice in the field. Yet how does this square with the buttoned-down notion that teams, if they're to be successful, must be strong up the middle (i.e., at the premium positions of catcher, shortstop, second base, and center field)? It's merely another baseball platitude that, it turns out, is largely fiction.

Teams—winners and losers alike—get the majority of their offensive production from the non-skill positions of first base, third base, left field, and right field. Lest this sound singularly obvious, I'll point out that this is true according to VORP, which, as detailed above, is adjusted for position and of decided benefit to hitters in the middle of the diamond. So even after correcting for positional scarcity, the corner spots for playoff teams (by a margin of 55 percent of the total offensive VORP to 45 percent and without including the DH) out-produce the up-the-middle hitters. For non-playoff teams, the margin is 57 percent to 43 percent for the corner hitters. While skill players for winning teams fare better than their less successful counterparts, they still don't measure up to their teammates manning the corners, even on a marginal level.

And speaking of imposing corner hitters, a player who's been given short shrift because of the untrammeled "panty raid" on the record book by Bonds and others is Schmidt. Observers generally recognize Schmidt as the greatest third baseman of all time, but that designation—as exclusive as it may be—doesn't rise to the level of his accomplishments. He's one of the greatest hitters ever to play the game.

Schmidt's legacy suffers because he spent the vast majority of his career in what was historically a low-scoring era by modern standards. That means runs were hard to come by, and, ergo, the individual offensive statistics weren't so immoderately distributed. Nevertheless, Schmidt excelled.

The Phillies drafted Schmidt with a second-round pick in 1971 out of Ohio University, where he had been an All-American shortstop and graduated with a degree in business. He spent only one full season in the minors (as a second baseman in the Pacific Coast League), and by 1973 he was in the major leagues for good. The Phillies had such faith in Schmidt as a prospect that they created a point of entry for him by trading away 25-year-old incumbent third baseman Don Money (who would go on to become a four-time All-Star in Milwaukee). In '73 Schmidt split time at third with Cesar Tovar; however, Schmidt foundered badly at the plate, batting only .196 and striking out in almost 40 percent of his at-bats.

That off-season, Schmidt, while playing on the team's orders in the Puerto Rican winter leagues, began making adjustments to his swing. He found something that, as he told *Sport* magazine, "made things happen."

The following season, Schmidt hit 36 homers, drew 106 walks, and led the league in slugging. More was to come. In '80, the season that ranks so high in the above lists, Schmidt belted 48 home runs, which set the mark for homers in a season by a third baseman, breaking by one the record set by Eddie Mathews in 1953. Over the years, Schmidt would lead his league in home runs eight times, which is a feat outdone by only Babe Ruth. Schmidt also hit at least 30 homers in 13 seasons (and nine consecutive). Only Hank Aaron has done that. Additionally, Schmidt reached the 35-homer mark in 11 seasons, a plateau reached more often by, again, only Ruth. By the time his career was over, Schmidt ranked eighth all-time in ISO relative to league average.

For all his triumphs as a hitter (not to mention his ten Gold Gloves at the hot corner), Schmidt was never fully embraced by the fans and writers in Philadelphia. Part of this is Philly's self-styled reputation for bestowing its athletes with only hard-won and grudging affection. Part of it is that Schmidt's game was often misunderstood. First, Schmidt was prone to strikeouts, which have unduly raised the hackles of the sport's followers since anyone can remember. Over his first four major league seasons, he averaged more than 150 strikeouts per season—a proclivity that prompted teammate Willie Montanez to nickname him "A-Choo!"

On balance, a strikeout is no different from any other out at the plate. In the modern era, strikeouts and outs by other means cost the team a little more than 0.01 run, and it hardly justifies as much kvetching as strikeouts seem to elicit. If you're a right-handed batter who's especially slow of foot (think Mark McGwire), give me strikeouts in place of ground balls so he's not hitting into 50 double plays a season.

There's also what logicians and pretentious people call the "confirmation bias." It's a phenomenon we're all prone to whereby we tend to notice, look for, or emphasize things that reinforce our preexisting beliefs. In Schmidt's case, those preoccupied with his strikeouts probably don't recall the countless times he struck out when it made no difference (at least relative to the other ways of making outs); rather, they fixate on the handful of times he whiffed with a runner on third and fewer than two outs. It's an understandable trap to fall into, but it clouds the reality that strikeouts are basically no worse than outs of other flavors.

Schmidt also suffered from the perception that he didn't perform in the postseason. This is an accurate perception (he hit .236 AVG/.304 OBP/.386 SLG in postseason series and .267 AVG/.380 OBP/.527 SLG for his career in regular season play), but it's likely not the result of some sniveling character flaw or an inability to handle pressure situations. I'm quite open to the idea that some players can wilt in especially urgent circumstances, but there's no evidence that Schmidt was of this stripe. I say that because his record of performance in the playoffs fluctuated more wildly than the stock-price chart of some high-beta outfit from the tech sector. In the first four postseason series of his career, he was ghastly. However, in the '80 World Series, which the Phillies won over the Royals, he posted a .462 OBP and slugged .714 over six games. He was strong again in the '81 division series and the '83 NLCS, but struggled in the '83 World Series. To buy into the notion of Schmidt's being or not being "clutch" based on his playoff travails would take a prescription-strength dose of credulity. He was decidedly nonclutch early in his career, but then, in 1980, summoned the necessary virtues to perform on the wide stage. Schmidt clung to those virtues through the penultimate series of the 1983 season (including a home run off Jerry Reuss in the Phils' 1–0 win over the Dodgers in game one), but then, in three days (from the end of the NLCS to the beginning of the World Series), he regressed into the malodorous layabout of yore. Value judgments, no. Sample size, yes.

In any event, Philadelphia's appreciation of Schmidt never rose to meet the gravitas of his accomplishments. However, when he retired not two months into the 1989 season, fans nevertheless responded by voting him in as the starting third baseman on the National League's

All-Star team. Schmidt declined the invitation. He was voted into the Hall of Fame in his first year of eligibility. That 96.5 percent of writers named him on their Hall of Fame ballots is historically impressive, but that 16 of those writers saw fit to leave him off reveals the strains of idiocy that still pollute the process.

Schmidt returned to Veterans Stadium, under reasonably amicable conditions, to throw out the first pitch before game three of the 1993 World Series. Just before going out to deliver the toss, Schmidt commented, "When I watch films of myself, I wish I had more fun playing. I wish I enjoyed myself more."

One player far more proficient at self-enjoyment was the Royals' George Brett. Brett was a California boy with honeyed, shaggy hair and a love of bacchanalian pursuits. He grew up in a family of gifted athletes (older brother Ken, who reached the majors as a 19-year-old, had a 13-year career, and two other brothers played in the minors). Brett made his major league debut in 1973 but struggled mightily in 13 games of action. The following year, he batted a respectable .282 but hit only two home runs on the season and slugged a paltry .363—inadequate power numbers for a corner defender. That off-season, Royal hitting coach Charlie Lau helped Brett concentrate on hitting to all fields and improve his pitch-recognition skills. How much credit Lau and his tutelage should get is hard to say, but Brett did indeed become a different hitter.

Over the years, Brett would bat at least .300 in 11 different seasons and claim three American League batting titles (one, in 1990, at age 37, which made him the first player in major league history to win a batting championship in three different decades). One of those batting titles, however, Brett claimed under questionable circumstances. Going into the final game of the 1976 regular season, the Royals were set to play the Twins. Two Royals, Brett and Hal McRae, and one Twin, batting titlist nonpareil Rod Carew, were in a dead heat for the league hitting crown. Going into the ninth inning, Brett and McRae both had two hits apiece and were due up in the bottom frame. Brett was first up, and, by partial dint of a Steve Brye misplay in left field, whipped an inside-the-park home run down the line. Brett's hit eliminated Carew from contention for the batting title, but McRae, if he were able to get a base hit, would claim the honor by percentage points. McRae grounded out and Brett had the title, but that was merely the beginning.

As he exited the field of play, McRae gestured angrily toward Twins manager Gene Mauch. Mauch returned the sentiment. McRae later accused Mauch of mandating that Twins defenders allow Brett to get a hit, which would help ensure that McRae, a black man, didn't win the batting championship. McRae never retracted his remarks, but later he, along with Carew, acknowledged that Brett deserved to win the title.

Three years later, Brett would begin a two-season dalliance with history. In '79 he became the first player since Willie Mays in 1957 to hit at least 20 homers, 20 doubles, and 20 triples in the same season. In 1980, the season you'll find him ranked on both adjusted percent of league SLG and adjusted percent of league ISO lists earlier in this chapter, he would fall narrowly shy of one of baseball's most hallowed benchmarks. As late as May 22 of that season, Brett was batting .255. Soon, however, he found his stroke and began cutting a swath through AL pitching. For the rest of the season, Brett batted .427 (including an imponderable .494 in July) and at one point set a franchise record by hitting safely in 30 straight games. On August 26 in Milwaukee, Brett stroked five hits to raise his average to a season-high .407. Not since Ted Williams in 1941 had anyone batted .400 over a full season.

Lau, Brett's hitting "Mr. Miyagi," said he felt like "Dr. Franken-stein watching his monster on the loose." When the calendar flipped to September, Brett's average stood at .403. However, he was bothered by a sore wrist, and a confluence of pressures was squarely upon him. The Royals, on September 1, led the AL West by an insurmountable margin of 19½ games, which meant they could play out the month with an eye toward resting their regulars for the playoffs. Nevertheless, Brett was acutely aware of the criticisms that would ensue if he were to make a light month of it and cosset away that .400 average. Also, he had missed 37 games before the All-Star break because of various injuries, and if he were to indulge in any rendezvous with history, he'd need to cobble together a qualifying number of plate appearances. So he appeared in 17 of the Royals' 26 games that month. Even with semi-frequent rest, his performance suffered, at least by "George Brett, 1980" standards. His last day above .400 was on September 19. Still, he finished the season at .390, the highest batting average since Williams in '41 and the best mark ever for a third baseman.

Brett's gripping chase for .400 was his personal story line that sea-son, but his work in '80 was special in other regards as well. His .466

average with runners in scoring position is, to this day, the highest ever recorded since the statistic began being tracked. As detailed earlier, I'm not a fan of the RBI as an analytical tool, but it certainly bears mentioning that Brett that year became one of the few players in baseball history to record more RBI than games played in a qualifying season. Besides winning the batting title in 1980, Brett also claimed the AL MVP and paced the loop in slugging and on-base percentage. In terms of power, he also dwelled in rarefied air. His adjusted slugging is the fourth best of any player I've studied for this book, and his adjusted isolated slugging—despite the fact that he hit .390 (recall that ISO is SLG minus AVG)—is the eighth-best mark from that same pool of hitters. Imagine if he hadn't been bothered by a bruised heel, a case of tendinitis, torn ligaments, and an injured wrist that season.

The glow of the postseason didn't dampen Brett's performance. In the ALCS win over the hated Yankees, he slugged a preposterous .909, and in the World Series loss to the Phillies he batted .375 with four extra-base hits in six games.

Years later, as the music swelled on Brett's career, he provided what was, for him, a rare example of bathos. On September 30, 1992, Brett, with his older brother Ken broadcasting the game for the Angels, became the first player in baseball history to reach the 3,000-hit threshold by collecting four hits in one game. However, immediately after notching hit number 3,000, he was picked off first base while idly chatting with Wally Joyner on a snap throw by lefty Tim Fortugno.

In the following season, which would be Brett's last, he regained his penchant for the dramatic. By this point in his career, his 21st season in the majors, he was strictly a DH, and the domestic tethers of his wife and new baby led many to speculate that 1993 would be his last go-round. Early in the season, Brett did his best to squelch the retirement rumors. However, in late September he told fans and media that he would retire from baseball following the '93 season. Brett hit four homers in the week following his announcement.

The final game of Brett's career, in Arlington, Texas, against the Rangers on October 3, was also the final game of Nolan Ryan's career. As Brett ambled to the plate for the final at-bat of his career, Ranger catcher Ivan Rodriguez rested a hand on his shoulder and told Brett to look for fastballs. It was indeed a 1–2 Tom Henke fastball that Brett laced up the middle for a base hit. He'd later score on a Gary Gaetti home run.

On January 4, 1999, writers named Brett on 98 percent of their Hall of Fame ballots, which was the fourth highest total in history. Later that year he was inducted into Cooperstown, alongside Ryan.

Since SLG has been revealed to be the most important of the traditional offensive measures in terms of run scoring, and since ISO is associated with winning teams, let's look at the best teams in terms of park-adjusted SLG and ISO relative to the league average. First SLG:

Ranking	Team	Adjusted Percentage of League SLG
1.	'82 Brewers	116.0
2.	'02 Giants	114.9
3.	'03 Braves	114.4
4.	'88 Mets	113.7
5.	'97 Indians	111.4
6.	'95 Indians	111.2
7.	'80 Yankees	110.7
8.	'96 Orioles	110.3
9.	'84 Tigers	109.9
9.	'85 Dodgers	109.9

And ISO:

Ranking	Team	Adjusted Percentage of League ISO
1.	'80 Yankees	148.6
2.	'82 Brewers	134.7
3.	'88 Mets	129.9
4.	'02 Giants	129.4
5.	'03 Braves	125.8
6.	'96 Orioles	123.8
7.	'84 Tigers	123.7
8.	'97 Indians	121.9
9.	'98 Braves	120.9
10.	'95 Reds	120.5

No team places as highly on both lists as the '82 Brewers. Fittingly known as "Harvey's Wallbangers" (in reference to manager Harvey Kuenn), the '82 Brewers rank as the best team in adjusted SLG and the second-best team in adjusted ISO—a genuine colossus of an offense. In '82 they flogged the opposition with 216 homers, 30 more than the next most powerful team and the highest team total in the American League since the '64 Twins tallied 221 (this was 16 years before the Brewers would be gerrymandered into the National League). You may have noticed that no '82 Brewer showed up on the individual lists, but five regulars hit at least 20 homers—Gorman Thomas (39), Ben Oglivie (34), Cecil Cooper (32), Robin Yount (29), and Ted Simmons (23). Paul Molitor added 19, and the aforementioned Don Money came off the bench to chip in 16. The Brewers that year also paced all of baseball with 891 runs scored. Relative to the league, that lofty run total made theirs the 12th most potent offense in baseball since 1900 and the best in the AL since the 1950 Red Sox. This, of course, was long before the playoffs expanded to three rounds of play, and the Brewers that season became the first team in major league history to play three "elimination" games in the same season. First, they won the final regular season contest over the Orioles, which determined the AL East title, then bested the Angels in the decisive game five of the ALCS. Finally, the Brewers fell to the Cardinals (whom they had outhomered by 149 in the regular season—an unimaginable mismatch in terms of power) in the seventh and final tilt of the World Series.

The "snow globe" version of Milwaukee's unseemly power that season occurred on June 5, when the Brewers persecuted the A's by the score of 11–3. On that day the Brewers hit back-to-back-to-back homers for the second time in a week, and all five 20-homer hitters in waiting—Thomas, Oglivie, Cooper, Yount, and Simmons—went deep.

Shortstop Robin Yount, who won the AL MVP in '82, had more to do with the Brewers' success that season than any single player. In 156 games he clouted 29 homers, which in those days was an astounding total for a shortstop. Additionally, he paced the AL in doubles (46), hits (210), total bases (367), and slugging percentage (.578). Also, with a .331 average, Yount finished second to Willie Wilson by a single point for the '82 AL batting title. Yount's 12 triples ranked third in the AL, and he won a Gold Glove.

Yount's 1982 was one of the greatest seasons ever for a shortstop. At the time, his SLG that season was the second best mark ever recorded by an AL shortstop, second only to Rico Petrocelli's .589 in 1969, and Yount's total base count was the highest ever for a junior-circuit shortstop. He became the first shortstop ever to lead the league in SLG and total bases in the same season, and he also became the first AL shortstop to hit more than .300 and tally at least 20 homers and 100 RBI in the same season. When the lights shone brightest in '82, Yount was at his best. In the decisive final game of the regular season against Baltimore, he launched a pair of homers off future Hall of Famer Jim Palmer, and in the World Series loss to the Cardinals, he batted .414 with a .621 SLG.

Yount was a lifetime Brewer who, in 1974, made the majors for good at age 18, thus becoming one of the youngest everyday players in major league history. He had learned the nuances of professional baseball from his older brother Larry, who spent eight seasons as a pitcher in the Astros' farm system. The younger Yount was a bally-hooed athlete at Taft High in Woodland Hills, California, and the Brewers made him the third overall pick of the 1973 draft (ahead of him, the Rangers selected David Clyde, and the Mets took John Stearns) and offered him a bonus sufficient for Yount to decline a base-ball scholarship to Arizona State.

In '75 and '76 Yount had the ineffable honor of playing alongside Hank Aaron, who spent the final two seasons of his career in Milwau-kee. By the '77 off-season, Yount found himself in a contract dispute with management. He walked out of spring training and, perhaps emboldened by a recent two-over-par round at Pebble Beach, threat-ened to join the PGA tour. Eventually, at the urging of his father, Yount returned to the Brewers in May 1978. He was introduced to his new double-play partner, a handsome young rookie named Paul Moli-tor. The two would anchor the Brewers for the next 15 seasons.

A chronic shoulder problem that he aggravated in 1984 eventu-ally forced Yount to the outfield, but he never stopped hitting. In 1986 he became the seventh-youngest player ever to record 2,000 career hits and also became the first player in AL history to lead the league in fielding percentage as an outfielder and an infielder. Three years later he won his second MVP Award and in doing so joined Stan Musial and Hank Greenberg as the only players to win an MVP at two different positions. While Musial and Greenberg did it as first basemen and corner outfielders, Yount garnered top honors while manning shortstop and center field—two of the most demanding positions on the diamond.

By the time Yount retired after the 1993 season, he ranked 14th on the all-time hits list with 3,142 (he's presently 17th) and 11th on the all-time doubles list (he now ranks 13th). Yount was inducted to the Hall of Fame in 1999 in the company of George Brett and Nolan Ryan.

First baseman Cecil Cooper in '82 helped the Brewer cause with a .313 average, almost 75 extra-base hits, and strong defense. Also impressive is that, as a corner defender who logged almost 700 plate appearances on the season, he hit into only four double plays.

Cooper came up with the Red Sox. For the first two years of his major league career the Sox toggled him between Boston and the minors, and once Cooper did arrive for good, he was relegated to spot duty in deference to Carl Yastrzemski, who was winding down his fabled career. Things reached critical mass in '75 after Yaz had been removed from the lineup because of injury (the result of his throwing a bat out of frustration). Manager Darrell Johnson told Cooper to replace Yastrzemski at first, but Cooper refused. On a certain level, it's possible to sympathize with Cooper's dismay, if not his insubordination; in 1975 he was manifestly a superior player to Yaz. Still, a dismal one-for-19 effort in the World Series loss to the Reds that October snuffed out Cooper's welcome in Boston for all intents and purposes. The winter after the '76 season, the Sox dealt him to the Brewers for George Scott and Bernie Carbo.

In Milwaukee came regular playing time and a more accommodating environment. And Cooper thrived. Beginning in 1978, his second year in Milwaukee, he gave the Brewers six seasons that ranged from solid to outstanding and seven straight seasons in which he hit .300 or better. The best year of his career came in 1980, when he batted .352 (most years worthy of a batting title, but that season second to George Brett's .390), finished fourth in the AL in slugging, topped the loop in total bases, swatted 25 homers, stole 17 bases, and tallied 219 hits. For his toils, he finished fifth in the AL MVP voting, made his second All-Star team, and won a Gold Glove. According to VORP, Cooper that season was far and away the most productive first baseman in the game. Cooper's 17-year career in the majors ended following the 1987 season. He was a five-time All-Star and four-time top-ten finisher in the voting for AL MVP.

Like Cooper, Ben Oglivie was another estranged Red Sock who unearthed productivity and contentment only after arriving in Milwaukee. A native Panamanian raised in the Bronx, Oglivie, nicknamed "Spiderman" for his rangy build and prevailing sense of physical awkwardness, struggled early in his career in Boston. He was a voracious reader and a devotee of Zen Buddhism, and he attended four different colleges in pursuit of his degree. That's to say, he was a bit of a pariah in "jock" culture, which probably contributed to the garden-variety fits and starts experienced by almost all young players. Following a .218 AVG/.269 OBP/.333 SLG season in 1973, the Red Sox traded him to the Tigers for second baseman Dick McAuliffe, who gave Boston 287 mostly useless at-bats after the trade.

Once in Detroit, the lefty-swinging Oglivie found a park more suited to his abilities, and his numbers improved. By '76 and '77 he was showing the rudiments of the power stroke that would later make him one of the most feared hitters in the league (five seasons he would rank in the top five for intentional walks). Still, he wasn't getting the playing time he warranted, as evinced by the fact that he led the AL in pinch hits in 1976. Despite the progress Oglivie showed in Detroit, the Tigers, following the '77 season, dealt him to the Brewers for pitchers Jim Slaton and Rich Folkers, whose very name is a bellowing phonetic assault upon society's upper strata. Once in Milwaukee, things changed immediately for Oglivie. In '78, his first season as a Brewer, he set career bests in AVG, OBP, SLG, extra-base hits, RBI, runs scored, and walks. Still, most of the time Oglivie was being spotted against lefthanders.

The following year, Larry Hisle, Oglivie's platoon partner, lost his season to an injured shoulder, and Oglivie was at last an everyday player—at age 30. He was at his best in 1980, his third year as a Brewer, when he batted .304/.362/.562 and led the AL in homers (41) and finished second to teammate Cecil Cooper in total bases (333). In '82, the season in question, Oglivie's production dropped notably (.244 AVG/.326 OBP/.453 SLG), but he did launch 34 home runs and set a career high in walks (70). Moreover, Oglivie, despite an otherwise lackluster postseason, launched a critical home run in game five of the ALCS and another in the final contest of the World Series.

Oglivie lasted for another four years of steady decline before signing a contract to play with the Kintetsu Buffaloes of the Japanese Pacific League. He spent two reasonably successful seasons with them before returning to sign a minor league contract with the Brewers in 1989—an arrangement that came to grief for both parties. Not long after agreeing to what was in effect a ceremonial agreement to return to Milwaukee, Oglivie retired from baseball for good.

Another vital contributor in 1982 was "Stormin' Gorman" Thomas. Thomas, whose lumberjackian mustache, vast swaths of hair (hair that formed wings coming out from under his cap and made Thomas look as though he were wearing Mickey Mouse ears on the field), and all-or-nothing style of play endeared him to the fans of Milwaukee, manned center field for the Brewers for five seasons and change in the late '70s and early '80s. Thomas played the field like a hydroplaning car and seemed to either strike out or homer in every at-bat. Such a novelty should be rented out for parties. "The fans come to see me strike out, hit a home run, or run into a fence," Thomas once observed. "I try to accommodate them at least one way every game."

In '82 Thomas batted only .245 and whiffed 143 times (only Reggie Jackson and Dave Kingman tallied more strikeouts that season), but Thomas's secondary skills were substantial. Besides capably manning a key defensive position, Thomas walked 84 times and tied Jackson for the AL lead in homers with 39. In the '82 postseason Thomas recorded only four hits in 41 at-bats, but the Brewers never would have gotten there without him.

Thomas was the first-ever draft pick of the Seattle Pilots; however, he never played a game for them. Before he could reach the majors, the Pilots went belly up and resurfaced as the Milwaukee Brewers under an ambitious young owner named Allan H. "Bud" Selig. The highly discernible (but overemphasized) flaws in Thomas's game kept him from being a full-time player until age 27, when he broke out with 32 homers, 73 walks, and a .515 SLG. The following season, 1979, was the best of his career. That year, Thomas led the AL in homers with 45 and ranked third in the league with 98 walks. Of course, his 175 strikeouts also topped the loop, and that unjustly detracted from what was, on balance, an excellent season. Over the five-year span from 1978 to 1982, only Fred Lynn had a higher total VORP among AL center fielders.

Midway through the '83 season the Brewers, perhaps sensing Thomas's looming decline, traded him along with Ernie Camacho and Jamie Easterly to the Indians for Rick Manning and Rick Waits.

Shoulder problems and age ended Thomas's days as a center fielder, and, other than a solid '85 with the Mariners, his offensive skills were squarely on the wane. Seattle released him in June '86, and the Brewers signed him as their DH. Thomas, however, had nothing left. He ended his career with the lowest career batting average (.225) of any player to log 2,500 at-bats. For his career, Thomas also struck out once every 3.49 at-bats—one of the worst ratios in history. However, it was his substantial secondary hitting skills that made him a near-great player for half a decade. Thomas wound up with 268 home runs for his career and 697 walks in 5,445 plate appearances. He hit for power, played an up-the-middle position for several years, and got on base at a solid clip—those are far more important than striking out too much or posting a low batting average. Thomas remains an underappreciated ballplayer.

And now for the worst power teams in terms of SLG to make the playoffs since 1980. These are the clubs that, obviously, won in spite of lackluster power numbers. In other words, they won by other means. When we examine winning clubs that underperform in a given statistical area, it generally means that they thrive at other elements that have been proved to be vital to winners. These clubs won not because an emphasis on "manufacturing runs" or whatnot ferried them to success, but because generally they prevented runs much better than they scored them. To the list:

Ranking	Team	Adjusted Percentage of League SLG
1.	'95 Red Sox	81.5
2.	'95 Yankees	89.2
3.	'95 Rockies	89.7
4.	'90 Red Sox	91.0
5.	'91 Blue Jays	92.6
6.	'82 Braves	92.7
7.	'87 Cardinals	93.4
8.	'02 A's	94.3
9.	'01 Yankees	94.6
10.	'83 White Sox	94.7

And now for the worst ISO playoff teams since 1980:

Ranking	Team	Adjusted Percentage of League ISO
1.	'90 Red Sox	78.5
2.	'87 Cardinals	80.4
3.	'95 Yankees	80.9
4.	'82 Braves	81.1
5.	'95 Rockies	82.1
6.	'82 Cardinals	83.8
7.	'88 Red Sox	85.6
8.	'01 Yankees	88.2
9.	'96 Cardinals	88.5
10.	'91 Blue Jays	88.7

As intimated earlier, the '82 Cardinals managed to win the World Series despite a terribly flaccid power attack. In fact, among the playoff teams ranked on the pair of lists immediately above, only the '82 Cards managed to run the postseason table. As I've already mentioned, St. Louis hit a paltry 67 home runs that season, which is the lowest total for a World Series–winning team since the 1942 Cardinals, who combined for only 60 circuit clouts. The '82 model hit the fewest homers of any team in baseball that year. In fact, they were the first team to win the World Series and finish last in home runs in the same season since the '65 Dodgers.

The Cardinal teams of the 1980s were, of course, famous for stealing bases and generally running wild on the basepaths. Stealing bases, however, was not the catalyst for their successes on offense. The '82 team, despite the fact that they easily paced the rest of the NL in steals, scored runs because they also led the league in OBP, which, to indulge in understatement, is ridiculously more important than stolen base totals. Considering how the front office and manager Whitey Herzog (who also served as general manager) constructed the team, it's hardly surprising that the Cardinals didn't show much power.

Outfielder George Hendrick led the team in home runs with 19 and in SLG with an equally modest mark of .450. Hendrick was one of only four Cardinal regulars that season to slug at least .400, and four lineup mainstays—Tom Herr, Darrell Porter, Ken Oberkfell, and Ozzie Smith—tallied fewer than 50 RBI, with Willie McGee having only 56.

Nicknamed "Silent George" for his Rifleman-like taciturnity, Hendrick (of whom teammate Clint Hurdle once said, "I don't think he even talks to his wife") spent 18 years in the majors and won two World Series rings, one with the '82 Cards and another as a young reserve on the '72 A's. Oakland had made Hendrick the top overall pick of the 1968 draft, but by the 1972 off-season, after Hendrick had put together two underwhelming auditions in the majors, the world champion A's shipped him, along with future pitching mahatma Dave Duncan, to the Indians for catcher Ray Fosse and infielder Jack Heidemann. However, Hendrick's time in Oakland was not without purpose; he often credited his Athletic teammate Joe Rudi for teaching him to play baseball at the highest level.

Once in Cleveland, Hendrick established himself as a capable regular by averaging more than 22 homers per season over his four years as an Indian. Despite the uptick in production, the Indians in the winter of '76 shipped him to the Padres for Johnny Grubb, Fred Kendall, and Hector Torres. The first year following the trade, Hendrick, despite playing half his games in run-suppressing Jack Murphy Stadium, put together a .311 AVG/.381 OBP/.492 SLG season, which placed him in the top ten in the league for AVG and SLG. Apparently, however, Hendrick's strong numbers in '77 didn't curry much favor with Padre brass; not two months into the 1978 season, they dealt him to the Cardinals for pitcher Eric Rasmussen. The 1980 season, his second full year as a Cardinal, brought Hendrick some overdue notoriety (although he still maintained a strict policy of nonengagement with the media). That year, Silent George batted .302 AVG/.342 OBP/.498 SLG, totaled 60 extra-base knocks, was selected to his third All-Star team, finished in the top ten for AVG, SLG, hits, homers, doubles, extra-base hits, and total bases, and placed eighth in voting for NL MVP.

In '82 Hendrick, as mentioned, paced the world champion Cardinals in every conceivable power indicator. However, he simultaneously failed to crack the NL top 15 for significant power indicators—SLG, ISO, extra-base hits, home runs, doubles, triples, and total bases. Following the 1984 season the Cardinals, in what turned out to be a tremendous trade for them, dealt Hendrick to the Pirates for lefty John Tudor and then-utility man Brian Harper. Tudor, of course, would be one of the best starters in baseball for the '85 pennant-winning Cardinals, while Hendrick, at age 35, began his slide out of baseball. He put together one final respectable season as a reserve for the AL West champion Angels in 1986, but he'd play sparingly over the next two seasons before retiring.

First baseman Keith Hernandez was famous for his deft glovework and on-base abilities. What he wasn't, however, was a power hitter. Despite playing a position where power is part of the required skills, Hernandez never hit more than 18 homers in a season. In '82 he batted .299 AVG/.397 OBP/.413 SLG, while the league-average first baseman in the NL hit .277 AVG/.346 OBP/.422 SLG. As you can see, Hernandez's SLG was worse than that of the average first baseman in 1982. However, he ranked third in the league in OBP and third in walks with an even 100. Additionally, that season "Mex," as his teammates called him—back in those happy days when you could get away with heritage-prompted nicknames—claimed one of his 11 career Gold Gloves (only shortstop Ozzie Smith, pitchers Jim Kaat and Greg Maddux, and third baseman Brooks Robinson collected more).

Hernandez was a native of the San Francisco Bay Area, and as a prep athlete he became the first student in the history of Capucino High School to be named all-league in baseball, football, and basketball. During his senior year of high school, Hernandez quit the baseball team because he was at loggerheads with his coach. The tarnish on his record caused him to drop to the 40th round of the June baseball draft in 1971. After signing with the Cardinals, Hernandez reached Triple-A in his first season as a pro—an exceedingly rare occurrence for a high school draftee. By the middle of the '75 season he was the regular first baseman in St. Louis.

He promptly established a reputation as a tremendously capable defender. For many years prior to Hernandez's arrival, first basemen were viewed as sluggard liabilities whose sole job was to receive the throws of other infielders. However, Hernandez's athleticism and defensive artistry reminded us of the capabilities of the position. Like Hal Chase and Ferris Fain generations before him, Hernandez made a habit of fielding sacrifice bunt attempts on the third-base side of home plate in an (often successful) attempt to extinguish the lead runner. He also defied convention with his preferred method of holding runners on. To make tags as quickly as possible, Hernandez, who threw left-handed and, hence, had his glove on his right hand, would position himself with both feet in foul territory and await a pickoff throw. Still, he was nimble and alert enough to get back into defensive position when a pitch was delivered.

Hernandez set an NL record by leading the league in double plays six times, the result of his devilish ability to turn the 3–6–3. His record for career assists by a first baseman stood until 1993, when Eddie Murray broke it. Such was Hernandez's feel for and intellectual grasp of the game that he often oversaw the positioning of his fellow infielders and occasionally called pitches from first base.

On the offensive side, Hernandez did everything but what you'd expect from a first baseman—that is, he hit for average, drew walks, showed power to the gaps, but didn't hit home runs. In 1979 Hernandez, even though he toiled for a third-place team, shared the NL MVP award with Willie Stargell thanks to a .344 AVG/.417 OBP/.513 SLG season. That year Hernandez paced the NL in AVG and doubles. He also ranked second in OBP, hits, and times on base, fifth in triples, and sixth in extra-base hits. It was also the only season of his career in which he slugged at least .500.

By the middle of the 1983 season Hernandez had fallen out of favor with manager-cum-GM Whitey Herzog and, in a trade that staggered and puzzled Cardinal Nation, he was traded to the last-place New York Mets for manifest nonentities Neil Allen and Rick Ownbey. After the trade, Allen and Ownbey accomplished nothing of consequence for St. Louis, while Hernandez helped ferry the Mets to near-dynasty status in the mid-to-late '80s. Herzog intimated that the trade was prompted by Hernandez's cocaine use. Hernandez responded by threatening Herzog with a libel suit; however, the ballyhooed MLB drug trials of 1985 vindicated Herzog and the Cardinals. As a result of his testimony, baseball threatened to suspend Hernandez for a full year. However, he dodged punishment by donating more than $150,000 to drug rehabilitation programs, submitting to periodic drug tests, and performing 100 hours of community service.

During his $5\frac{1}{2}$-year run in New York, Hernandez won a second World Series and endeared himself to Met fans of all stripes with his leadership and broad skills. In 1989, his final season in New York, Hernandez posted a career low in AVG, notched his worst OBP and SLG since his rookie season, and lost more than two months to a broken kneecap. That winter the Mets allowed him to depart via free agency. Hernandez signed a two-year contract with the Indians. In his first season in Cleveland he didn't hit and made three trips to the disabled list with an injured calf muscle. After missing all of 1991 while recovering from back surgery, Hernandez attempted a comeback in '92 but found little interest in his services, so he retired. Because of his astonishing defensive skills and 2,182 career hits, Hernandez gained modest traction as a Hall of Fame candidate, although he never approached the vote total needed for election.

Although the Cardinals in '82 were productive in their own ways, they stand as outliers. That's because they didn't hit for power, which distinguishes them from most other great teams throughout the modern era. It's certainly possible to assemble a winning offense around speed and on-base abilities, as the Cardinals did, but it's not how most great teams score their runs. Imagine, for instance, a Cardinals amalgam featuring the pitching and defensive chops of the '80s models and the Albert Pujols–, Scott Rolen–, and Jim Edmonds–powered versions of the aughts.

CHAPTER 2

The Ace

(or, What Really Makes a Rotation)

The great Oriole teams of the '60s and '70s are well regarded for trotting out rotations of imposing depth and strength. In 1971 they famously boasted four 20-game winners in Jim Palmer, Mike Cuellar, Dave McNally, and Pat Dobson. Over the next several years, hurlers such as Ross Grimsley, Mike Torrez, Mike Flanagan, Steve Stone, and Dennis Martinez would be critically productive for them. Heck, manager Earl Weaver even wrung a 20–7 season out of Wayne Garland, who was 35–59 throughout the rest of his career. In each of Weaver's first 13 seasons as Oriole manager, the team produced at least one 20-game winner, which still stands as a record. Over the years, Weaver and longtime pitching coach George Bamberger would husband 22 seasons of at least 20 wins from nine different pitchers. In part this phenomenon was owing to the fact that O's fielded great teams for many of those years. However, part of it was also Weaver's predominant adherence to the four-man rotation during a time when it was otherwise beginning to fall out of fashion in baseball. And part of it was Bamberger's ability to flesh out repertoires and persuade his charges to alter their pitch sequences.

The anchors of the '83 staff, Scott McGregor and Mike Boddicker,

are other notable examples of this particular facet of the "Oriole way."
The Yankees made McGregor, a high school teammate of George
Brett in El Segundo, California, the 14th overall pick of the 1972 draft.
Coming up through the system, the lefty quickly established himself as
a control artist who made hay with a tremendous curve. However, in
1976, just as McGregor was becoming seasoned enough for the
majors, the Yankees parted ways with him. On June 15 the Yankees
held a firm 10½-game lead over the Red Sox, but with an eye toward
October, they wanted to add veterans. So they packaged McGregor
with pitchers Rudy May, Tippy Martinez, and Dave Pagan, and
catcher Rick Dempsey to Baltimore for catcher Elrod Hendricks
(whose most notable skill was probably his ability to serve as transla-
tor between Weaver and Cuellar) and veteran hurlers Doyle Alexander, Ken Holtzman, and Grant Jackson. The deal would turn out to be
one of the best ever for the Orioles. Martinez would go on to become
one of the best lefty relievers of the late '70s and early '80s (and would
once pick off three Toronto Blue Jays in a single inning), and Dempsey
would be the O's regular catcher for more than a decade. Following
the 1977 season, Baltimore traded May in a six-player deal with the
Expos, and another starter, Grimsley, signed with the Expos as a free
agent. That left two vacancies in the rotation. One would be filled by
Dennis Martinez, and the other would go to McGregor. Bamberger
worked with McGregor on placing his fastball higher in the zone, and
the improvement was immediate. Beginning in '78, McGregor would
peel off seven straight winning seasons, making him the only pitcher
in the majors to do so over that span.

In McGregor's first season as a rotation regular, some chicanery by
Weaver would secure McGregor one win that otherwise would never
have happened. On August 13, in a home game against his former
team the Yankees, McGregor carried a shutout into the seventh inning.
However, in that frame New York reached him for five runs and a 5–3
lead when the rains began. As the rains started, Weaver commenced
with the stall tactics. Some conspicuously bumbling groundskeepers
helped out, and since the game was called in the middle of an inning,
the score reverted back to the last completed frame. The result was a
3–0 win for McGregor and the Orioles.

The 1979 campaign would see McGregor throw a shutout against
the Angels in the pennant-clinching win in game four of the ALCS.

However, his October prowess that year would be short-lived. In game seven of the World Series and with the O's up 1–0 in the sixth, McGregor surrendered a one-on, one-out homer to Willie Stargell. It would prove to be the game-winning hit, as the Pirates went on to win 4–1 and take the Series.

The 1980 campaign would be McGregor's only 20-win season of his career, and he wasn't able to win number 20 until the final game of the season, in which he allowed one run over seven innings in a 7–1 win over the Indians. McGregor suffered arm maladies in '82, but he would come back strong the following year and make the 1983 season the best of his career. His park-adjusted ERA was 24 percent better than the league average, and he finished fifth in the AL in ERA, innings, and complete games. Of course, he struck out a trifling 86 batters in 260 innings, which comes to less than 3.0 per nine innings. That means a great many balls in play, and, as we'll soon see, positive outcomes under those circumstances may have more to do with good defense and good fortune than anything else. The season culminated happily for McGregor, who won the fifth and final game of the World Series by tossing a five-hit shutout against the Phillies.

The '83 season was McGregor's last effective one. He would hover around the 200-inning mark for the next three years, but he'd never again, in park-adjusted terms, best the league-average ERA. In 1987, the wheels came off. Over the next season and a half, McGregor would work barely 100 innings in total, post seasonal ERAs of 6.64 and 8.83, respectively, and win only two games. The steep decline prompted his retirement following the 1988 season.

The Orioles drafted Mike Boddicker, an undersized righthander, out of the University of Iowa with a sixth-round pick in 1978. The following season, Boddicker set a Southern League record by striking out 18 batters in an 8–2 win over Knoxville. He made his major league debut in 1980, but it wasn't until '83 that he became a rotation regular. That season, Boddicker worked 179 innings, led the AL in shutouts (despite not making his first start of the season until May 5), placed second in ERA, and finished with the seventh-best strikeout-to-walk ratio in the league. In the postseason he set an ALCS record by whiffing 14 batters in a shutout win over the White Sox, a performance that helped him win ALCS MVP. In his only World Series start, Boddicker pitched a three-hit complete game win over the Phillies.

The following season, Boddicker paced the AL in wins and ERA and finished second in the league with 16 complete games. However, his pitching cratered over the next two seasons, and midway through the 1988 season (the one the Orioles began 0–21), Baltimore traded him to the Red Sox for a pair of young minor leaguers named Curt Schilling and Brady Anderson. Boddicker would pitch well in Boston, but nevertheless it was a terrible trade for the Red Sox.

Boston has an unfortunate history in making deals. Notably, they've swapped Babe Ruth to the Yankees for cash (for the moment we'll define the trade as an exchange of commodities rather than an exchange of players) and sent Red Ruffing to the Yankees for reserve outfielder Cedric Durst and $50,000. (Pitcher wins and losses have substantial weaknesses as evaluative tools, but consider that Ruffing was 39–96 as a Red Sock and 234–129 as a Yankee.) There's also the Larry Andersen-for-Jeff Bagwell colossal misplay in recent history. In fact, researchers Dave Studenmund and Mike Carminati, writing for the Hardball Times Web site, found that according to the Bill James Win Shares statistic, the Red Sox were the worst team in baseball in making trades during the 1961–2002 period. Observe that two of the worst trades in franchise history—the Ruth and Ruffing swaps— occurred prior to '61. As for recent times, it's worth pondering whether the Boddicker trade was actually more costly in terms of talent squandered than the Bagwell deal, despite the scores of Red Sock lamentations that have followed the latter.

The numbers show that the Bagwell trade was more damaging to the organization, but not by a terribly wide margin—only about $2\frac{1}{2}$ wins, in fact. So yes, the Bagwell-Andersen trade is the worst of the modern era for Boston, but let's not give short shrift to the cost exacted by acquiring Boddicker.

Nevertheless, Boddicker got off to a quick start in Boston. For the balance of the '88 season he worked 89 innings after the trade and posted a 2.63 ERA. The following season he logged $211\frac{2}{3}$ innings for the Sox with an ERA a few ticks better than the league average. In 1990 he formed a tandem with Roger Clemens that narrowly missed ranking as one of the great duos of the modern era. That season, Clemens topped all of baseball in SNLVAR (I'll explain this acronym shortly), and Boddicker ranked 12th. For the year, Boddicker posted a 3.36 ERA, ranked in the top ten for innings and starts, and won his first and only Gold Glove award. He signed with the Royals after that season and began a three-year pattern of decline that would land him

in Milwaukee two seasons later and force him from the league following the '93 season.

The notion of the "one-two punch"—that is, a pair of certifiable aces in
the rotation—is often pointed to as being of critical importance once a
team has already reached the postseason. In a short series, the idea
goes, having a pair of dominant starters confers a sizable advantage. In
this book, however, my concern is how these teams get to the postseason. This leads me to ask: how critical is it to have a one-two punch in
winning the division or claiming a wild card spot?

To probe a bit more deeply into this matter, I'll use a *Baseball
Prospectus* statistic that's clunkily and bureaucratically named support-
neutral lineup-adjusted value added for pitchers, or, for the sake of
sanity and sentence construction, SNLVAR. SNLVAR expresses how
much a value a pitcher would have, in terms of wins and losses, over
the previously detailed "replacement level" player, given league-
average run support. Additionally, SNLVAR is adjusted to reflect the
strength of the opposing lineups the pitcher has faced during the season and the tendencies of his home park.

Of the 124 teams I've examined, 60 have had at least two starters
among the major leagues' 25 best in SNLVAR for that particular season. Stated another way, a narrow majority *doesn't* have what can be
reasonably referred to as a potent one-two punch. On average, the best
starters for these 124 teams have an average SNLVAR ranking of 14.4
(that's in all the majors, not just their respective leagues). The second-
best starters on these teams, meanwhile, have an average ranking of
28.6. Again, on average, great teams over the past quarter century or
so haven't had two rotation stars among the 25 best in the game. The
vaunted one-two punch is certainly desirable, but the numbers say it
isn't a prerequisite to success.

Now let's turn to the extremes. What follows are rankings, according to SNLVAR, of the best tandem aces of the contemporary era.
They'll be ordered by their total ranking. For instance, in 1983 White
Sox starters Rich Dotson and Floyd Bannister ranked fifth and 11th,
respectively, in the majors in SNLVAR that season. So their total ranking would be 16 (5 + 11). Obviously, the lower the total ranking, the
better. Now for the best:

Ranking	Pitchers	Total SNLVAR Rank
1.	Randy Johnson, Curt Schilling ('01 Diamondbacks)	3
2.	Greg Madduz, Tom Glavine ('98 Braves)	6
3.	Barry Zito, Tim Hudson ('02 A's)	8
4.	Greg Maddux, Tom Glavine ('93 Braves)	9
5.	Mike Witt, Kirk McCaskill ('86 Angels)	10
6.	Greg Maddux, Tom Glavine ('97 Braves)	11
6.	Greg Maddux, Tom Glavine ('00 Braves)	11
6.	Bret Saberhagen, Charlie Leibrandt ('85 Royals)	11
9.	Doyle Alexander, Dave Stieb ('85 Blue Jays)	12
9.	Scott McGregor, Mike Boddicker ('83 Orioles)	12

Johnson and Schilling (despite the blight upon the land that are Arizona's market-tested, "fashion forward" uniforms), who placed first and second in SNLVAR respectively, that season, rank as one of the most imposing tandems ever. Maddux and Glavine, to no one's surprise, occupy four of the above spots, and Barry Zito and Tim Hudson of the '02 A's also rank high. In the case of Maddux and Glavine, in those four seasons they graced the Braves with almost 2,000 total innings and a combined ERA of 2.72, with every frame coming during and after the 1993 offensive explosion. NL teams in '93 averaged 4.49 runs per game, which was the highest in the senior circuit since 1961. That's the lowest they've been since then. In 2000—another Maddux-Glavine season to make the cut—run scoring levels reached 5.00 in the NL for the first time since 1930. Not only have Maddux and Glavine put up tremendous numbers, but they've also done it in an era that squarely benefits the hitter. Furthermore,

Maddux's best two seasons—1994 and 1995—didn't make the cut. In '94 Maddux worked 202 innings with a 1.56 ERA, and his park-adjusted ERA relative to the league average was the best NL mark of the twentieth century. The following season Maddux logged a 1.63 ERA in 209⅔ innings, but Glavine ranked "only" 13th in SNLVAR that season. However you frame it, it's difficult to overstate the brilliance of Maddux and Glavine as a duo.

As demonstrated above, it's not terribly essential for a winning team to have a pair of aces. So how vital is it to have one certifiable top-shelf starter? Of the 124 teams I'm looking at, 68—or 54.8 percent—have at least one starter in the top ten SNLVAR rankings for that particular season. And recall, SNLVAR rankings encompass both leagues, so it's marginally more common for a team to have one top-ten pitcher than it is for a team to have two top 25 pitchers. Expand the "lone ace" cut-off to top 20 in SNLVAR, and 73.4 percent of teams qualify. Stated another way, only 26.6 percent of playoff teams since 1980 have failed to place at least one starting pitcher in the SNLVAR top 20. You can get by without a two-headed ace, but, generally speaking, you do need at least one veritable force in the rotation. You're probably not thunderstruck by this finding, but in an industry that cherishes its articles of faith, almost anything's worth the trouble of verifying.

Given enough run support, almost any pitcher can look like an ace to the undiscriminating observer. In reality, a select few teams have thrived despite a decidedly unimposing front of the rotation. They won, variously, with offense, defense, and perhaps a potent bullpen, such as the teams that make up this list of the highest and, ergo, worst, tandem rankings:

Ranking	Pitchers	Total SNLVAR Rank
1.	Kevin Ritz, Bryan Rekar ('95 Rockies)	229
2.	Phil Niekro, Rick Mahler ('82 Braves)	100

3.	Ken Forsch, Mike Witt ('82 Angels)	94
4.	Johan Santana, Brad Radke ('03 Twins)	91
5.	Mike Mussina, Orlando Hernandez ('02 Yankees)	90
5.	Kerry Wood, Steve Trachsel ('98 Cubs)	90
7.	Andy Ashby, Joey Hamilton ('96 Padres)	86
8.	Charles Nagy, Orel Hershiser ('97 Indians)	85
9.	Kelly Downs, Atlee Hammaker ('87 Giants)	84
9.	Pete Vuckovich, Mike Caldwell ('82 Brewers)	84
9.	Masato Yoshii, Orel Hershiser ('99 Mets)	84

The first thing to leap off the page in the "ten worst" list above is the execrable performance of the '95 Rockies. Before you're tempted to dismiss this as Coors Field statistical mangling, recall that SNLVAR values are all park-adjusted. So the Rockies' rotation that season was really that inferior, even in a neutral context. Notional "ace" Kevin Ritz was fairly effective by Coors Field standards (4.21 ERA); however, since he ranked only 24th in the NL in innings pitched, his SNLVAR ranking falls accordingly. Bryan Rekar, the team's second-best starter according to SNLVAR, logged only 83⅓ innings as a starter. The far-flung innings dispersal of the '95 Rockies has much to do with why none of their starting pitchers fares well in SNLVAR. Only Ritz and Bill Swift logged at least 100 innings that season (with Swift coming in at only 105⅔), and although the '95 season was only 144 games in length, the Rockies hopscotched through 20 different pitchers that season, and 12 different hurlers made at least one start. In some ways this embodies the "let God sort 'em out" approach to assembling a pitching staff that's become somewhat endemic to baseball at one mile above sea level.

. . .

The '82 Braves were a team of oddities. As you'll see in a later chapter, they fielded one of the youngest gaggles of position players of any playoff team; they opened the season at an NL record 13–0 (then lost five straight); and, as you see above, the front of their rotation was conspicuously weak. Fronting that rotation, however, was future Hall of Famer Phil Niekro (35th in SNLVAR), and behind him was Rick Mahler (65th in SNLVAR). In many ways Niekro's 1982 season is an object lesson in the silliness of pitcher win-loss records (the idea of ascribing a win or a loss to any one player for any given game has always seemed terrifically stupid to me). For the year, the 43-year-old Niekro put together a bright and shining 17–4 record. However, his ERA was only a few notches better than the league average and ranked a middling 24th among NL qualifiers that season (but younger brother Joe ranked 2nd).

Phil Niekro spent 24 years in the majors, and, like fellow Hall of Famers Don Sutton and Gaylord Perry, was one of those who assembled his credentials as a legend at a seemingly glacial pace—the wins and accolades came gradually, intermittently, quietly. When he broke into the majors in 1964, the Braves were still in Milwaukee, and the league leader boards were peppered with iconic names such as Mantle, Koufax, Drysdale, Mays, Wills, and Spahn. Niekro retired following the 1987 "campaign" and he spent part of his final, late-season sinecure with the Braves imparting wisdom to a young lefty named Tom Glavine.

When Niekro, a boyhood friend of basketball legend John Havlicek, was only 10 years of age, his father, a pitcher for a local industrial league, threw him a knuckleball—as a joke, the story goes. However, young Niekro was captivated by the fluttering, improbably slow nature of the pitch and beseeched his father to teach it to him. His dad, a rough-hewn type from the Appalachian coal country of eastern Ohio who relied on the stouthearted fastball, blanched at first, but Niekro insisted. That insistence would pay off. By the time Niekro was in high school, he had such command of the knuckleball that his father could no longer catch him (it's the bassackward nature of the knuckler that a catcher's inability to receive it properly can be sign of mastery by the hurler).

Niekro's amateur days came during a time when knuckleballing starters were out of fashion. In the '50s, those pitchers who did feature the knuckleball—Hoyt Wilhelm and Gene Bearden being the two most prominent examples—did so mostly as relievers. That was the case, by and large, from the time New York Giant manager Leo Durocher converted Wilhelm into a reliever in 1952 (the 1949 season was the last in which Bearden would make more starts than relief appearances) to when Niekro himself became a predominant starter in the majors in 1968. Once Niekro established himself and disabused managers of the notion that knuckleball pitchers were best deployed as relievers, many others followed. In a sense, Niekro heralded the knuckleballer-cum-starter renaissance that's still with us today in the form of Tim Wakefield (granted, as renaissances go, it's been a mild one of late).

In any event, the Braves thought enough of young "Knucksie" to sign him out of high school in 1958 to a $500 bonus. That turned out to be quite a bargain. Adjusting for inflation, these days that figure comes to a little more than $3,000, or roughly the manner of bonus commanded by an afterthought drafted in the 40th round or so and having no other meaningful life options to leverage in his favor. The days when players were hoodwinked chattel seem a world removed these days, but they were once very much with us.

Throughout much of his minor league career Niekro was confined to mop-up duty in games that had long been decided. He also struggled to control his pet pitch, and his fastball and slider weren't anything more than "show" pitches. Gradually, however, he harnessed the knuckler. He made the majors to stay in 1965, but manager Bobby Bragan kept him in a relief role for the first two seasons. In '67 Niekro still worked primarily in relief, but he also made 20 starts, mostly because of a serious injury to Tony Cloninger. Regardless of how Niekro was deployed that season, he was excellent. In 207 innings he posted a league-leading 1.87 ERA and gave up only nine homers. It was his first of 20 seasons in which he pitched at least 200 innings. In 1969 the Braves, in the inaugural season of division play, took the NL West title thanks almost entirely to Niekro and Hank Aaron. That season Niekro worked 284⅔ innings, posted a 2.56 ERA, completed 23 games, finished second in the voting for the NL Cy Young Award, and made his first of five All-Star teams (although, for his career, Niekro would log only 1⅓ All-Star innings, mostly because managers didn't want him throwing the knuckleball to unfamiliar catchers). In the postseason Niekro lost the first ever NLCS game to Tom Seaver of the Mets, who went on to sweep the Braves and best the Orioles in the World Series.

The following season, Niekro had one of the least effective years of his career, as he posted an ERA just a whisker better than the league mean and gave up 40 homers in 229⅔ innings. After Niekro developed arm soreness, Braves manager Eddie Mathews moved him back to the bullpen to start the 1973 season. However, he was eventually returned to the rotation, and on August 5 of that year he tossed a no-hitter in a 9–0 win over the Padres. Because of his durability, he'd make desultory relief appearances from time to time, but from that point forward he was never again lifted from the rotation.

The first of Niekro's four 300-inning seasons came in 1974, when he tallied a league-leading 302⅓ frames and finished second in the loop with a 2.38 ERA. During these years, however, the Braves as a team were getting progressively worse, which meant that Niekro's occasionally brilliant pitching was veiled by an inferior supporting cast and, hence, middling won-loss records. In '77 Niekro succumbed to the capricious nature of the knuckleball; his 164 walks on the season were the third most in the NL since 1900. Still, there were high points of note. In the sixth inning of a game against the Pirates on July 29, Niekro, thanks to a Biff Pocoroba passed ball, was able to whiff Dave Parker, Bill Robinson, Rennie Stennett, and Omar Moreno and thus become the ninth National Leaguer ever to strike out four batters in the same inning. Niekro for the season posted a park-adjusted ERA 11 percent better than the league mean and paced the NL in strikeouts. Nevertheless, he tied Jerry Koosman of the Mets for the league "lead" with 20 losses (that was mostly because the Braves lost 101 games and finished last in the NL West). The 1977 season began a four-year run in which Niekro would lead the NL is losses. In each of those seasons, however, he bettered the league ERA. In 1978 he won the first of his five Gold Gloves, and he finished with a 2.88 ERA, a second-place strikeout total, and a rather bizarre 19–18 record. Speaking of rather bizarre, the following season Niekro became the first pitcher since 1906 to win *and* lose at least 20 games in the same season. That year, the Braves once again finished last, which made Niekro the most recent pitcher to win 20 for a last-place team. Additionally, he set career single-season benchmarks in '79 with 342 innings pitched and 23 complete games. That innings total is the third highest in the NL since 1920, and his complete-game tally marks the last time any NL pitcher has logged more than 20 in a season. Niekro that season also won the Lou Gehrig Award for outstanding character, a nod to his tireless charitable efforts in the Atlanta area.

In '82 the Braves returned to the postseason, and Niekro finished fifth in the NL Cy Young voting. As mentioned, however, his 17–4 record that season obscured his solid yet unspectacular job of pitching. Throughout the vast majority of Niekro's career, his teammates were generally derelict in their duties when he was on the mound. In fact, with 49 career shutout losses, Niekro trails only Nolan Ryan and Walter Johnson in that ill-fated category. The 1982 season, however, was a happy outlier for Niekro. That season, the Braves lavished him with an average of 5.5 runs of support in his 35 starts, which most assuredly helped pad that eye-grabbing record of his. In Niekro's lone NLCS start against the Cardinals, he pitched well—two earned runs in six innings of work—but the Braves fell and were eventually swept by St. Louis. Following a fairish season in '83, the Braves cut bait on Niekro, who, at age 44, signed a two-year contract with the Yankees. In '84, his first season in the Bronx, the gray-haired Niekro ranked fourth in the AL in ERA and led the staff in innings. The following year, he regressed to mediocre status, and the Yankees opted not to re-sign him. Still, '85 saw Niekro win his 300th game in a start against the Blue Jays on the final day of the season. But Phil Niekro wasn't quite Phil Niekro on that day in Toronto; he spun a four-hit shutout but didn't throw the knuckleball until he faced the final batter of the game, when he struck out Jeff Burroughs with three straight knucklers. With that win, he also became, at age 46, the oldest pitcher ever to throw a complete game shutout.

The 1986 season, which he'd spend in the employ of the Indians (he was signed mostly to tutor Tom Candiotti in the ways of the knuckleball), would be his final tolerable one. Niekro was 47 years old that year, and the music was swelling on a major league career that lasted almost a quarter century. He opened the '87 season back in Cleveland, but after 123⅔ ineffective innings, the Tribe dealt him to the Blue Jays for Don Gordon and Darryl Landrum. However, 22 days, 12 innings, and 11 runs later, the Jays cut him loose, which allowed him to sign once again with the Braves for one final outing, which came on September 27. Niekro, pitching against the Giants in Atlanta–Fulton County Stadium, lasted only three innings and left the game with the bases loaded. The Braves would go on to lose the game 15–6.

Unfitting ending notwithstanding, it was a remarkable career, and one that ended only 18 months from Niekro's 50th birthday. Niekro won 121 games after age 40—a record. He also holds the records for wins at age 45, 46, 47, and 48. He and younger brother Joe won a combined 539 games in the majors, ten more than Gaylord and Jim Perry and a record for siblings. Another record Phil Niekro holds, but one he surely doesn't hold dear, is for most major league seasons—24—without appearing in a World Series. In retirement, Niekro gained further notoriety by managing the short-lived Colorado Silver Bullets, the first all-female professional baseball team. He was voted into the Hall of Fame in 1997, his fifth year of eligibility.

It's interesting to note that our list of "worst" aces actually contains a pitcher who won the Cy Young for his work during that particular season. That pitcher is Pete Vuckovich of the '82 Brewers, who, along with Mike Caldwell, ranks as the ninth least imposing duo I've studied.

Vuckovich was a three-sport standout at Conemaugh Valley High School in Pennsylvania and went on to play at nearby Clarion University. After an impressive amateur career, he was chosen by the White Sox in the third round of the 1974 draft. He spent barely a year in the minors before being called up to Chicago, where he worked primarily in relief for a season and change. In 1976 the freshly minted Toronto Blue Jays nabbed Vuckovich in the second round of the expansion draft. In '77 he made only eight starts in 53 appearances, but one of those starts—a win over Jim Palmer and the Orioles on June 23—was the first shutout ever thrown by a Blue Jay.

Despite making low-grade history, Vuckovich was jettisoned to the Cardinals that winter along with outfielder John Scott for pitchers Tom Underwood and Victor Cruz. In 1978, Vuckovich's first season in St. Louis, he pitched primarily as a starter for the first time in his young career, although he also made 22 relief appearances. On the year, Vuckovich ranked third in the league in ERA, seventh in the league in strike-out-to-walk ratio, and third in strikeouts per nine innings. Vuckovich's work in '78 certainly didn't garner the attention that his '82 season would, but it was plainly a better year, as you'll soon see. Based on the strength of his pitching in '78, Vuckovich became a rotation regular and would remain there for the rest of his career. His meaningful indicators declined the following year, but his 15 victories gave him the cachet needed to brand himself a winner. Following another winning yet generally mediocre season in 1980, the Cardinals shipped him to Milwaukee in one of the biggest trades of the year. Vuckovich, catcher Ted Simmons, and closer Rollie Fingers (who had come to the Cardinals only four days prior in an 11-player leviathan with the Padres) went to the Brewers for slugging outfielder Sixto Lezcano, putative phenom David Green, righthander Lary Sorensen, and lefty Dave LaPoint. The trade, while not a disaster for St. Louis, was costly. Lezcano was a liability in his lone year as a Cardinal; Green never came close to realizing his promise; Sorensen gave them one unremarkable season; and LaPoint, on balance, was suboptimal during his first Cardinal tour of duty.

Milwaukee's swag, meanwhile, gave them a front-line starter, regular catcher, and relief ace. All would be key components of the almost-great Brewer teams of the early '80s. During the abbreviated '81 season, Vuckovich compiled a 14–4 record and tied for the league lead in wins despite a park-adjusted ERA that was below the league average. Milwaukee made the playoffs that season by winning the second-half AL East title. In the postseason, Vuckovich blanked the Yankees for 5⅓ innings in game four of the Division Series, but New York prevailed in five games. The following season was Vuckovich's Cy Young campaign and the one in which the Brewers won their first and only pennant.

As the '82 season wore on, however, Vuckovich began to break down. Shoulder soreness hampered him in the second half, but in a division that would eventually be decided by a single game, he took a flurry of cortisone shots to permit him to soldier on. Showing the solemn resolve of a cockroach infestation and pitching with what would turn out to be a torn rotator cuff, Vuckovich threw five complete games over his final 10 starts, including an 11-inning outing against the Red Sox on September 20. In the postseason, however, he posted a 4.45 ERA in four starts. His shoulder was never the same and, as a result, neither was his pitching. Over the next four years Vuckovich would throw a total of 159⅔ innings before retiring at age 33.

For the 1982 season, Vuckovich ranked 25th in SNLVAR, while Caldwell ranked 59th. What's prominent about this tandem is that although they combined for 35 wins on the season, they also teamed up to strike out only 180 batters in 481⅔ innings. That comes to a piddling 3.4 strikeouts per nine—a thoroughly afflicted figure for two front-of-the-rotation talents. So Vuckovich and Caldwell relied overmuch on a below-average Milwaukee defense. In Vuckovich's case, that defense (or good fortune) certainly came through for him. Despite striking out—or, if you prefer, taking care of his own business—just more than four batters per nine innings, Vuckovich managed to rank sixth in the AL with a 3.34 ERA. Look behind that ERA, however, and you see a different rendering of his season. First, Vuckovich allowed 13 unearned runs on the season, which, despite the "unearned" qualifier, are also the fault of the pitcher. Second, on the season he struck out 105 batters and walked 102. That comes to a beastly strikeout-to-walk ratio of 1.03 (the worst such mark ever for a Cy Young winner). That's one of the most important traditional pitching statistics we have, and in '82 Vuckovich, among AL qualifiers, ranked 46th in it. He wasn't doing his job, low ERA notwithstanding.

The fact that Vuckovich won the Cy Young in '82 is largely because his record on the season was 18–6. He finished first in the league in winning percentage and second in wins. As has been emphasized ad nauseam, judging a pitcher by wins and losses is like judging a late-model Rockefeller by his bank account—only a bantam fragment of it has anything to do with genuine ability. The thunderous Brewers offense scored 5.3 runs per start for Vuckovich, and he faced losing teams in 17 of his 30 starts. All of this leads me to ask: is Vuckovich the worst Cy Young winner ever? To explore this question, I'll use VORP rank (SNLVAR evaluates only starters, and since relievers have won the award, we need a metric that assays them both). The problem is that adequate play-by-play data are available only back through 1972, so we'll have to recast the question as this: is Vuckovich the worst Cy Young winner since 1972?

Ranking	Year	Winner	VORP Rank
1.	1987	Steve Bedrosian, Phillies	90
2.	1979	Bruce Sutter, Cubs	66
3.	1989	Mark Davis, Padres	59
4.	1984	Rick Sutcliffe, Cubs	45
5.	1992	Dennis Eckersley, A's	37
6.	2003	Eric Gagne, Dodgers	32
7.	1977	Sparky Lyle, Yankees	26
8.	1974	Mike Marshall, Dodgers	19
9.	1978	Gaylord Perry, Padres	18
10.	1981	Rollie Fingers, Brewers	15

. . .

Notice a pattern? No Vuckovich (he was 14th in VORP in '82, so he would have ranked 11th on this list had it run long enough to accommodate him), but we do have closers/ace relievers in nine of the top 10 spots. In fact, every reliever to win the Cy Young since 1972 save for Willie Hernandez of the '84 Tigers appears on this docket of the least deserving. The merits of VORP with regard to how it evaluates pitchers can be debated, but that it's rarely a good idea to vote for a reliever for the Cy Young is beyond reproach. They have a vital role, but when thrown into the same population as starters, they simply don't have the innings to compare in terms of value.

Even so, VORP probably gives more credit to Vuckovich than he warrants. For VORP, insofar as it applies to pitchers, the rubber hits the road with runs allowed and innings pitched. While Vuckovich certainly kept runs off the board, his success in that regard exceeds what *should have* transpired given his poor supporting statistics. But is it fair to excoriate Vuckovich for having such a dreadful strikeout-to-walk ratio when he otherwise did a fine job? Yes, it just might be.

At this juncture in the field of baseball analysis, there are no inventions, only discoveries. However, one of those discoveries that's so staggering it seems to border on invention belongs to a researcher named Voros McCracken. In January 2001, McCracken wrote a piece for *Baseball Prospectus* that created something of a tectonic shift in the way we think about a pitcher's true abilities. McCracken found that pitchers, generally speaking, had negligible control over what became of a ball once it left the hitter's bat. More specifically, the fate of a ball in play (i.e., a ball hit into fair territory that's not a home run) had more to do with the fielding skills of the defense behind the pitcher and blind luck than it did with any indigenous pitching skill. Needless to say, McCracken's findings countervailed decades upon decades of entrenched thought. It's not surprising that his research and its implications caused—and still causes—many a kerfuffle in the baseball world.

McCracken's discoveries took the form of what he called "defensive-independent pitching statistics," or DIPS. DIPS attempted to isolate those elements of the game over which pitchers exerted almost absolute control. Those elements are walks, strikeouts, home runs allowed, and hit batsmen. In the case of homers, there's the occasional over-the-fence grab or Jose Canseco cranial-induced bomb, but by and large, homers allowed constitute a genuine and isolated skill of the hurler. Those measures that are highly defense- and luck-dependent include wins, losses, innings, runs, earned runs, hits allowed, sacrifice hits, and sacrifice flies. By examining year-to-year trends among these statistics, McCracken discovered that, in his words, "there is little if any difference among major league pitchers in their ability to prevent hits on balls hit into the field of play."

A number of specific findings led McCracken to his bold conclusion. To wit, pitchers who are among the best in the game at preventing hits on balls in play in one season are often among the worst in the following season; there's scant correlation between what a given pitcher does in one season with regard to preventing hits on balls in play and what he does in another; you can better forecast a pitcher's hit rate on balls in play by using his teammates' rates during that same year than by using his rate from the previous season; the range of career hit rates for pitchers logging a significant number of innings is about what you'd expect from random chance, and when you adjust for park and league, that range becomes even narrower.

Subsequent research by Clay Davenport and Nate Silver of *Baseball Prospectus*, Tom Tippett of Diamond Mind Baseball, and McCracken himself revealed the original findings to be overstated and flawed. To cite a pair of examples, knuckleballers do appear to have some ability to prevent hits on balls in play, while lefties seem to be modestly worse in this regard than their right-handed counterparts. Additionally, there's strong reason to believe that pitchers at the major league level have a small but statistically significant ability to prevent hits on balls in play. However, the overarching point remained strong and surprising: pitchers, in general terms, simply don't have nearly as much control over the fate of a ball batted into the field of play as we once thought. The upshot is that we can now come reasonably close to isolating the performance of a pitcher by focusing on his "DIPS" metrics—strikeout, homer, HBP, and walk rates. By running a series of calculations, we can come up with a DIPS ERA for pitchers. This is the ERA the pitcher "deserved" based on his defensive-independent peripheral statistics.

When we compare how these teams fare in DIPS ERA and standard ERA, we find there's a stronger trend of success with regard to the latter. In the aggregate, the 124 teams under this particular micro-scope have bested the league-average DIPS ERA by 5.3 percent and the league average ERA by 11.96 percent. However, those figures don't adequately impart the strength of the associations. This does: a whopping 82.3 percent of all playoff teams since 1980 (excluding the '81 season) have bested the league mean for DIPS ERA, and an even more whopping 90.3 percent of those same teams have come in under the league ERA.

In other words, pitchers on these teams—be they relievers or starters—strike guys out, exhibit good control, and keep the ball in the park.

However, the more notable success in ERA suggests that these teams—whether by dint of defense, some low-grade skill of the pitcher, or reining in that quisling called luck—have done at least a passable job of turning batted balls into outs. To put numbers to the assumptions, let's examine how these playoff teams compare to the league average in terms of batting average on balls in play (BABIP):

- Our 124 teams, on average, have allowed a BABIP of 1.55 percent less than the league average.

- Of these teams, 68 (54.8 percent) have logged a BABIP of better than league average, 32 (25.8 percent) have been exactly at the league average, and 24 (19.4 percent) wound up worse than the league average.

- While the positive associations aren't that strong, more than 80 percent of the 124 teams have a BABIP of league average or better.

So we have strong links to DIPS ERA, ERA, and weak ones to BABIP. Since, in grossly oversimplified, nonmathematical terms, DIPS ERA = ERA − BABIP, we can conclude that the pitching staffs for these winning teams succeed most notably at recording strong strikeout-to-walk ratios and keeping the ball in the park. In these elements, they're quite successful. In the missing component of traditional ERA, which is BABIP, they're only narrowly better than the herd.

One vital element that's not addressed in the seminal DIPS research is a pitcher's ground-ball/fly-ball tendencies. Whether a ball is lofted or skips through the infield grass has something to do with the hitter's proclivities, but the primary determinant is the pitcher. These tendencies also have a bearing in how a pitcher fares with balls in play. Ground-ball pitchers tend to yield higher batting averages on balls in play, but they also tend to allow a lower slugging percentage on balls in play. After all, other than the rare grounder that scoots down either foul line for extra bases, almost all ground balls that make it past the infield are singles. Additionally, ground ballers, as you'd expect, tend to give up far fewer homers than their fly-ball counterparts. Those with fly-ball tendencies often have balls hit to the outfield. These are generally turned into outs more often than infield grounders, but those that aren't can find the gaps, land beyond the reach of an outfielder, or turn into souvenirs. Broadly speaking, given equal skill sets, you'd rather have a ground-ball pitcher than one with fly-ball habits.

This brings us to how these 124 teams stack up against their less successful peers in generating ground balls. As it turns out, not too well. The teams I've studied, as a group and viewing staffs as a whole, posted a GB/FB ratio only 1.5 percent higher than the league average. Additionally, only a Calista Flockhart–thin majority of teams (63 of 124, or 50.8 percent) have bettered the league mean in GB/FB ratio. While having a staff that tends toward the ground-ball end of the continuum makes intuitive sense, winning teams in the modern era have barely and narrowly done so.

Ground-ball tendencies and having a potent one-two punch appear to be substantially less important than thriving, as a staff, in the statistical elements most under the absolute control of the pitcher alone.

One pitcher who time and again asserted himself as a veritable force for a playoff team is Pedro Martinez. By all rights, Martinez, for his part, deserves to make the above tandem list, but at all turns he was shanghaied by his less worthy wingmen. Between 1998, Martinez's first season in Boston, and 2003, the Red Sox made the playoffs three times. In those three seasons, Martinez has ranked fifth, first, and second, respectively, in all of baseball in SNLVAR. As for his help, Bret Saberhagen ranked 26th and 20th, respectively, in '98 and '99, and Derek Lowe ranked 65th in 2003. In analyzing Martinez's career, many will point to the 1999 season as his best ever. That has much to do with the fact that he went 23–4, pitched his team to the ALCS, won the Cy Young Award, and finished second in the MVP voting. However, his 2000 season was not only his personal best, it was also one of the best seasons in history by a starting pitcher.

In 2000 Martinez went 18–6, worked 217 innings, and posted a 1.74 ERA. In those 217 frames he struck out 284, walked only 32, and gave up only 17 homers. Martinez also paced the AL in 2000 in a heaving bevy of categories: ERA, shutouts (four), strikeouts, opponents' OBP (.213), opponents' SLG (.259), hits per nine innings (5.31), homers per nine innings (0.71), AVG vs. left-handed batters (.150), AVG vs. right-handed batters (.184), opponents' AVG with runners in scoring position (1.33), strikeout-to-walk ratio (8.9), and quality starts (25).

In an article I wrote for the *Baseball Research Journal* a few years ago, I explored how some of Martinez's 2000 numbers fared in historical terms. Here's some of what I found:

- As mentioned, Martinez's league-leading ERA was 1.74. Placing second in the AL that season was Roger Clemens with a comparatively lofty 3.70 ERA, more than twice Martinez's mark. In fact, Clemens's ERA is closer in number to the 35th-best ERA in 2000, which belonged to Rolando Arrojo, than it is to Martinez's. Never before has there been such a gap between the top two spots.

- Martinez's park-adjusted ERA was an implausible 192 percent better than the league average, the best such mark of the 20th century. (Yes, the year 2000 was, for doctrinaires of the calendar, part of the 20th century.)

- Martinez's opponents' batting average of .167 bests Luis Tiant's 1968 mark of .168 for tops all-time. Of course, Tiant's mark came in the "Year of the Pitcher," when the mammoth strike zone suppressed run-scoring levels to historic lows. In contrast, Martinez's mark came during a season in which the AL posted its third-highest league ERA of the 20th century.

- Martinez's 8.9 strikeout-to-walk ratio is the third-best mark of the century, behind only Bret Saberhagen's 11.0 gold standard of 1994 and Curt Schilling's 9.6 ratio in 2002.

- If we coin a stat called strikeout-to-walks + hits ratio, we find that Martinez's 1.8 is easily the best ever.

- Martinez's base runners per nine innings figure of 6.64 is the best ever.

- On the road in 2000, Martinez was 12–1 with a 1.66 ERA and .190 OBP allowed.

- In his six losses that season, Martinez had a 2.44 ERA, which, of course, still would have led the league by a comfortable margin. In fact, if we park-adjust his ERA *in only the games he lost that season* and compare it to the league average, it would rank in the top 30 all-time.

So yes, the signposts are everywhere: Martinez's 2000 season was probably the greatest ever by a pitcher. You can make a case for Tim Keefe's work back in 1880. However, in his day, the ball was larger and heavier, there was no groundskeeping to speak of, many parks had no outfield fences or barriers, pitchers delivered the ball from 50 feet, and batters wouldn't face overhand pitches for another four seasons. In other words, as sound and elucidating as our statistical contortions are, it's hard to put a great deal of faith in the translations when making comparisons to what was, in essence, a significantly different game. Moreover, Keefe worked only 105 innings that season. So with apologies to Mr. Keefe, I'm comfortable placing the single-season pitching laurel wreath on the head of Pedro Martinez.

How, then, did he manage not to win the MVP Award in 2000? The '99 AL MVP vote is generally regarded as being more controversial. That year Martinez, who won the Cy Young Award, garnered more first-place votes than Ranger catcher Ivan Rodriguez, the winner of the MVP. So how did he come up short? The answer is George King of the *New York Post* and La Velle Neal of the *Minneapolis Star Tribune*. These two voters left Martinez off their ballots entirely. Only Neal bothered to explain himself. "I feel a pitcher should just not be an MVP," Neal said. "To win that award, it should be someone who's out there every day battling for his team. It's nothing personal against Pedro."

Neal's sentiment has the foundations of sensibility, and it's a highly common one in mainstream circles. However, ideologies carried blindly to extremes serve only to make one look like a fool. Great hitters, in general, are more valuable than great pitchers, but that's not a hard-and-fast proclamation. King's and Neal's hijacking of the process not only wrenched the honors away from Martinez, but the voters also overlooked hitters more deserving than Rodriguez, such as Roberto Alomar, Manny Ramirez, and Nomar Garciaparra. In 2000, however, the real injustice occurred. Jason Giambi won the award, but Carlos Delgado and Alex Rodriguez were both more valuable. Martinez, however, was more valuable than anyone. Take the misleading luster of 20 wins and better teammates away from him, and, despite having the forces of history behind his season, Martinez finishes fifth in the MVP voting, not garnering a single first-place nod. The work he did over the span of that remarkable year deserves better.

CHAPTER 3

The Glove Man

(or, There Are Worse Things Than Making Errors)

As previously detailed, in terms of run prevention the process of decoupling what's attributable to pitching and what's attributable to fielding is sometimes freighted with difficulties. In the embryonic days of modern statistical analysis, it was acceptable to dismiss defense as a minor part of the game. John Thorn and Pete Palmer, writing in *The Hidden Game of Baseball*, first published in 1984, surmise that defense accounts for 6 to 15 percent of the game, depending on the year. This faulty notion became fashionably subversive in 1990s, and many stathead circles began rather loudly denouncing the importance of team defense. This results in something I like to call the "Skateboarder's Paradox," whereby conformity and nonconformity, at a certain point, become indistinguishable. What was once edgy is now banal, and no one's exactly sure at what point the change occurred. But there it is.

Billy Beane's early teams in Oakland embodied the belief that defense was of tertiary import (for instance, the '99 A's had the torpid likes of Ben Grieve and Matt Stairs manning the outfield corners), and Michael Lewis's *Moneyball* shed further light on Beane's seeming affection for endomorphs. This was certainly true at the time, but the "fat guy" approach was a fleeting meme in Oakland. The more contemporary—and more successful—A's teams have been crafted with a high regard for team defense. In recent seasons, Beane's decisions to acquire and/or heavily deploy players such as Chris Singleton, Mark Kotsay, Mark Ellis, Scott Hatteberg, and Damian Miller were, to a large degree, motivated by a desire to buttress the team's fielding capabilities.

When ruminating on the success of the A's, many will drone on in tedious M.B.A. patois about "undervalued commodities" and "corrected markets" and the like. In my opinion, this betrays a Ptolemy-like misunderstanding of how Oakland has evolved as an organization. I think the changes you've seen in the way the A's have made personnel decisions have more to do with comfort levels and a connoisseurish obsession with details than with ballplayer P/E ratios or finding "virgin timber." By that I mean that as Oakland has cultivated a better understanding of how to quantify and project defensive performance, they've become more willing to make million-dollar decisions in the name of good fielding. In the late '90s they very much had a handle on evaluating offensive performance (back when "OBP = good" was still a rousing and provocative idea), and they acquired players who fared well according to their chosen metrics. Now the A's have a great deal of faith in their proprietary system of evaluating defense, and it informs many of their decisions. Oakland is now a team that cares little for the tragicomic defensive stylings of someone they can't stow away at DH, and that, I believe, is because they now trust that they can identify good glove men better than other organizations can. It's not because the market for talent gives short shrift to capable defenders. If you don't believe me, just ask me.

There always has been and probably always will be a peculiar opacity in the nature of pitching and defense. However, as the work of Voros McCracken, for all its flaws, has shown, fielding has more to do with run prevention than most of us thought. The thing to realize is this: every ball in play (i.e., any batted ball that's not a home run or fouled out of play) is a potential out for the defense. Whether they make those outs by way of positioning, range, or sure-handedness is immaterial; just make the out. As such, it's sensible to evaluate defense on the team level by examining how proficient said team is at converting batted balls into outs. By and large, this isn't what we do.

Most often, analysts of most stripes judge a player's defense by looking at his fielding percentage, which, of course, depends upon his error totals. This is a flawed method of assessing defense. A high fielding percentage is a good thing, but it's not an all-encompassing touchstone of defensive excellence.

The assigning of errors by official scorekeepers is also problematic. What's an error under one set of conditions isn't under other conditions. The foibles of the human eye, scorer bias, amorphous mandates from the rule book, and other factors make it a highly irregular process. Of course, on some plays (e.g., a harmless fly ball dropping lamely between two incommunicado outfielders) an error, by rule, isn't assigned even though there's no question that it was squarely a defensive lapse. Errors also don't account for fielding range. I could conceivably go out there and man shortstop while (lend me your blind credulity for a moment) putting up an error total within hailing distance of, say, mid-'80s Ozzie Smith. (In point of fact, I can't do this—even the "Plato's world of forms" version of myself couldn't do this—but work with me. Picture the nerdy kid in gym class dodgeball, diving away from every ball that comes at him.) However, what those comparable fielding percentages don't tell you is that Ozzie got to, oh, 500 more balls than I did during a season. Fielding range—or a defender's ability to put himself in position to make a play—is vitally important, yet fielding percentage is heedless of it. After all, you can't make an error on a ball you didn't even get to. The ability to make the routine plays, which is what fielding percentage measures, is certainly meaningful. However, without some mechanism to assess range, we don't have a way of making cogent evaluations of defensive performance. There's also evidence to suggest that the ability to avoid errors is unrelated to a defender's fielding range. It's often assumed that the more range one has, the more errors one is likely to make. This doesn't appear to be true, which suggests that the two skills are mutually exclusive. Sure-handedness is a virtue all its own, as is the ability to reach batted balls near and far. Assessing both skills is important in making judgments about a player's, or a team's, defensive aptitude.

On the team level, we can do this with a Bill James concoction called defensive efficiency rating (DER), which is simply the percentage of balls in play that a team converts into outs. As addressed previously in this book, pitchers may have a limited amount of control over what becomes of a ball in play, but it's mostly the work of the defense and blind luck. As is the case with any other statistic, DER is prone to the mannerisms of the various playing environments. That's why all the DER numbers you're about to see will be park-adjusted, which is done by establishing a ratio of home DER to road DER for each team. Of our 124 teams, 67 (54.0 percent) finished with a park-adjusted DER of better than league average, 54 (43.5 percent) finished worse than league average, and three (2.4 percent) were at exactly league average. In the aggregate, these playoff teams have an average park-adjusted DER that's 1.1 percent better than the league mean.

As you can see, most successful teams have been better than the league mean in terms of defense, but the correlation isn't a jaw-dropping one. So, summarily speaking, a strong team defense is common among winning ball clubs, but other elements of the game are more important.

So what does an Oreck-quality defense look like? To explore this question, let's look at the best team defenses in terms of percentage of the park-adjusted, league-average DER:

Ranking	Team	Percentage of Adjusted League DER
1.	'99 Mets	104.2
2.	'91 Blue Jays	104.1
2.	'84 Padres	104.1
4.	'98 Red Sox	103.7
5.	'93 Braves	103.4
6.	'02 Angels	103.2
7.	'01 Mariners	103.0
8.	'98 Braves	102.8
8.	'99 Red Sox	102.8
10.	'03 Giants	102.6

The '99 Mets were conspicuous in their defensive excellence, breaking the '64 Orioles' record for fewest infield errors in a season, with only 33 misplays for the entire year. We've already detailed the evaluative weaknesses of errors and fielding percentage, but in the case of the '99 Mets they also excelled at other aspects of defense. As such, they rank, according to park-adjusted DER relative to the league, as the best-fielding team of any I've studied.

Third baseman Robin Ventura claimed one of the team's two Gold Gloves that season and the sixth and final one of his career. According to fielding runs above average (FRAA), which is a *Baseball Prospectus* measure that evaluates a player's defense, Ventura's '99 season was one of his best ever with the glove. That year, his first after signing a free agent contract with the Mets the previous winter, Ventura batted .301/.379/.529, which made him the third most productive third baseman in baseball that year, behind only Chipper Jones and Fernando Tatis. Throw in Ventura's defensive contributions, and he's second only to Chipper. It was likely the best single-season performance by a third baseman in Met franchise history.

By the time the White Sox drafted Ventura with the tenth overall pick of the 1988 draft (behind talents such as Bill Bene, Monty Fariss, Willie Ansley, and Ty Griffin), he was already a collegiate baseball pantheon dweller. At Oklahoma State, Ventura logged a 58-game hitting streak during his junior season and set the school record for career hits despite playing only three seasons in Stillwater. The summer after his junior year, he batted .409 in the Seoul Olympics and led the U.S. team to a gold medal. For his efforts, *Baseball America* named him their College Player of the Decade for the 1980s and tabbed him as the third baseman on their All-Time College All-Star Team. Needless to say, by the time he arrived in Chicago after only one season at Double-A Birmingham, he was already a much-ballyhooed talent. However, he struggled early. During his rookie season, Ventura abided a ghastly 0-for-41 cold streak that saw him go hitless in 16 straight games. On the season, he slugged only .318 and, according to VORP, ranked as the next-to-worst qualifying third baseman in the AL (only Minnesota's Gary Gaetti was less delectable). Even so, Ventura was already putting up impressive defensive numbers, and the next season his offensive game began to improve.

In '91, his second season in the bigs, Ventura won AL Player of the Month for July, claimed his first Gold Glove, smacked 23 homers, and drew 80 walks. The following season was another fine one for him. His numbers on a raw level (.282/.375/.431, 16 homers) may not appear especially strong at first blush, but this was 1992—one year before offensive levels would drastically increase. It was the best season of Ventura's career with the glove, and he claimed his second Gold Glove and was selected to the first of his two career All-Star Games (he had two hits in the midsummer classic, which occurred on his 25th birthday).

In 1993 he earned headlines of another sort. During a game in Arlington on August 4, Ventura charged the mound after taking a 96-mph fastball in the back. Pretty pedestrian stuff on most days, but on the mound was Nolan Ryan—homespun, ageless (stupendously over-rated), and wildly popular in his native Texas. Ryan deftly caught the onrushing Ventura in a firm headlock and, to hear the adoring media tell it, ferociously pummeled some respect into him. To hear the highlights tell it, he sprinkled Ventura with a few dainty schoolyard noogies. Of course, that doesn't square with the prevailing idolatry of "Sheriff Ryan," so it'll forevermore be reprised as the story of how Ventura got his ass whupped up on. Ah, well . . .

The 1996 season was another fine one for Ventura. That year he slugged .520; clouted 67 extra-base hits; drew 78 walks; and, sayeth VORP, finished behind Jim Thome as the best offensive third baseman in the junior circuit. In 1999 Ventura, besides anchoring the best team defense in recent history, provided the Mets with one of their most cherished postseason moments. In game five of the NLCS against the Braves (a series the Mets would eventually lose in six games), Ventura launched a 15th-inning walk-off grand slam. However, that grand slam was but an RBI single in the box score, as Ventura's jubilant teammates swarmed him at second base, and he never made it home.

Speaking of grand slams, Ventura ended his career after the 2004 season with 18 in his career, which ties Hall of Famer Willie McCovey for third on the all-time list, trailing only Eddie Murray and Lou Gehrig. Ventura also ranks tenth all time for career home runs by a third baseman.

First baseman John Olerud was also a critical member of the generally successful Met squads of the late '90s. Despite an early brush with tragedy, Olerud's promise as a young ballplayer was undeniable. At Washington State he was twice named NCAA Player of the Year by *Baseball America*, and he set single-season WSU records with a .462 average; 23 homers; and, on days when he pitched, a 15–0 record on the mound. However, Olerud almost lost his life to a brain aneurysm just prior to his senior season. As a result, for the rest of his career Olerud, as a protective measure that became a grim calling card of sorts, would wear his batting helmet while in the field. Even so, Olerud convalesced in time for a strong senior season, and the Toronto Blue Jays made him their third-round pick of the 1989 draft. If not for those serious health concerns, Olerud surely would have been a high first-rounder.

Nevertheless, Olerud became, at that time, only the 16th player since the draft was instituted in 1965 to go from the amateur ranks to the majors without playing a single game in the minor leagues. By '92 he was entrenched as the Jays' starting first baseman, and was the fourth best in the league at his position in offensive production. The Jays, of course, won the World Series that season, and en route Olerud batted .365 and slugged .565 in the ALCS win over Oakland. The next season, however, Olerud would become a star. In '93 he garnered attention for chasing a .400 average for much of the season. In fact, on August 2, a 1-for-4 day in the Bronx left his average at exactly .400. It would be the last time he'd see .400 that season. The next day, still facing the Yankees, Olerud went hitless in three at-bats, dipping his average to .397.

It was nevertheless a season for the ages. For the year, Olerud batted .363 AVG/.473 OBP/.599 SLG, claimed the batting title, paced the AL in OBP, and ranked fourth in SLG. Additionally, his 54 doubles led the majors, and he also bested the league in times on base. According to VORP, he was the most productive hitter in the AL (and second to only Barry Bonds in the majors), and with the glove Olerud saved eight runs more than the average first baseman. He also became only the 20th player in major league to history to rack up at least 200 hits and 100 walks in the same season. In spite of those extraordinary numbers (all put up on the AL's best team during the regular season), Olerud somehow managed to finish behind Frank Thomas and teammate Paul Molitor in the race for AL MVP. He was better than both.

The Jays, perhaps tantalized by Olerud's numbers of '93, began to fiddle with his hitting mechanics in the hopes that he'd become more of a pull hitter. Over the next three seasons he continued to display strong on-base skills, play good defense, and hit for gap power; however, he never evolved into the 30-homer force the team hoped he'd be. In part because he had failed to reach the heights of his '93 campaign, in part because they failed to recognize his other merits, and in part because of his $6.5-million salary, Toronto began to sour on him. So at the '96 winter meetings GM Gord Ash sent Olerud (and enough cash to defray the cost of much of his salary) to the Mets for boiler-plate righthander Robert Person. Jays manager Cito Gaston even went so far as to predict that the soft-spoken and introverted Olerud (who was tongue-in-cheekly nicknamed "Gabby" by his teammates) would wilt under the jewelry appraiser's scrutiny of the New York media and wind up retiring. Well, in roughly a season's worth of work spread over three years, Person would allow more than 6½ runs per game as a Blue Jay, while Olerud would not only dodge an early pension but also renaissance nicely in Gotham. Not only that, but Olerud, miracle of miracles, seemed to enjoy playing in New York. He rented an apart-ment on the Upper East Side, regularly took in the opera and theater, and even cultivated a salty rapport with the media.

In his first season as a Met, Olerud posted a .400 OBP for the first time since '93, and he lashed 34 doubles and 22 homers. The next year, as the Mets posted back-to-back winning seasons for the first time in almost a decade, he had what still stands as the second-best season of his career. Despite playing half his games in hitter-unfriendly Shea, Olerud mashed to the tune of .354 AVG/.447 OBP/.551 SLG, finishing second to Larry Walker (who, in contrast, spent half his time on Planet Coors) for the batting title and second to Mark McGwire in OBP. Incidentally, his .354 average broke Cleon Jones's franchise record (.340 in 1969), and Olerud just missed another 200-hit, 100-walk season.

The following season, Olerud's AVG and SLG took a dive (though not below acceptable levels), but his OBP of .427 was good for fifth in the NL. With the leather, Olerud, according to FRAA, had one of the best seasons of his career. Olerud, as men-tioned, was long regarded as an especially capable glove man. Of course, he's a first baseman, which, we're generally told, is the least important defensive position on the diamond. That's certainly true in terms of how many balls are hit within the fielding zones of first base-men, but it neglects an important element of the job: fielding bad throws. Certainly, putout totals are available for first basemen, but what those numbers don't reflect is how adept a first baseman is at fielding poor throws from other infielders and, in effect, turning errors into outs. Olerud was particularly adept at this. One admittedly flawed and somewhat crude way to assess his skills in this regard is to examine error totals for the other infielders before, during, and after his tenure as a Met.

Since Olerud spent three seasons with the Mets, let's break the categories down into three-year spans and look at the error patterns for Met second basemen, third basemen, and shortstops (those who are most often making throws to first):

Period	Total Errors by 2B, 3B, SS
Before (1994–1996)	192
During (1997–1999)	129
After (2000–2002)	181

The "Before" period covers the three seasons prior to Olerud's arrival, the "During" period comprises his years as a Met, and "After" includes the trio of seasons following his departure for Seattle. As I said, this method of evaluating a first baseman's "scoopabilities" is somewhat problematic. To wit, throwing errors aren't isolated from other kinds of errors, and changes in personnel (other than Olerud) aren't accounted for. Still, the differences are stark enough that it's safe to assume Olerud was making a substantial impact in terms of rescuing his fellow infielders from throwing errors. Note in particular that non–first base infield errors decreased by 32.8 percent after Olerud arrived on the scene. Now consider that the 1994 labor stoppage, which affected the '94 and '95 seasons, means that the "Before" period contains a substantially smaller sample of games played. Nevertheless, the "During" period saw 63 *fewer* 2B/3B/SS errors despite the fact that the Mets played 68 *more* games over that span. Furthermore, once Olerud ceased to be a Queenslander, those same error totals trampolined once again.

Olerud anguished over the decision to leave the Mets, but ultimately the three-year, $20 million offer made by the Mariners and the prospect of being near his wife, son, and parents were too much to resist. Back in Seattle, where he was reunited with college teammate Aaron Sele, Olerud continued to hit for adequate power, get on base, and play sound defense, at least for his first three seasons as a Mariner.

. . .

The 1984 San Diego Padres won 92 games, a modest total for a World Series team, but because no other team in the NL West managed a winning season, they breezed to the division flag by 12 games over the second-place Braves. The Padres were a balanced ball club that season, finishing fourth in the NL in runs scored and fifth in runs allowed. The team ERA was a fairly nifty 3.48, but among senior circuit clubs, only the Cardinals' staff struck out fewer batters. (For instance, fourth starter Mark Thurmond in $178\frac{2}{3}$ innings that season struck out only 57 batters—an unthinkably low total for a regular member of a rotation pitching in the modern era.) That means Padre pitchers were surrendering quite a few balls in play, and Padre fielders were turning a high percentage of those balls into outs.

No '84 Padre won a Gold Glove that season, but the club did boast two aging defensive warhorses, first baseman Steve Garvey and third baseman Graig Nettles, and a future one in young right fielder Tony Gwynn.

Born in Tampa, Garvey was the grandson of a Brooklyn native and ardent Dodger supporter. His father would drive the Dodger team bus while the club was in spring training at nearby Vero Beach, and the younger Garvey would tag along. A Dodger from the womb, it seemed. Garvey wound up at Michigan State on a dual football-baseball scholarship and graduated with a bachelor's degree in education. According to divine plan, the Dodgers chose him in the secondary phase of the 1968 draft. While his new teammates were inelegantly decked out in T-shirts and jeans, Garvey showed up at the rookie league facilities in Ogden, Utah, in a suit and tie, signed autographs, and even kissed grandmothers and babies. His catalog-model good looks, preponderant smarminess, and seeming embrace of those very traits set debutante hearts athrob and earned him the nicknames "Senator" and "Mr. Clean." (Only later would the tawdry appropriateness of the former and the bald irony of the latter be revealed.)

By late 1970, Garvey had arrived in Los Angeles as the Dodgers' starting third baseman. However, he struggled defensively, and by 1973 his already poor throwing arm in tandem with a serious injury to his right shoulder forced him across the diamond. There, mostly because of his penchant for avoiding errors, he crafted a reputation as a stellar defender, winning four straight Gold Gloves from 1974 through 1977. Deserved? He was certainly a master of the routine play. Garvey went the entire '84 season in San Diego without committing an error and set major league records for first basemen by playing 193 straight games without an error and logging a career fielding percentage of .996. On the downside, Garvey was famously reluctant to throw to second base on force attempts, and he almost never lobbed a fielded ball to the pitcher covering first, instead preferring to beat the runner to the bag with ball in hand. The latter presumably wouldn't be a glaring negative; however, most infield coaches prefer that their first baseman make such throws so the pitcher gets in the habit of covering first any time a ball is hit to the right side of the infield. Otherwise the pitcher might not be there when he's truly needed.

As for the former shortcoming—Garvey's preternatural reluctance to make throws on potential force plays at other bases—it's an important one. Bill James, in his 2002 book *Win Shares*, observes that whenever a first baseman notches an assist by throwing to someone other than the pitcher, it's almost always a vital play. In 3–4 assists, he's likely fielding a bunt and snuffing out the lead runner. In the instance of the 3–6 assist, he's most often cutting down the man going to second, thus keeping a runner out of scoring position and getting an out and perhaps starting a double play. If it's a 3–5 assist, he's doing the same, except the extinguished runner otherwise would have been at third. When you see a 3–2 assist in the books, the first baseman's throw has turned a run into an out. In terms of making these essential plays, Garvey was notoriously lacking. James points to a study by researcher Mike Emeigh, who found that Keith Hernandez, who was famous for his abundant skills in this regard, fielded a ground ball with a runner on first and fewer than two outs on 206 occasions from 1979 through 1983. Hernandez managed to start a double play 49 times (or 24 percent of the time) under those conditions. Garvey, meanwhile, had that identical opportunity 113 times over the same five-year span and managed to start only three 3–6–3 twin killings, or just 2.7 percent of the time—a terrible figure. Additional research by James finds that Garvey ranked at or near the bottom of the league in first-base assists minus pitcher putouts (an approximation of first-base assists to second base, third base, and home plate) from 1975 through 1985. The conclusion is that while Garvey was an adroit defender in terms of making routine fielding plays, he nevertheless had a serious deficiency in his defensive game: he couldn't throw and, as a result, cost his teams valuable outs.

Overrated defender or not, Garvey was entrenched in L.A. Along with Ron Cey, Bill Russell, and Davey Lopes, Garvey became part of the longest-running infield in major league history, as each player manned his respective position as a starter from 1973 to 1981. Garvey's carefully guarded image also paid off with the lucre of popularity. In 1973 he became the first player to start an All-Star game as a write-in selection, in '78 he became the first player to receive 4 million All-Star votes, and in Southern California they even named a junior high school after him while he was still an active player. Yes: a junior high. While he was still playing.

Obscuring Garvey's offensive abilities were the era and park he played in. Dodger Stadium of the '70s and '80s was squarely a run-suppressing environment, but Garvey nonetheless put up quality numbers from time to time. On the other hand, Garvey, somewhat counterintuitively, put up notably better power numbers at home for the latter part of his Dodger career. In '80 and '81, for instance, Garvey slugged, respectively, .406 and .403 on the road—not the kind of power numbers you want from a first baseman regardless of what contextual adjustments go in his favor. Garvey never slugged .500 for a full season, but he did log at least 200 hits in six of seven seasons from 1974 to 1980. His most glaring weakness, however, was his lack of plate discipline. His career high for walks in a season was 50 in 1976, and 11 of those were intentional. In '79, Garvey managed to play all 162 games while drawing only 21 unintentional walks. Three seasons later, Garvey again played in every game and drew only 10 (!) unintentional walks for the entire year. Rare is the hitter who can thrive with such a lack of selectivity at the plate.

As Garvey aged and his ability to hit for average and power began to wither, he didn't have the complementary skills to remain a productive player. In '84, the season of interest, he hit a measly .284 AVG/.307 OBP/.373 SLG and, according to VORP, was the least productive qualifying first baseman in the NL. Still, in game four of the NLCS, with the Padres facing elimination against the Cubs, Garvey drove in five runs, including a two-run, ninth-inning bomb off Cubs closer Lee Smith. Garvey made marginal improvements in '85, but the following year his OBP dropped to .284. A shoulder injury and lapsing numbers forced him into retirement in '87.

Off the field, Garvey was also caught in a spiral of decline. Late in his Dodger days, he and pitcher Don Sutton brawled in the clubhouse after Sutton insulted Garvey's wife, Cyndi. The couple would later divorce, and Garvey would be further embarrassed by his ex-wife's wonderfully indiscreet book about their relationship. Tax problems followed, and then came the stunning revelation that "Mr. Clean" had fathered a handful of illegitimate children. While Garvey's oat-sowing wasn't enough to make Bob Marley look like the avatar of Victorian reserve, it still came as quite a shock. Garvey's carefully guarded yet crumbling public image endured another blow when his second wife, Candace, filed for separation, citing years of harassment by the first Mrs. Garvey. To top it off, Garvey's once seriously regarded Hall of Fame candidacy (deservedly) foundered. On the upside, the Ninth U.S. Circuit Court of Appeals in 2000 overruled a previous arbitration decision and awarded Garvey $3 million—his overdue share of the penalty owners paid for their collusive efforts in the '80s.

Third baseman Graig Nettles was another veteran glove man on the '84 Pads. "Puff," as he was called, was a fourth-round choice of the Twins out of San Diego State in 1965—the first such draft in baseball history. After being called up to Minnesota in '67, he played only sparingly in his three seasons as a Twin and spent most of his time in the outfield (in deference to third baseman Harmon Killebrew). At the '69 winter meetings, the Twins packaged Nettles with outfielder Ted Uhlaender and pitchers Dean Chance and Bob Miller to the Indians for righthanders Luis Tiant and Stan Williams.

In Cleveland, Nettles would settle in as the team's regular third baseman and tally 71 homers in three seasons. He also emerged as a top defender. In 1971, his second year with the Tribe, Nettles set the AL records for assists and double plays by a third baseman. The following season he again paced the league in assists. That combination of power and defense made Nettles a commodity, and the Indians, coming off a fourth consecutive losing season, cashed him in. In the winter of '72, they sent Nettles and reserve catcher Jerry Moses to the Yankees for four hitting prospects—John Ellis, Jerry Kenney, Charlie Spikes, and Rusty Torres. None would achieve anything of consequence at the highest level.

Nettles, meanwhile, became a star in New York. His deft glovework at third, timely power, and self-deprecating wit (his vanity license plate read "E-5") all played quite well in baseball's largest market. His first season as a Yankee, however, was a bit of a struggle. Superficial difficulties at the plate (fans and media fixated on his .234 batting average) along with some fits and starts with the glove made Nettles look like a bust. Two homers against the Royals in the ALCS helped his cause, and the following season he curried further favor with Yankee fans by smashing 11 homers in April (including four against the Tigers in an April 14 doubleheader). On September 14 of that same year, Nettles and younger sibling Jim became only the fourth pair of brothers in major league history to homer in the same game. In 1976, his fourth season with the Bombers, Nettles, taking advantage of the user-friendly right-field porch in Yankee Stadium, became one of only four third basemen in history to lead the AL in home runs (Bill Melton, Al Rosen, and Frank Baker were the others). Thanks in large part to Nettles' production, the Yanks won their first pennant in 12 years. The following season, Nettles would win his first Gold Glove and put up the best offensive numbers of his career. He batted only .255, but he supplemented that low average with a career-high 37 homers (second only to Jim Rice's 39 that season) and 68 walks. As for the team, the Yankees claimed their first World Series title since 1962.

In '78, Nettles put up another strong season at the plate and claimed the second and final Gold Glove of his career. However, he's most remembered for his World Series glovework that year and an LCS brawl with George Brett of the Royals. In game four of the ALCS at Yankee Stadium, Brett slid hard into third after smacking a triple, tumbling Nettles on top of him. As the two players untangled, Brett gave Nettles an elbow to the head, and Nettles responded by kicking Brett in the face. Then the punches flew. In the resulting scrum, however, Brett was spared further abuse by, of all people, gruff Yankee captain Thurman Munson. "Graig [Nettles] and I are throwing haymakers at each other, and the next thing I know I'm on the bottom," Brett remembered. "And Thurman is lying on top of me with his catching gear on and saying, 'Don't worry, George. I won't let anybody hit you when you're down.' And he didn't."

If Nettles showed the requisite grit in the LCS, then in the World Series his grace afield was on vivid display. With the Yankees down two games to none to the Dodgers, Nettles made four stunning plays in the field, twice pilfering hits from Reggie Smith. The Yankees rallied to win four straight and their second consecutive World Series. In 1980, Nettles was diagnosed with hepatitis and played in only 89 games on the season. However, he returned in time to play in the Yankees' loss to the Royals in the ALCS. The publication of Nettles' fittingly titled book *Balls*, in which he candidly blistered owner George Steinbrenner and several of his managers and teammates, helped him fall into gradual disfavor in the Bronx. In spring training of '84, the Yankees sent him to the Padres for pitcher Dennis Rasmussen and prospect Darin Cloninger, who would never make the majors. In San Diego, Nettles rejoined former Yankee teammate Goose Gossage, who had signed a free-agent contract with the Padres that January.

Nettles was a central, if not vitally important, part of the pennant-winning Padres in '84. His numbers rebounded in '85, as he set a career high for walks and tallied 39 extra-base hits in 137 games of action. Two years later, the Padres cut him loose, and Nettles had pinch-hitting tours of duty with the Braves and Expos before retiring after the 1988 season. He retired with 319 homers as a third baseman, an American League record for the position, and 390 total for his career.

It may surprise some to see two Red Sox teams on the above list. In searching for reasons to explain the franchise's serialized failures, a historic collection of supposedly poor defenses is often pointed to. However, this overlooks the fact that Fenway is a tough park for fielders. To cite but one conspicuous feature of the park that hamstrings defenses, Fenway, more so than any other venue, produces balls in play that can't possibly be fielded. The famous Green Monster in left field stretches 37 feet above the playing surface and runs 240 feet long. Because of the Monster's lofty height, balls quite often parabola off of it, making contact far out of the reach of fielders. In other parks, quite a number of these balls would be either flyouts or home runs—either helping or not affecting DER numbers. Things as they are, however, these unplayable balls get counted against the Red Sox defenses, at least until DER is adjusted for park effects. Once those adjustments are made, the team fares better.

Even so, glancing over the roster of the '98 Red Sox, we find a team peopled with many notional defensive liabilities. Catcher Scott Hatteberg would eventually be forced to vacate the position because of his poor throwing arm. First baseman Mo Vaughn was an excellent hitter in his prime, but he played defense like an ice sculpture. Nomar Garciaparra is a player of many merits, but his defense was mediocre at best. So how'd they do it? For starters, when dealing with DER, it's impossible to remove completely luck and whatever rimming influence pitchers have over balls in play from the calculus. So there's some of that involved. However, the Red Sox also had a particularly skilled defensive arrangement in the outfield that season. Darren Lewis was not an accomplished hitter, but he could pick it in center (four years earlier, he won a Gold Glove as a Giant). And Darren Bragg, the primary right fielder for Boston that season, was for most of his career a reasonably accomplished fourth outfielder and was coming off a season in which he logged 118 games in center. In essence, the Red Sox regularly started two center fielders in 1998.

This "hydra-headed center fielder" approach appears to be a fairly common one among great defensive teams. Of the ten best park-adjusted DER teams listed above, all ten of them followed this approach by deploying a pair of "true" center fielders in the outfield. All ten of them.

Range in the outfield is important. Whereas most hits through the infield result in singles, those that find the outfield gaps often go for extra bases. A fleet-footed outfield corps affords much flexibility in terms of positioning. Those who get great reads or have the wheels to compensate can play shallower to cut down on bloop singles and effectively reduce doubles and triples by winnowing down the gaps with their exceptional range. This is especially critical if a team's staff has fly ball tendencies.

The '99 Mets used Brian McRae/Darryl Hamilton and Roger Cedeno (to be fair, it's somewhat charitable to refer to Cedeno as a center fielder, despite the fact that he played a number of games there in his career). The '91 Jays had Devon White in center and manning right was Joe Carter, who, in the three previous seasons, had played a total of 370 games in center. The '84 Padres had Kevin McReynolds in center and in right a young, svelte Tony Gwynn, who would see occasional time in center over the next decade. In 1993 the Braves had Otis Nixon in center (with a chaser of Deion Sanders) and Ron Gant in left. Two years prior, Gant had been the everyday center fielder for the first Braves team to win the pennant since 1958.

In 2002, the Angels' center fielder was Darin Erstad, who had one of the great individual defensive seasons of all time, while Garret Anderson, who was the club's primary center fielder in 1999, 2000, and 2004, patrolled left. For the 2001 season, the record-abusing Mariners had Gold Glove winner Mike Cameron in center and Gold Glove winner Ichiro Suzuki in right. Ichiro, of course, was an accomplished center fielder in Japan before signing with Seattle prior to the '01 campaign. The Braves of '98 boasted the inestimable Andruw Jones up the middle, and Michael Tucker, who saw spot duty in center for years, was in right. The '99 Red Sox had Darren Lewis back in center and Trot Nixon, who two years later would play 70 games in center, in right field. Finally, the 2003 Giants had Marquis Grissom in center and Michael Tucker in right.

Let's frame this trend another way and see what we can learn from the worst teams, in terms of fielding, in the study population. Among these teams, you'll find a number of squads famous for punishing the ball, which suggests that teams who can't field are often assembled with an eye toward offense. "If he hits, then we don't care about his glovework," the thinking probably goes. So now for the least competent defensive teams I've studied, ranked according to percentage of league-average, park-adjusted DER:

Ranking	Team	Percentage of Adjusted League DER
1.	'01 Yankees	96.6
2.	'83 Phillies	96.8
3.	'99 Rangers	97.0
4.	'98 Padres	97.2
5.	'01 Indians	97.3
5.	'87 Tigers	97.3
7.	'87 Giants	97.4
8.	'95 Mariners	97.5
9.	'00 A's	97.6
9.	'03 Marlins	97.6
9.	'02 Yankees	97.6

Going through these, we find that only four of 11 (36.4 percent) employed the dual-center fielder alignment. Those clubs are the '83 Phillies, '87 Tigers, '95 Mariners, and '03 Marlins. I'm certainly not going to suggest that such an arrangement is essential to winning (after all, every one of these teams was a winner), but the better defensive teams do seem to have this element in common. Ideally, they'd deploy the more skilled of the two in center, but that hasn't always been the case.

Little surprise to see the 2000 A's here with their outfield "defense" of Ben Grieve, Terrence Long, and Matt Stairs (tastes like . . . triples!). Two Yankee models make the 10-worst list, and a pair of others narrowly miss. Whenever the merits or demerits of the Yankee defense are discussed, shortstop Derek Jeter inevitably becomes the flash point. The mainstream media have long delighted in genuflecting before Jeter and his dowry of intangibles. At the other end of the continuum we have some of the shriller corners of the Sabermetric world who stay relentlessly on-message in pointing out what an awful defender he is, even when he makes an undeniably brilliant play. The mainstream viewpoint is informed mostly by subjective observation and regnant hero worship. The problems with the latter are obvious, but less so with the former. When we watch a defender make what appears to be a dazzling play afield, we don't know whether the play was genuinely brilliant or whether—because of a poor first step, faulty positioning, or inferior range—the play was at its heart a routine one made to shimmer falsely. Unless one is a gifted and seasoned observer, the eyes, in terms of evaluating defense, aren't to be trusted.

On the other side, many statistically inclined analysts pillory Jeter's defense because of how he fares in certain flawed defensive metrics. The reality, at least according to the more useful defensive statistics, is that Jeter is a below-average to solidly below-average defensive shortstop—certainly not the virtuoso he's made out to be, but he's not an outright abomination with the glove, either. In any case, Jeter has company in helping make the recent Yankee teams defensive train wrecks. According to Ultimate Zone Rating, which is a defensive statistic (and probably the best one currently at our disposal) invented by a brilliant researcher named Mitchel Lichtman, the Yankees have had problems at more than one key position of late. From 1999 to 2002, Jeter ranked as the worst regular or semiregular shortstop in baseball in terms of defense. (However, it should be noted that the Yankees in recent years have habitually shaded their third basemen and shortstops toward the middle of the diamond. This phenomenon certainly hurts Jeter in the sundry zone-based defensive measures.) Additionally, center fielder Bernie Williams shakes out as the fourth-worst at his position over that same span. Alfonso Soriano and Paul O'Neill, who were Yankee regulars for much of that time, also rank in the bottom tier of second basemen and right fielders, respectively. In some years, that's half the defensive unit that—to be frank and inelegant—sucks. As such, it's not surprising that the above list of forgettables is bookended by two Yankee models.

Despite being one of the teams that utilized the two-center fielder outfield, the '87 Detroit Tigers nevertheless rank as one of the worst defensive playoff teams since 1980. The team isn't remembered as one of the greats, mostly because of their ALCS loss in five games to the Twins, but the '87 Tigers won 98 games, the sixth-highest total in team history. The Tigers that season also had a number of the most historically neglected players in baseball. Actually, I'd say roughly half their lineup gets much less adoration than they should. That shortstop Alan Trammell and second baseman Lou Whitaker should be in the Hall of Fame is, in my mind, an ineluctable conclusion. This is especially the case once their offensive numbers are considered in light of the premium positions they played (and played well) and, to a lesser extent, the era in which they toiled. Trammell doesn't appear to have much of a prayer, and Whitaker, inexplicably, didn't receive enough support to stay on the ballot longer than a single year.

Here are Trammell's credentials: six-time All-Star, four Gold Gloves, World Series MVP in '84, and three times in the top 10 for AL MVP. Among shortstops, Trammell is in the top 10 for career hits, extra-base hits, home runs, and total bases. In Whitaker's case, he won three Gold Gloves and made the All-Star team for five consecutive years. Among second basemen, he ranks in the top 10 for career hits, extra-base hits, doubles, home runs, total bases, and walks. Trammell's case is modestly stronger, but both are Hall of Famers as far as I'm concerned. Of course, Trammell and Whitaker weren't the only overlooked Tigers on the '87 team.

Chet Lemon was a gifted center fielder for much of his career. By 1987 he was 32 and had lost a step, but he was still above average with the glove. A first-round choice of the A's in 1972, Lemon came to the pros as an infielder. In June of 1975, the A's traded their third baseman of the future along with lefty Dave Hamilton to the White Sox for veteran starter Stan Bahnsen and lefty reliever Skip Pitlock. It turned out to be one of the best swaps in White Sox history.

The organization, believing that Lemon's athleticism and instincts were best suited for center field, moved him there for good. By 1976 he was the White Sox's starter in center, fleetly patrolling the vast swaths of outfield green in Old Comiskey while his cap seemingly hovered over his far-reaching Afro. It was a wise transition for the team to foist upon the young ballplayer. In 1977 Lemon set the AL record for putouts by an outfielder (512) and chances for an outfielder (524). According to FRAA, Lemon graded out as no worse than an above-average center fielder for every season from 1976 through 1987. Lemon was also an underrated force with the bat. Although he spent most of his career in a pitcher's era and in a pitcher's park, Lemon's numbers hold up quite well, particularly by the standards of up-the-middle defenders. His chief skill was getting on base. In five seasons he batted at least .285. He also drew at least 50 walks in eight different seasons and finished in the top 10 in the AL for OBP in three different seasons, and Lemon currently ranks 17th on the all-time list for hit by pitches.

Additionally, Lemon clouted 215 homers in his career (thrice breaking the 20-home run mark for a season), and four times he ranked in the top 10 in the AL for doubles, leading the league in 1979 with 44 two-baggers. Lemon's best season was probably the strike-shortened '81 season, when the then two-time All-Star batted .302 AVG/.384 OBP/.491 SLG for the White Sox and, of course, provided excellent glovework at a critical position. Nevertheless, the White Sox traded Lemon, still only 26 years of age, to the Tigers for outfielder Steve Kemp. Kemp, the top overall pick of the 1976 draft and a player long yenned for because of his power potential, would founder away from Tiger Stadium, while Lemon would go on to have a number of productive seasons in Detroit.

For the 1982 season, Lemon's first with the Tigers, he agreed to move to right so the more popular—yet defensively inferior—Kirk Gibson could play center. However, the two wisely swapped positions beginning in '83. The 1984 Tigers, who started that season an astounding 35–5, were one of the great teams of all time, and that year Lemon made the All-Star squad for the third and final time of his career. In '84, Lemon hit .287 AVG/.357 OBP/.495 SLG and smacked 60 extra-base hits. In '87, when the Tigers returned to the postseason, "The Jet" chipped in with another fine offering: .277 AVG/.376 OBP/.481 SLG, 70 walks, and 20 homers. In the '84 playoffs, Lemon had struggled, but in the '87 ALCS, despite the losing effort, he hit two bombs and slugged .611 for the series. Injuries and age began to stem his production over the next three seasons, and he opted to retire following the 1990 campaign.

Lemon, like everyone else, retired to Florida, where he became a high school baseball coach in Eustis. He won a state championship at the school in 2003, but an especially vocal cabal of parents forced him to resign with (as of yet uncorroborated) allegations that Lemon recruited players from out of the district—a common yet forbidden practice in major prep athletics. Not long after leaving his coaching job, Lemon began to be pained by agonizing cramps in the muscles of his extremities. After navigating a maze of tests and specialists, Lemon was diagnosed with a rare hematological disorder that causes the body to produce too many red blood cells. Doctors were able to treat his disease into remission, but after a recurrence he underwent major surgery. Healthy once again, Lemon went on to head Florida's AAU baseball program.

Whereas Lemon was one of the most underrated players of his vintage, another '87 Tiger deserves to be mentioned, if not alongside, then just south of names such as Dick Allen, Bobby Grich, Bert Blyleven, Ron Santo, and Minnie Minoso as one of the most underrated in the annals of the game. That's Darrell Evans.

The A's originally drafted Evans in 1967, their final season before moving to Oakland from Kansas City; however, they lost him the following year to the Braves in the Rule 5 draft. (As an aside, Evans joins Roberto Clemente, George Bell, and Johan Santana as the most successful Rule 5 picks of all time.) It was a move that would pay off for Evans and the Braves. Although he would go on to hit 414 homers in his career, Evans, at the outset of his professional career, wasn't regarded as much of a power threat. However, once he was Braves property, they paired him with roving instructor and Hall of Fame slugger Eddie Mathews, and Evans's production soared. As Evans himself put it, "I was strong enough, but I didn't know how to pull the ball. Mathews taught me how to do it. . . . He did more for me than anyone else in my career."

By working with Evans on shifting his weight and rotating his hips at the proper time, Mathews taught him to yank the ball down the right-field line. Evans was also a deeply patient hitter, a habit that he credited to reading Ted Williams's hitting manifesto *The Science of Hitting*. (Probably also beneficial was that Evans began wearing contact lenses in 1971.) After three seasons of being ferried between Atlanta and the minors, Evans landed a regular role as the Braves' starting third baseman in 1972. During that season he batted only .254, but he padded that low average with 19 homers and 90 walks. The following season, Evans exploded. He played in every Braves game that season and mashed 41 homers, slugged .556, and led the league in walks. That year Evans, Davey Johnson, and Hank Aaron became the first trio of teammates to each hit at least 40 home runs in the same season. In his four years as a Brave regular, Evans totaled 107 home runs and twice topped the loop in bases on balls. He was on first base in 1974 when Aaron laced his historic 715th home run into the Atlanta–Fulton County Stadium bullpen just beyond the left-field wall. In spite of Evans's accomplishments and relative youth, the Braves in June of '76 packaged him along with infielder Marty Perez to the Giants for Willie Montanez, Craig Robinson, Mike Eden, and Jake Brown.

In San Francisco, Evans continued to play well, but Candlestick Park, with its swirling winds and mercurial weather patterns, was especially ill suited for his offensive game. Only once in his seven full years as a Giant did Evans hit more than 20 home runs in a season. He continued to draw walks and make consistent contact, but the power just wasn't there. This changed in 1983, his final season in San Francisco, when, at age 36, he tallied 30 homers (including three in one game against the Astros on June 15), set a career high with 29 doubles, and posted his highest SLG in a decade. Evans shifted to first base prior to the '83 season, so the slackened defensive responsibilities may have helped him rediscover his stroke. To hear Evans tell it, he recouped his chops at the plate after he and his wife sighted what they believed to be a UFO in the summer of '82. I don't know when exactly during that summer Evans spotted the UFO, which prevents me from obtaining accurate pre- and post-UFO statistical splits. All I have to go on is that Evans claimed he saw the UFO in the summer of 1982, but nevertheless . . .

His SLG in '82 peaked at .486 on April 19, which, as you are no doubt aware, is more than two months before the annual summer solstice on June 21. From that point, Evans's power numbers wavered on a general downward trend to his season-long SLG of .419. The autumnal equinox, which marks the end of summer and, in the Northern Hemisphere, occurs on about September 22, is also to be considered. Evans's post–summer solstice low SLG is .409, which occurred on June 22. That means, from that point forward, his SLG rose only 10 points the rest of the way. Hardly a quantum leap. By the time the season ended on October 3, autumn was already upon Evans. If the

"UFO as batting coach" theorem is to be believed, then one of two things must be true: one, the historians have it wrong and Evans's sighting actually occurred over the off-season; or, two, there's a lag time between the UFO's proffering of wisdom and the manifestation of its teachings at the plate. Failing either of those, we must conclude that Evans was at least temporarily dippy. Or, I suppose, it's possible he was broken out of his decade-long slump by a misidentified weather balloon. I'll bet on "temporarily dippy."

Nevertheless, Evans's career did turn around at that point. Eligible for free agency and his street cred as a slugger restored, Evans, over the winter, was pursued by a whopping 18 clubs. In the end, he inked with the Tigers and thus rescued himself from the number-choking tendencies of Candlestick. His first season in Detroit was a disappointment (Exhibit B against Coach UFO), but only in terms of personal performance, as the Tigers stormed to a World Series title. The following year, Evans launched 40 bombs and, at age 38, became the oldest player in major league history to win a home run title. In '86 he hit 29 homers, and the following season, for the team that appears on the above list, Evans broke Hank Sauer's record for most home runs by a player at age 40. In 1957, Sauer set the record with 26 as a Giant—their final year in New York. Thirty years later, Evans broke the record with 34 homers. His production declined significantly in '88, and after one final season in Atlanta, in 1989, Evans retired.

As for his defensive abilities, FRAA rates him as a very capable third baseman through '75 and then, for most seasons, narrowly above average through '80. By '83, when the Giants moved Evans to first base, he was very much in decline with the glove, so the shift seemed to be a sensible one. According to FRAA, Evans was a good fielder at first for almost the rest of his career. In '87 he rates as 11 runs—or more than a full win—better with the glove than the average AL first baseman that season.

As for why Evans hasn't been recognized as the near great he was, it has much to do with his flavor of production as a hitter. First, he never hit for high averages (Evans's .248 career batting average is the same, incidentally, as that of Graig Nettles), which is bound to get you ignored by those who don't know any better. As a result, Evans was sometimes thought to be a sloppy hitter. This is ridiculous on its face; he was a deeply patient batter who, for his career, walked almost 200 times more than he struck out. Still, Evans, despite his high OBPs and 400-plus homers, wasn't able to overcome the gaggle of stigmas that go along with a sub-.250 lifetime average. Second, he played on a number of lousy teams and only two clubs that made the postseason, which tends to sully one's reputation by association. Third, he spent more than a third of his career in San Francisco and half of those games in Candlestick, which served to dampen his numbers. Fourth, many of his best seasons occurred when his career should have been winding down and after some of his epitaphs and eulogies as a ballplayer had been written. I don't think Evans is a Hall of Famer, but he's earned more recognition than he seems to get. In any event, he'll probably never get the chance to make a Cooperstown acceptance speech and thank, among others, Eddie Mathews and a certain gracious spacecraft.

CHAPTER 4

The Closer

(or, Why the Old and the New Both Have It Right . . . and Wrong)

Not so many years ago, the relief ace was the one who entered the game during a middle- to late-inning crisis or when the starter began to falter and the score was close. The relief ace would regularly work multiple innings at a time, in situations the manager deemed most crucial. He often eclipsed the 100-inning mark in any given season, and he was used to snuff out rallies rather than tick off saves. "Firemen" these aces were called in the '60s and '70s, and larding their statistical records wasn't their raison d'être. If the game was in peril, save situation or not, firemen such as Goose Gossage, Sparky Lyle, and Tug McGraw would be called upon.

That's not the case now. Over the years, the fireman has become the closer—one whose primary job is to finish games rather than face whatever emergencies arise in the earlier innings. Now he works predominantly in save situations, thus reducing his innings load and his number of multi-inning outings. So it follows that the save has become synonymous with value in the eyes of many of the game's decision-makers. It's a puzzling trend, but it's one that has indisputably been de rigueur for several years. I say puzzling since any kind of objective analysis leads to the conclusion that though relief aces are more coveted than ever, their true value is not all that it could be.

Some especially heady teams realize this, and are taking steps to restore maximum value to the relief ace in particular and the bullpen in general. Still, the trend holds, and it's one the origins of which can be traced back to the afternoon of April 3, 1987.

It was on that date—just before opening day—that the Chicago Cubs traded an aging, stringy-haired starter who was coming off one of the worst seasons of his career, and whose coif and mustache made him look more like a bassist for a Foghat cover band than an elite professional athlete. Along with utility infielder Dan Rohn, the aging starter went to the Oakland A's for minor leaguers Brian Guinn, Dave Wilder, and Mark Leonette. The Cubs also agreed to pay a substantial portion of that aging starter's $3 million salary.

The pitcher in question was, of course, Dennis Eckersley, and those three prospects the Cubs received in return would never play a day in the majors. In what might pass for irony to a television reporter, Eckersley had shut out the A's in 1976 in his first start in the major leagues, for the Cleveland Indians. Now he himself was an Oakland Athletic.

"Eck" was nothing if not embattled and resilient. Traded from the Indians to the Red Sox at age 22, Eckersley told his young wife that they were moving to Boston, but his wife, already disillusioned by the peripatetic life of ballplayer, instead filed for divorce. Years later, in Chicago, Eck was waylaid by a shoulder injury and a grievous drinking problem. But he beat both. By 1987 it looked like the music was swelling on his fine, but not stellar, career as a starting pitcher.

Once in Oakland, Eckersley made only two starts before a sore arm sidelined reliever Jay Howell. At the behest of manager Tony La Russa, Eckersley then began a transition that would turn what should have been his swan song as a ballplayer into a lengthy succoring of his Hall of Fame credentials. He became a reliever.

In the beginning, he worked as a long reliever—the neglected middle child of the major league bullpen—but by the 1988 season he was La Russa's closer. Eck's unassailably brilliant pitching (thanks mostly to his legendary slider) over the next few seasons in tandem with La Russa's new usage schema would revolutionize the closer role. What La Russa did, and what no other manager before him had done, was deploy his closer with strict adherence to the dictates of the save rule.

You might think the save is about as old as baseball itself. You'd be wrong. Chicago sportswriter Jerome Holtzman concocted it in 1960 to reward the reliever who enters the game with tying or go-ahead runs on base or at bat and finishes with the lead intact. In 1975, the truly modern notion of the save was implemented. Since then, a pitcher earns a save when he, one, finishes a game won by his team, two, is not the winning pitcher, and three, meets one of the following criteria: (a) enters the game with a lead of no greater than three runs, and pitches one complete inning, (b) enters the game with the possible tying run on base, at bat or on deck, or (c) pitches effectively for at least three innings.

La Russa used Eckersley in keeping with all the aforementioned conditions, save for 3c. The idea was that Eckersley—or any relief pitcher, for that matter—could better perform with tightly structured roles and predictable workloads. No three innings for Eck. And without blurring the edges of causation and correlation, it's apparent that Eck did indeed thrive in this role. La Russa thus changed the way managers handled their bullpens. But was he right?

Eckersley was Oakland's closer for its 1988, '89, '90, and '92 playoff teams. In those four seasons he led the AL in saves twice and finished second once and third once. Combine a team that wins a lot of games with La Russa's by-the-book closer usage, and that's almost bound to happen. Eckersley's nominal pinnacle came in 1992, when he became only the third AL reliever ever to win both the Cy Young and MVP awards. While he was truly great that season, 1992 was plainly not his best year as the A's closer. That was 1990. In '90 Eck pitched $73\frac{1}{3}$ innings, logged 48 saves, and posted a sublime ERA of 0.61. Moreover, his strikeout-to-walk ratio of 18.25 was outrageously strong, and his park-adjusted ERA was an unthinkable 506 percent better than the league average. The latter mark is the best of any of the 124 closers studied here, and the former mark is outdone (narrowly) by only Eck himself in the prior season. Baseball's trophy-giving habits are often approximated by the motion picture industry's Thalberg Award—sorry it's taken so long for us to get around to recognizing you; here's your award. Insofar as it *was* an inferior season, that and two additional saves are probably what garnered Eck all his 1992 plaudits.

Of course, he wouldn't have deserved it in 1990, either. Closers, no matter how highly leveraged their innings may be, simply don't do enough in the way of preventing runs to ever justify MVP honors. They just don't pitch enough; it's the nature of the relief pitching in general and the modern closer in particular. La Russa may have revolutionized the closer role, but some revolutions are better left in the penumbras of the imagination (see also Cuba, Chile).

Still, credit where credit is due. Piecemeal changes in the use of relief aces had begun even before Eck was dealt to Oakland. In 1985, the Blue Jays used their primary closer, Bill Caudill, as a one-inning reliever. In previous seasons, playoff-bound relievers had never averaged less than 1.31 innings per appearance, but that year Caudill averaged just barely more than one inning per appearance. The next season, Dave Smith of the Astros worked just more than an inning per game while pitching only 56 innings on the season. Additionally, Smith logged 64.7 percent of the Astros' team saves (33 for the season). While that percentage wasn't unprecedented at the time, it was comfortably above the mean. Two years later, Eckersley would push the margins even farther.

By the time the 1990s arrived, closer deployment in baseball was La Russa's approach writ large: fewer total innings, fewer multi-inning appearances, and usage patterns dependent upon the strictures of the save rule. Putting numbers to the ideas, an Eck-style closer has these four characteristics that distinguish him from those of a generation earlier:

- fewer than 85 innings pitched per season;
- fewer than $1\frac{2}{3}$ innings per outing;
- at least 70 percent of team's total saves;
- a save recorded in at least 65 percent of appearances.

Prior to 1990, not a single closer for any team making the postseason met all of the above criteria. From 1990 onward, 55.7 percent of closers from postseason clubs met or exceeded those same criteria. From 1998 and beyond, that figure increased to 64.6 percent. So recent history has seen an upward trend in the number of closers used in relentless observance of the Eckersley model.

It's not that closers, since the 1990s, have become drastically less valuable than their predecessors (although this is something you'll hear parroted in a many a stathead echo chamber); rather, it's that the contemporary closer isn't used in an optimal fashion. Over time, an ace reliever's level of performance has become conflated with his ability to rack up saves. Needless to say, there's a serious disconnect between the two. For instance, it takes very little skill—at least relative to the skill of the garden-variety major league reliever—to record three outs while holding a two- or three-run lead. The research of Keith Woolner of *Baseball Prospectus* shows that fewer than three runs are scored in 94.6 percent of all innings, and fewer than two runs are scored in 87.8 percent of all innings. Yet this is how many ninth innings have been approached: preserving the relief ace for a situation with staggering odds of success rather than using him at some earlier point of crisis. I do believe that the pressure of pitching the final frame is something to be considered, but major league relievers who can't regularly protect three-run leads have no business being major league relievers.

Still, the '90s changed everything. It's when the free agent and trade markets began valuing relievers who supposedly proved their mettle by hoarding saves. It follows from the establishment of saves as a value determinant that closers and their representatives now have financial incentive to lobby for save opportunities; in effect, that means they're applying internal pressure to continue the trend of inefficient deployment. Because of this dynamic, it's been recent baseball orthodoxy to believe that closers are more nature than nurture. You have to be tough like Billy Wagner, not a sniveling wuss like Calvin Schiraldi. Heck, this might even be true. Nevertheless, those who do have the requisite fortitude for ninth-inning detail can be better wielded.

Here's what we have Dennis Eckersley's success to thank for:

- faulty deployment of ace relievers in low-leverage situations;
- a prevailing decrease in ace reliever workloads;
- throughout the baseball industry, wrongheaded valuation of relievers with high save totals.

So how have these changes really affected the game?

Bill James, most notably, has written about the inefficient use of the modern closer. His findings suggest that many critical relief situations occur in nonsave circumstances. In particular, despite the fact that it's common practice to bring in the closer in the ninth inning even with a three-run lead, it's a terribly inefficient way to use the man who's presumably your best reliever.

Using data available at Tangotiger.net, we find that, from the sixth through ninth innings (when a valued reliever would typically be used), there are for a hypothetical home team no fewer than 368 base-out-run differential states that are more critical than the ninth-inning/three-run-lead situation that so often results in a save. Yes: 368 other situations are more vital to the outcome of the game. Once more for maximum emphasis: 368 other situations.

What's more is that the same holds true for a two-run lead with no outs in the ninth inning: no fewer than 368 situations. Even in the case of a one-run lead with no outs in the ninth there are 163 scenarios from the sixth inning on that are more dangerous for the home team (although the idea of using your best reliever to protect a one-run lead or even a two-run lead against a potent offense is eminently defensible to me). All of this is to say: closers are not used to maximum efficiency these days.

Perhaps the very word "save," with its connotations of heroism, rescue, and valor, has imbued the statistic with far more admiration than it merits. That modern managers are so beholden to it when determining bullpen division of labor does not speak highly of their ability to think independently or their sense of history.

Once again, to draw upon the fireman metaphor (and perhaps beat it senseless), it's as though the fire department, normally on the ready whenever an emergency may arise, decided to patrol your neighborhood only during certain hours. Should you happen to heave a Molotov cocktail into the hayloft when the FD isn't on duty, you'd best make do with the garden hose. In a sense, that's what most contemporary managers are hoping for—convenient and timely emergencies—when they insist on using their best relievers only in the ninth inning.

Yet look at what winning teams usually do. Historically, playoff teams since 1980 haven't worried overmuch about rolling up indecent saves totals. Closers on these teams, on average, rank between fifth and sixth in the league in saves, which is unspectacular for an ace reliever on a team graciously purveying save opportunities. Set that against the fact that the same group of closers have posted a park-adjusted ERA, on average, 70 percent better than the league mean. It's not the saves that the winners are looking for, whether they realize it or not; it's the quality innings.

As you can see, the entire La Russan model of closer usage is dependent upon the occasionally fallacious idea that critical mass in any particular ball game occurs, ipso facto, in the ninth inning.

Common sense tells you this isn't true. By no means is this lost on all contemporary managers in all situations. Take, for instance, Yankee manager Joe Torre and how he wields his closer, the inestimable Mariano Rivera, once the calendar flips to October. Among contemporary closers, none—not even Eck— matches the accomplishments of Rivera, who, as you'll see later in this chapter, is responsible for exactly one-fourth of the greatest closer seasons studied here.

Rivera, a native of Panama, cut his teeth in the majors first as a starter in 1995. After some early struggles and an injured shoulder, the Yankees almost traded him to the Tigers for David Wells. But once Rivera was healthy again by the playoffs, manager Buck Showalter moved him to the bullpen, where he thrived. The Yankees even opted to place him on the postseason roster. In the ALDS he struck out eight and gave up no runs in five innings against the Mariners. Most notably, Rivera tossed $3\frac{1}{3}$ scoreless frames in the white-knuckled, 15-inning Yankee win in game two. The following season, Rivera labored as a setup man to John Wetteland. Rivera that season would strike out more batters than any reliever in Yankee history (130), and would provide Yankee brass with the impetus they needed to let Wetteland depart via free agency. Rivera was granted the closer's job going into the 1997 season, a year in which he'd finish second in the AL in saves and register a 1.88 ERA. Five years later, he would be a Yankee pantheon-dweller.

Although the 1999 season was "only" Rivera's third best, it's arguably the one that cemented his legend. Over its final three months, he allowed not a single run. In the '99 postseason he was without peer, tossing $12\frac{1}{3}$ scoreless innings, striking out nine, walking one, and picking up six saves and a pair of wins. As great as he was in the regular season, it was in the Yankee haunts of October that Rivera forged his luminous reputation. In 96 playoff innings through the 2003 season, Rivera went 7–1, saved 30, and posted a minuscule ERA of 0.75 and a strikeout-to-walk ratio of 5.83.

What distinguishes Rivera in October, and what makes the larger point here, is how Torre (Rivera's skipper for 58 of his 61 postseason appearances) deployed him. Since becoming the Yankees' closer in 1997, Rivera has averaged 1.10 innings per appearance in the regular season and recorded saves in 64.4 percent of his outings. In the post-season, however, over that same span he has averaged 1.53 innings per appearance and posted saves in only 60 percent of his appearances. Torre altered his usage of Rivera in the playoffs to fit what he intuitively knows to be true: the most critical situations in a game don't always intersect with save chances, and it often behooves a manager to use his ace reliever for more than one inning at a time. It's the same recognition that was pervasive in baseball before the days of Eckersley and La Russa.

Today's closers also no longer take on the Rubenesque workloads of the firemen of the '70s and '80s. Dan Levitt and Mark Armour in their book *Paths to Glory* argue persuasively that La Russa is responsible for dovetailing closer usage with the dictates of the save rule, and in the process they document the declining usage patterns of the ace reliever.

Armour and Levitt discovered that total bullpen workload has increased only marginally over the past 35 years. Over that same span, the number of relievers used per game increased markedly, and the percentage of that bullpen workload shouldered by the fireman/closer, in most instances a team's best reliever, decreased greatly. Consider these additional findings from the pool of closers studied here:

- from 1980 to 1990, closers for playoff teams averaged 104.9 innings per season;
- from 1990 onward, closers for playoff teams averaged 65.5 innings per season, a decrease of 37.6 percent;
- from 1980 to 1990, closers for playoff teams averaged 1.49 innings per appearance;
- from 1990 onward, closers for playoff teams averaged 1.07 innings per appearance, a decrease of 28.2 percent.

The upshot is that more relief innings began going to, generally speaking, inferior pitchers. The fireman/closer, meanwhile, became less valuable as a result of this sea change.

Men of the fireman generation were famous for their willingness to pitch whenever they were needed, no matter how frequently, no matter how long. Managers today might say that change was necessary— the more innings pitched, the greater chance of injury. To this I ask, why the embrace of the opposite extreme rather than some sensible midpoint on the usage continuum? Levitt and Armour, backed by an informal study, speculate that the workloads of the traditional fireman may have led to a glut of injuries among top-tier relievers. At the same time, their research suggests that the modern closer can withstand higher innings loads and that the optimum usage pattern may be that of the closer-fireman hybrid of the mid-'80s. I certainly don't advocate the imprudent reliever workloads of thirty years ago—I do believe those lead to injuries in most pitchers, save for those genetic outliers such as Gossage. In the '80s, for example, Willie Hernandez and Dan Quisenberry racked up innings totals that seem positively criminal—with good reason—by today's standards.

Hernandez won fame in his native country for pitching for the first Puerto Rican national team to defeat a U.S. team. Although Hernandez never pitched until age 18, legendary Phillies scout Ruben Amaro was quick to sign him in September of 1973. Less than three years later, the Phillies lost him to the Cubs in the Rule 5 draft.

In Chicago, Hernandez established himself as a durable and reasonably effective setup man to closer Bruce Sutter. But the Cubs, at times vexed by his "give me saves or I'll take a hostage" attitude, traded him back to Philadelphia early in the 1983 season for Dick Ruthven and Bill Johnson. With the Phillies, Hernandez pitched well in front of closer Al Holland and even had three scoreless appearances in the '83 World Series. However, Hernandez still wanted to close, and after signing a three-year extension with the Phils, importuned them to that end. Fearful of internal strife, the Phillies dealt him along with Dave Bergman to Detroit the following spring for John Wockenfuss and Glenn Wilson. In Detroit, Hernandez got his chance to close.

In 1984, Hernandez's deep repertoire of sharp breaking stuff and jittery fastballs overwhelmed the American League. For his efforts, he was rewarded with the AL's Cy Young, and he became the first reliever to win an MVP Award since Jim Konstanty of the Phillies in 1950. Although Hernandez didn't deserve the AL MVP in '84, he did have a legitimately great season—the greatest of any closer on a playoff team since 1980, as you'll soon see. Hernandez's stat line as a closer in 1984 looks unspeakably strange in light of how we've been conditioned to think of the role in the here and now: 140.1 innings (!), 1.75 innings per appearance, 32 saves in 80 games. Truly, Hernandez was being used in a manner bearing scant resemblance to

the post-Eck closer. The workload may not have been entirely prudent, but his ability to go almost two innings every time he took the
mound contributed greatly to his value that season. We may never see
his kind again.

The late Dan Quisenberry is another '80s closer who regularly
hefted burdensome workloads. "Quiz," as he was known by adoring
Royal partisans, was a soft tosser who relied on a sinker and soft-
breaking slider to get his outs. Never thought highly of by scouts,
Quisenberry relied on great control and a ground-ball-inducing repertoire to pass muster. His delivery, an unlikely mix of effortlessness and
awkwardness, couldn't have looked odder if he'd been wearing leder-
hosen on the mound. Nevertheless, Quisenberry was one of the premier firemen of the 1980s. His durability and exacting control allowed
him to be effective despite posting basement-level strikeout rates for
much of his career.

After a reporter once asked John Wathan, Quisenberry's catcher
for most of his best seasons, how Quiz could work so unflaggingly,
Wathan responded, "There's nobody there to get tired. It'd be like asking a broom if it was getting tired."

Broomlike or not (I have no idea what that means—but I like it),
Quisenberry cobbled together three amazing seasons for Royal playoff teams. The greatest of these, 1985, saw Quiz rack up 129 innings,
post a 2.37 ERA, lead the AL in saves with 37, and average more than
1.5 innings per outing. Quisenberry struck out only 54 batters that
season, which is an astonishingly low total for an elite reliever pitching almost 130 innings, so he did rely heavily on his defense to make
outs for him. However, he walked only 16 and kept the ball in the
park. In Kansas City's other two full-season playoff appearances of
the decade, 1980 and 1984, Quiz would work 99 and 129.1 innings,
respectively.

The Royals released Quisenberry midway through the 1988 season, just as the sea change in closer usage was taking place. Duane
Ward of the Blue Jays embodies this transition nicely. Ward was
groomed in the Braves' organization as a starter, but after a trade to
Toronto he moved to the bullpen. Once there, he became one of the
best middle relievers ever.

From 1988 to 1992 Ward filled what would have been classified as
a fireman's role a decade earlier. Over those five years, he averaged

roughly 113 innings and 15 saves per season—workloads not unlike a Quisenberry seasonal offering a few years earlier. Ward also consistently bested the league ERA, posted a 2.41 strikeout-to-walk ratio, and was notoriously stingy with homers over that span.

Following the Jays' World Series triumph in '92, they let closer Tom Henke depart for Texas via free agency and promptly installed Ward as his replacement. With the more prominent job description came reduced value. In 1993, Ward worked as a strict post-Eckersley closer. His innings tumbled from 101.1 to 71.2, and his saves vaulted from 12 to 45 (the latter mark led the AL that season). Because of the innings decline and narrowly defined usage, Ward was, you could muster the case, a less important pitcher in 1993 than he had been a year earlier, through no fault of his own. But his Herculean efforts were not without cost.

After his headline-grabbing season in 1993, Ward missed the entire '94 season with torn cartilage in his shoulder. His comeback attempt in 1995 came to grief, and he was forced to retire after logging only $2\frac{2}{3}$ innings that final year. His final major league victory came in game six of the 1993 World Series, when Joe Carter's historic clout off Mitch Williams vanquished the Phillies and led the Jays to a second straight world championship.

So how do, say, Willie Hernandez, Dan Quisenberry, and their high-inning ilk stack up against Eckersley and the post-Eckersley brand of closer? First we need the proper tool to answer such a question.

An excellent way to assess, in one metric, the quality of a reliever (or any player, for that matter) is to determine how many runs he prevented (or contributed, in the case of hitters) relative to a conceptual being called the "replacement player." As we learned with VORP, in statistical parlance, the replacement player has nothing to do with labor strife or scab workers. Rather, it refers to a hypothetical level of player who's readily available to all teams (e.g., the waiver claim, the B-list prospect, the minor league veteran, the bench player). So, by using a stat called Pitching Runs above Replacement (PRAR), which, like VORP, was developed by *Baseball Prospectus*, we can determine how many runs a reliever is keeping off the board.

PRAR also allows us to determine which individual performances have been the most valuable. Here are the top 20 PRAR seasons among closers on playoff teams since 1980:

Ranking	Closer	Team	PRAR
1.	Willie Hernandez	1984 Tigers	76
2.	Dan Quisenberry	1985 Royals	75
3.	Trevor Hoffman	1996 Padres	70
4.	Byung-Hyun Kim	2002 Diamondbacks	68
4.	Mariano Rivera	1997 Yankees	68
4.	Mariano Rivera	2001 Yankees	68
7.	Keith Foulke	2003 A's	67
7.	Tom Gordon	1998 Red Sox	67
9.	Dennis Eckersley	1992 A's	66
9.	Trevor Hoffman	1998 Padres	66
11.	Mariano Rivera	1999 Yankees	65
12.	Dennis Eckersley	1990 A's	64
13.	Mariano Rivera	2003 Yankees	63
14.	Dan Quisenberry	1984 Royals	62
15.	Jose Mesa	1995 Indians	61
16.	Dan Quisenberry	1980 Royals	60
16.	Mariano Rivera	2000 Yankees	60
18.	Billy Wagner	1999 Astros	59
18.	Todd Worrell	1987 Cardinals	59
20.	Robb Nen	2000 Giants	58

Not one of Eckersley's seasons ranks higher than ninth. That's where his innings deficit comes into play. As great as he was, his work load was historically light at the time. For instance, Eckersley in most years pitched roughly half as many innings as Hernandez did in his MVP and Cy Young season of 1984—the top-ranked season on the list. In light of this, it may seem counterintuitive that, although closers were broadly more valuable prior to the late-'80s paradigm shift, this list is mostly littered with post-Eck closers: 15 of 20 spots, in fact, are occupied by closers of the late '80s and beyond. But contemporary closers occupy the margins at both extremes, which, in this instance, makes their net value slightly less than that of ace relievers of previous generations.

Examining the closers from each playoff team from 1980 to 2003, we find that the average closer saves his team 44.2 runs in a season.

What we also find is that, as can be expected, the average closer PRAR declines after Eckersley's emergence. Prior to Eckersley's first season as closer for a playoff team in 1988, closers averaged 46.2 PRAR per season; after that point, their value declined to 43.5. That's a drop, but it's only a 5.8 percent decline in runs saved on average.

There's also leverage to be considered. By leverage we mean the critical nature of an appearance. If a reliever comes in with a one-run lead, no outs, and runners on second and third, those are obviously highly fraught circumstances. On the other hand, if a reliever works the ninth with a six-run cushion, that's not a situation of critical mass. To assess just this, *Baseball Prospectus* uses a Leverage Score. We can examine leverage trends by breaking the numbers down into five-year increments and determining the average leverage score for each time period (the higher the score, the more perilous the appearance). Our reliever population will comprise only save leaders for each team—playoff and nonplayoff teams included—since 1980. Here's how things shake out:

Time Period	Average Leverage Score/Saves Leader
1980–1984	1.53
1985–1989	1.62
1990–1994	1.66
1995–1999	1.70
2000–2004	1.69

Given all the harrumphs coming from some corners, these aren't the results you'd expect, and they sunder the notion that the closer model sacrifices leverage. In terms of deploying closers/relief aces/firemen in high-leverage situations, managers have gotten progressively better at it. There are incontrovertible flaws with the usage of modern closers, but as far as leverage goes, things were demonstrably worse in the past. Analysts who assail the use of the modern closer need to be mindful of this fact.

The worst season of any contender's closer since 1980 belongs to Norm Charlton of the '97 Mariners. Charlton's PRAR for the season was exactly zero, meaning he was precisely replacement level. In 69⅔ innings that year, Charlton led the team in saves with 14 (the lowest team-leading total for an AL playoff outfit since someone called Eric King paced the '87 Tigers with only nine saves), but Charlton's ERA was a grisly 7.27. Not only does Charlton have the lowest PRAR of any closer in the lot, but he also boasts the worst park-adjusted ERA (38 percent below the league average) of any closer on a playoff team from 1980 onward.

Such was Charlton's fecklessness that Seattle GM Woody Woodward, flailing about for someone resembling a passable reliever, was driven to execute the most self-immolating trade in team history. On July 31, Woodward traded catcher Jason Varitek and righthander Derek Lowe to Boston for the since reviled Heathcliff Slocumb. What did Woodward see in Slocumb? Saves. Slocumb had logged 63 saves over the previous two seasons as closer for the Phillies and Red Sox and was on pace for his third consecutive 30-save season. What Woodward presumably didn't see was that Slocumb's peripheral skills were lacking and that he had, at the time of the trade, a 5.79 ERA. A reliever with an ERA of almost 6.00 isn't a closer; he's an opener. But Woodward saw only the saves and parted with two fine young ballplayers to get them.

Slocumb was middling for the balance of '97 and awful in 1998. Varitek and Lowe, meanwhile, have gone on to distinguished careers as centerpieces of the fine Boston teams of the early 2000s.

The historical struggles of teams such as Seattle to find capable ace relievers have led many to believe that closers have some preternatural ability to handle the intrinsic pressures of the job. There's probably some legitimacy to that viewpoint. Whatever the case, some organizations seem to dig up effective closers almost annually.

The Braves of the '90s and the aughts, the greatest non-Yankee dynasty in baseball history, are a prominent example of this phenomenon. From 1991 to 2003, the Braves made the playoffs in every completed season. Over that same span, they had ten different relievers lead the team in saves. Ten.

While the Braves' rotation was a bastion of stability during the 1990s, the team's architects quite clearly viewed the closer role as fungible and the closer himself as utterly replaceable. Additionally, the Braves also found these ace relievers from an array of sources and prototypes. The secret to their dynamism is that they were swayed not by save totals but rather by underlying performance.

In 1991, the year of Atlanta's improbable worst-to-first pennant run, they primarily used Juan Berenguer as their closer. At the time of his elevation to closer, Berenguer, always possessed of a Falstaff-like build, was 36 years old and had 14 career saves in 13 seasons. "Senor Smoke" (better nickname incorporating both his porcine build and unproven closer mettle: "The Trial Balloon") responded to the call to duty with 64$\frac{1}{3}$ innings, 17 saves, and a 2.24 ERA. As the season wound down, a lingering arm injury finally caught up to Berenguer, and he was finished for the year. General Manager John Schuerholz's rejoinder to his closer's injury was to trade a pair of lesser lights to the Mets for Alejandro Pena. It was a sage move.

Pena, working as closer down the stretch, converted all of his 11 save opportunities and posted a 0.51 ERA. He picked up three saves in the NLCS, but took the loss in the wrenching game seven of the World Series in Minnesota. It was Pena's first loss as a Brave.

The very next season, Atlanta, bound for the World Series for a second consecutive season, once again turned to Pena. In what seemed a replay of the previous year, the Braves' closer went down with an elbow injury. Pena still led the team in saves, but eventually missed not just the end of the 1992 season but the entire '93 season as well.

Seemingly in yet another quandary, the Braves turned to lefty Mike Stanton, who'd toiled as the club's primary left-handed setup man. That season Stanton ranked seventh in the NL with 27 saves. However, he was a bit of an oddity as a closer in that he was the worst regular reliever on the team. In spite of filling such a putatively critical role with a pitcher whose ERA was comfortably worse than the league average, Atlanta won 104 games and their third straight division title.

Dissatisfied with Stanton's efforts, the Braves turned to Greg McMichael for the strike-snuffed 1994 season. But it was the hard-throwing Mark Wohlers, performing yeoman's work in middle relief, who turned heads for the future. Wohlers had been the presumptive future closer in Atlanta ever since 1991, when, at age 20, he pitched two innings of a combined no-hitter with Kent Mercker and the afore-mentioned Pena. Although he was a September call-up that year, Wohlers made the postseason roster and logged five scoreless appear-ances in the playoffs.

It would be another four seasons before Wohlers would settle in as closer. His first season would be his best. Wohlers in 1995 was unqual-ified excellence. In 64$\frac{2}{3}$ innings he struck out 90, walked 24, yielded only a pair of homers, and posted a sparkling 2.09 ERA. After saving a pair of games and notching a 1.80 ERA in the World Series, Wohlers appeared well on his way to a career as an elite closer.

In the 1996 regular season, Wohlers was impressive once again: $77\frac{1}{3}$ innings, 100 strikeouts, 21 walks, eight homers, 39 saves (a franchise record at the time), and a 3.03 ERA. Then came the World Series. While it's possible, perhaps even likely, that the critical home run Wohlers surrendered to Jim Leyritz in the eighth inning of game four and Wohlers' subsequent decline aren't causally related, that perception remains to this day. The Yankees, of course, were down two games to one at the time and trailing by three runs. Leyritz's clout tied the game, which the Yankees went on to win. They also went on to win the Series, four games to two. And Wohlers would never be the same pitcher again.

In 1997 Wohlers saved 33 games, but his peripheral numbers declined notably, and his ERA rose to 3.50. In particular, he began to lose his control. Wohlers opened the 1998 season by walking an astonishing 33 batters in $20\frac{1}{3}$ innings. Shortly thereafter, the Braves placed him on the disabled list for the most damning of reasons: "an inability to pitch."

They once again showed their willingness to eschew the idea of a seasoned closer by giving the job to Kerry Ligtenberg, a rookie who'd recorded exactly one save above the Double-A level. Ligtenberg rewarded the club's departure from convention by saving 30, posting a 2.71 ERA, and striking out 79 in 73 innings. It once again appeared that the Braves had a top-shelf closer for the foreseeable future. However, Ligtenberg tore an elbow ligament the following spring, and Atlanta was once again navigating familiar shoals.

They turned to John Rocker. Rocker had debuted in Atlanta the previous season as a fireballing lefty middle reliever. The organization loved his classic closer's arsenal—mid-'90s fastball and hard slider.

With his sprint to the mound and tortured facial contortions, Rocker quickly became the object of opposing fans' scorn and ridicule. But he could pitch. That season he saved 38 games, struck out 104 batters, and logged a 2.49 ERA—one that was 74 percent better than the league average, after adjustments for the home park. Rocker was dominant in the postseason, striking out 18 and not allowing a run in 13 innings. The winter, however, wouldn't be so accommodating, for reasons of his own making.

By this point in his career, he was a star (and therefore unlike most of the other Braves closers), and the media found him good copy. Then in December of 1999, Rocker granted an interview to *Sports Illustrated* writer Jeff Pearlman. During the course of the interview, Rocker vomited up a misanthropic, hate-sodden rant that offended immigrants, gays, single mothers, AIDS victims, polyglots, counterculture denizens, ex-cons—just about anything carbon-based. Asked about his, until then, seemingly innocuous rivalry with New Yorkers, Rocker held forth on what it was like to ride the No. 7 train to Shea Stadium: "You're next to some kid with purple hair next to some queer with AIDS right next to some dude who just got out of jail for the fourth time right next to some 20-year-old mom with four kids. It's depressing."

And he wasn't done. "The biggest thing I don't like about New York are the foreigners," Rocker fumed. "I'm not a very big fan of foreigners. You can walk an entire block in Times Square and not hear anybody speaking English. Asians and Koreans and Vietnamese and Indians and Russians and Spanish people and everything up there. How the hell did they get in this country?"

A chorus of enmity followed Rocker's diatribe. Outrage came from places as disparate as the NAACP and the afterthought of a rock band Twisted Sister, whose song "I Wanna Rock" was Rocker's favored entrance music. Commissioner Bud Selig ruled to suspend Rocker for the first month of the 2000 season, but after the Players' Association appealed, the punishment was reduced to a fortnight.

Suffice it to say, Rocker, from that point forward, was a bit of a firebrand. Nonetheless, he was again the Braves' closer in 2000, but his performance declined (much to the delight of immigrants, gays, single mothers, AIDS victims, polyglots, counterculture denizens, ex-cons, and New Yorkers the world over). He was still dominant at times, but he walked 48 batters in 53 innings of work that season.

Rocker was still Atlanta's closer in 2001. But his performance degraded further, and after another spate of peccadilloes his presence on the team became a gargantuan distraction. By June the Braves had traded him to Cleveland for a pair of middle relievers. He was never the same.

After jettisoning Rocker and trying out Steve Karsay as closer, the Braves uncharacteristically turned to an already famous player. John Smoltz had been a highly effective starter for Atlanta since 1989, but his chronically injured elbow finally caught up to him in 2000. Beset by arm problems for the better part of four years, Smoltz changed to a three-quarters delivery to provide some relief to his ailing elbow. However, that only delayed the inevitable: reconstructive elbow surgery, which Smoltz underwent in the spring of 2000.

In May of 2001, Smoltz attempted to come back, but pain in his surgically repaired elbow forced him back on the DL. Once he was able to return again, in July, the Braves were without a closer. Smoltz spent the better part of a month in middle relief, but by mid-August he was closing games regularly. The experiment began as a way to acclimate Smoltz's mended wing to the rigors of pitching. However, that soon changed. The closer void in tandem with Smoltz's fine performance as a reliever and concerns about his ability to abide a starter's workload led the Braves to make an improbable decision: Smoltz would be the closer for good.

And so he was. In 2002, his first full season as a closer, he was outstanding: $80\frac{1}{3}$ innings, 85 strikeouts, 24 walks, 55 saves (breaking Trevor Hoffman's NL record), and a park-adjusted ERA 27 percent better than the league average. While there was apparently some internal vacillation on whether Smoltz would remain the team's closer, the Braves opted to keep him there despite his stated desire to return to the rotation. Late in 2003 Smoltz reinjured his elbow, but that didn't prevent him from putting together an incredible year. Although he was outshined by Eric Gagne's Cy Young plaudits in Los Angeles, Smoltz still put together one of the best seasons of any modern closer. In $64\frac{1}{3}$ innings Smoltz fanned 73 and walked only eight, which comes to an outstanding 9.13 strikeout-to-walk ratio. He also finished second to Gagne in saves and posted a subatomic ERA of 1.12—271 percent better than the league mean when adjusted for park effects.

In analyzing the Braves' decision to keep Smoltz in the bullpen, I'm forced to wallow in the hypotheticals. If Smoltz were able to remain healthy and absorb the abuse a major league starting pitcher faces in any given season, then the decision was unwise. If, however, returning to the rotation would have gravely compromised his health, then morphing him into an elite closer was a fine bit of damage control. Considering the organization's imposing pitching dossier, it's probably best to give them the benefit of the doubt.

So what does this decade-long history of Braves' closers tell us? The Braves maintained a dynastic level of play for more than a decade despite constant upheaval in the closer role. Whether their closers left them in the lurch by dint of injury, ineffectiveness, or a faulty moral compass, Atlanta faced the same dilemma time and again. The club responded with resourcefulness and creativity, and always with an understanding that a quality reliever, most of the time, is a quality reliever—often just as capable at dousing flames in the middle innings as he is at racking up oodles of Jerome Holtzman's quasi-useless statistic.

That's a lesson GM Billy Beane and the Oakland Athletics learned quite well (pre–Octavio Dotel, anyway), but for different reasons. The A's under Beane mustered four consecutive playoff appearances, from 2000 to 2003, in spite of a hermetically sealed budget. Part of their success was in realizing how best to spend the few dollars they had. One of the determinations made by the Oakland brain trust was that they couldn't be wastrels when it came to paying relievers. This meant that parting with closers who were pending free agents or on the verge of their high-salary years became standard operating procedure.

In 1999, the season before the A's unforeseen playoff run was to begin, they used Billy Taylor as their closer. Taylor, however, was in the midst of his fifth season of major league service and already making $2.5 million. By the trade deadline Oakland, despite being in the throes of contention, opted to deal their closer to the Mets for a tattered young arm by the name of Jason Isringhausen.

Isringhausen, along with Paul Wilson and Bill Pulsipher, formed the Mets' ballyhooed troika of young pitchers in the early 1990s. Nicknamed "Generation K," Isringhausen, Wilson, and Pulsipher stole column inches around the country and bolstered Met fans' hopes for another minidynasty. But whether it was bad luck or the reckless usage of their tender young arms by manager Dallas Green (although Wilson was largely spared any problematic workloads), the three pitchers were run to seed before realizing their substantial promise at the highest level.

It was Isringhausen, however, who was able to salvage the most from his once limitless abilities. Early in his career, "Izzy" found ways to hurt himself that went beyond those of the standard-issue injury-prone ballplayer. Besides undergoing three major surgeries on his pitching arm, he also broke his wrist punching a garbage can, stabbed himself in the thigh while trying to open a package with a kitchen knife, grappled with a case of tuberculosis, and suffered a concussion after falling off a three-story building (doctors told him if he hadn't been drunk at the time, his tensed muscles probably would have rendered his injuries fatal).

In spite of Isringhausen's abundant medical rap sheet and a lifetime 4.67 ERA, the A's and Billy Beane installed him as the Oakland closer. He had only one career save at the time. The Mets and manager Bobby Valentine never seemed willing, in their view, to squander Izzy's potential as a starter by shifting him to a relief role. Isringhausen's tremendous minor league performance and his rookie showing (14 starts, 9–2, 2.81 ERA in 1995) certainly made that a defensible stance, but it's also true that his grim history of arm trouble made untenable the prospect of maintaining effectiveness in the face of a starter's workload. The A's wisely realized this and believed that despite Isringhausen's never having been a closer, a good pitcher is a good pitcher.

Their faith was rewarded. Isringhausen, down the stretch in 1999, didn't allow a run in his first seven innings as an A and converted all eight of his save opportunities. In 2000, when the A's would make the postseason for the first time since 1992, Isringhausen saved 33, which was good for seventh in the AL, and posted a 3.78 ERA. The following season, which was Isringhausen's free-agent walk year, he was one of the best closers in the game. His 34 saves ranked sixth in the loop, but it was the strides he made with his command that were most notable. His 3.22 strikeout-to-walk ratio was easily the best of his career, and the A's also showed some willingness to expand his role beyond that of the typical modern closer: Isringhausen averaged more than one inning per outing and logged a save in only 52 percent of his appearances. Of the top ten finishers in saves in the AL that season, only Mariano Rivera and Keith Foulke pitched more innings.

But the A's didn't hesitate to let Isringhausen go once he filed for free agency and demanded more than they were willing to pay someone who pitches only 70 innings per season. To plug the hole, Beane dealt two youngsters, third baseman Eric Hinske and pitcher Justin Miller, to the Toronto Blue Jays for Billy Koch, who'd saved exactly 100 games over the previous three seasons. Miller's career, at this writing, has been insignificant. Hinske, meanwhile, hit 24 homers and drew 77 walks for the Jays in 2002 and also garnered Rookie of the Year hosannas in the AL. While Koch's lone season in Oakland didn't merit parting with a 24-year-old third baseman with power and patience, he was effective in the role (his 44 saves placed second in the league), and his handlers in Oakland moved him even farther from the traditional closer's regimen.

In particular, Koch's workload—93$\frac{2}{3}$ innings—looked like something culled from the age of the fireman 20 years earlier. The last closer on a playoff team to pitch 90 innings and log at least 30 saves was Todd Worrell of the Cardinals in 1987. Raising the bar a bit, the only other closer on a playoff team since 1980 to record at least 40 saves and pitch at least 90 frames was Quisenberry of the 1984 Royals. In what's also something of a rarity these days, Koch, as closer, pitched more innings than the club's primary setup man, Chad Bradford.

But with Koch set to make $4.25 million the following season, the A's opted to trade him to the White Sox for Keith Foulke, the deposed closer who, despite his perceived struggles in Chicago, had some of the strongest peripheral numbers of any reliever in the game. So rather than take the all-too-common path to conspicuous consumption, Beane and the A's dealt for a reputedly fallen closer who'd saved only 11 games the previous season. What the A's saw, however, was that Foulke had command, durability, and a record of success, the saves category notwithstanding. In 2003 they got all that plus the saves. Foulke led the junior circuit in saves with 43 in 86$\frac{2}{3}$ innings, posted an outstanding 4.4 strikeout-to-walk ratio, and logged a park-adjusted ERA 105 percent better than the league average. In the AL, only Mariano Rivera was better. Koch, meanwhile, struggled mightily in Chicago.

After the 2003 season, Foulke signed a lucrative free-agent contract with the well-heeled Red Sox, and Oakland, once again poised for contention, was without an ace reliever. This is where their deft touch ended. The A's turned to Arthur Rhodes, formerly of Seattle, who was coming off a nominally disappointing season; however, Oakland, as they did with Foulke, saw that Rhodes's surface-level struggles (i.e., a high ERA) masked underlying skills that were still fairly strong. Even so, Rhodes failed to adapt to his new role. It's possible the role was not a comfortable one for him, or it's possible age-related decline (he was 35 during the 2004 season) or the ankle injury he suffered the previous season hampered his effectiveness. Then they turned to Octavio Dotel, whom they acquired near the trade deadline, and he was no more effective than Rhodes. Nevertheless, Oakland's successes in finding a closer on the fly far outnumber their failures. Like the Braves, there was an element of demystification in the way they approached the closer. Despite frequent turnover, both teams, by dint of viewing the closer as a system of deployment rather than so much chimerical *je ne sais quoi*, were able to fill the role almost every time a need arose.

When Theo Epstein was named general manager of the Red Sox in 2002, he became at age 28 the youngest GM in the history of the game. He had built his reputation as an executive, like Sandy Alderson before him and contemporary peers such as Billy Beane and Kevin Towers, willing to eschew baseball orthodoxy when necessary. An especially noisy example of this—and the one that best embodies Lincoln's famous admonition "The dogmas of the quiet past are inadequate to the stormy present"—was his regime's handling of the Boston bullpen.

Not long after ascending to the Boston GM-ship, Epstein announced to assembled media that, under his watch, the Red Sox would shirk traditional principles of bullpen usage. In particular, the closer role would be redefined. The Boston media, already rankled by Esptein's age and his lack of a traditional baseball pedigree, seized upon the approach as being pedantic and needlessly subversive. They even mischaracterized it as a "closer by committee" arrangement, which it plainly wasn't. A better moniker might have been "properly leveraged stopper," but that lacks the vaguely dismissive, bureaucratic element that the word "committee" evokes. Forms signed in triplicate and all that.

The season before, Ugueth Urbina had finished third in the AL with 40 saves. Accordingly, that priced Urbina, if not out of Boston's budget, certainly beyond what they were willing to pay for him. So Epstein allowed Urbina to depart via free agency and sign with the Rangers for $4.5 million. Then the Red Sox signed presumably capable relievers such as Ramiro Mendoza, Mike Timlin, Chad Fox, and Brandon Lyon to join returnee Alan Embree in the pen.

But an already unpopular idea got off to a most unfortunate start. On Opening Day, against the Devil Rays, Embree and Fox each gave up two-run homers in the ninth to turn a Pedro Martinez near-gem into a Red Sox loss. The very next night, Bobby Howry coughed up a game-tying homer in the eighth, forcing the Sox to finally eke out a victory in a 16-inning war of attrition. After pair of untimely struggles, the media scrutiny intensified.

"When we say we're not going to have a closer," Epstein attempted to explain to the *Sporting News* that following winter, "it doesn't mean that we don't want a dominant pitcher in the pen. Of course we do. Usage pattern is the key. We want to get to anoint where the most critical outs are pitched by the best pitchers for that situation, be it in the seventh, eighth, or ninth inning."

Esptein's clarification made perfect sense. What the Sox were attempting to do was strike a balance between the closer model and the fireman—use their best arm in the most crucial situations and maximize the usage of their more effective relievers. That meant paying more attention to run-expectancy charts than to the criteria of the save rule. Ultimately, however, Epstein's plan was shanghaied not by the concept, but by the relievers he chose to execute his plan. To wit, Fox was never able to harness his control, and Boston finally released him. Mendoza, a putatively vital acquisition plucked from the Yankees, was in various states of disrepair for most of the year and wound up as the least effective pitcher on the entire staff.

As the season wore on, the fourth estate's orchestrated wrath toward Epstein's vision continued. Overly credulous observers bought into the notion that it was the design and not the personnel that was the problem. But while Boston often toggled relievers among various roles and brought in different arms over the course of the year, they rarely reverted to saves-driven decision-making. After trading third baseman Shea Hillenbrand to the Diamondbacks for the sidearming Byung-Hyun Kim, the Sox installed Kim, following a brief but successful trial as a starter, as their nominal closer. Although by season's end he did lead the Red Sox in saves (with 16, good for only 10th in the AL), Kim was not used by manager Grady Little in a strict post-Eckersley manner. Kim logged only 0.36 saves per outing, the lowest among closers for junior-circuit contenders since Derek Lowe, also of Boston, in 1999. Kim also averaged more than one inning per relief outing. By the playoffs it was Scott Williamson, acquired from the Reds just before the July 31 trade deadline, working the most crucial innings.

While the perceived failure of the Boston bullpen perestroika and the inveighing against it by the mainstream media no doubt had chilling effects, Epstein and company mostly stayed the course. A few weeks prior to spring training 2004, Epstein, in an interview with *Baseball Prospectus*, reflected upon his derided experiment. "In retrospect, if I could do last year's bullpen over again, for starters I hope I'd do a better job putting together quality relievers," he lamented. "I didn't do a very good job. No matter what we said about it, I didn't have the right guys in here to get the job done."

Epstein worked quickly and earnestly to change that. Going into the 2004 season, the Red Sox garrisoned their bullpen with Keith Foulke, who'd served as Oakland's closer the season prior. To hear many in the media tell it, the Foulke signing signaled a tacit admission by the Red Sox that the bullpen experiment of the previous season was a failure. That may well have been the thinking, since during their World Championship season of 2004 the Sox mostly reverted to a traditional arrangement. Things might have gone better for them the season before had they had better relievers and proceeded with the experiment sans grand pronouncements. Still, a thorough razing of the closer paradigm isn't required. As we've seen, closers are better leveraged than their fireman/ace reliever predecessors, but tweaks to the model are in order. For one, the ninth-inning save with a three-run lead should go the way of the wine cooler—used only when no one's watching, if at all. Additionally, the ninth-inning save with a two-run lead can be avoided against teams with especially weak offenses. Furthermore, teams, in my mind, should *modestly* increase the workloads of their best relievers. The post-Eckersley closer model has been pilloried overmuch in many quarters, but there's no reason why improvements can't be made.

CHAPTER 5

The Middle Reliever

(or, A Closer Does Not a Bullpen Make)

We've already spent a great deal of dead tree on the evolving role of the closer, and now to complete our tour of the bullpen we'll take a closer look at the setup corps. The middle reliever—he who bridges the middle innings so that the relief ace can close the game—is ignored or undervalued only at a team's peril. While they're often viewed as the "uneaten marshmallow peeps" of the bullpen, setup men are indeed valuable; in some cases, they're more crucial than their team's closer. As the numbers show, winning teams tend to have strong middle relief units.

On average, our 124 teams have posted a middle relief park-adjusted runs-per-game 6 percent better than the league average. For this chapter we're defining middle relief innings as any relief frame logged by someone other than the team's leader in saves for the season. In most instances this will isolate middle relief innings. Overall, 84 of these teams (67.7 percent) have bettered the league average for park-adjusted runs per game by middle relievers—a solid trend and a definite indicator that good teams have good bullpens.

Before delving further, the use of runs per game (R/G—meaning runs surrendered per nine innings) rather than ERA provides a tidy jumping-off point for a discussion of why R/G is a superior measure to

ERA. While ERA isn't as misleading as, say, RBI—I use ERA from time to time in this book—it's still a significantly flawed statistic and provides no better than a thumbnail measure of pitching quality.

The earned-run rule has been around for almost 120 years, so its place in the statistical pantheon certainly isn't imperiled. But it should be. What ERA aims to do—isolate pitching from defense—is a worthy aim, and it's a notion analysts are just beginning to get their heads around. However, ERA falls miserably short of accomplishing its goal. That's because it depends upon fielding errors to define earned and unearned runs, and, as touched upon previously, fielding errors provide only imperfect strobe-lit glimpses of true defensive perform-ance. The blemishes of fielding percentage as an evaluative tool of defense undermine ERA as an evaluative tool of pitching. Fielding percentage, as previously explained, pays no mind to fielding range. Therefore, by using fielding errors to construct ERA, you're absolv-ing those pitchers who play in front of a defense that commits errors but not those pitchers who play in front of a defense encumbered with limited range. Additionally, the scoring of errors is a process riddled with inconsistencies and biases. I maintain: we'd be better off elimi-nating the error altogether.

However, even if errors were the heaven-sent indicator of defen-sive performance, ERA would still be a deeply flawed measure. Implicit in the logic behind the earned-run rule is that the pitcher's job ends once an error is committed. As anyone who's ever watched a game knows, this is the case only within the confines of the scorecard. To cite one example, take the fairly common situation in which an error is scored on a play that otherwise would have been the third out of an inning. Two outs, man reaches on error, next man up hits a two-run homer. Neither of those runs counts against the offending pitcher. It's as though the second batter hit the home run off a ghost. It's on the scoreboard, but it's no one's fault. Removing unearned runs from a pitcher's record assumes that preventing unearned runs entails no skill of the pitcher. Of course, that's patent nonsense.

Research by Michael Wolverton of *Baseball Prospectus* has shown a firm correlation between a pitcher's ability to prevent earned runs and a pitcher's ability to prevent unearned runs. Also, Wolverton found that of the top 50 pitchers in career park- and league-adjusted ERA, 46 of them ranked better than average in keeping unearned runs off the board. Additionally, Wolverton's research shows that knuckleball pitchers tend to be significantly worse at preventing unearned runs than more conventional hurlers. The obvious explanation is that knuckleballers induce an exorbitant number of passed balls, and passed balls count the same as errors on the scorecard.

For all these reasons, R/G is a vastly superior measure of pitching than is ERA, especially when adjusted for the nuances of park and league. R/G still doesn't optimally extricate pitching from the influence of team defense, but it's time we move it ahead of ERA in the queue of traditional pitching statistics. Moving along . . .

As I did in chapter 4, "The Closer," I'll use Pitching Runs above Replacement (PRAR) to sort out middle relief wheat and chaff. So, culled by PRAR, let's look at the top 20 individual middle-relief offerings from playoff teams since 1980:

Ranking	Reliever	Team	PRAR
1.	Mariano Rivera	'96 Yankees	60
2.	Duane Ward	'91 Blue Jays	53
3.	Duane Ward	'92 Blue Jays	51
3.	Jeff Zimmerman	'99 Rangers	51
5.	Steve Bedrosian	'82 Braves	49
5.	Rob Dibble	'90 Reds	49
5.	Jesse Orosco	'86 Mets	49
5.	Dave Smith	'80 Astros	49
9.	Tom Niedenfuer	'83 Dodgers	48
10.	LaTroy Hawkins	'03 Twins	46
10.	J. C. Romero	'02 Twins	46
12.	Mike Henneman	'87 Tigers	45
13.	Jeff Nelson	'95 Mariners	44
13.	Arthur Rhodes	'97 Orioles	44
13.	Mike Stanton	'01 Yankees	44
16.	Aurelio Lopez	'84 Tigers	43
17.	Bobby Ayala	'97 Mariners	42
17.	Mike Remlinger	'99 Braves	42
17.	Jeff Robinson	'87 Giants	42
20.	Steve Karsay	'02 Yankees	41
20.	Joe Nathan	'03 Giants	41

For a long time, middle relief has been viewed as proving grounds for regular closing detail. Indeed, 12 of the 21 names on the above list would one day work as closers at the highest level. Of those, Rivera, Ward, Smith, and Niedenfuer would go on to close for playoff teams, while Ayala and Stanton had previously toiled as closers for teams that made the postseason.

Speaking of Rivera, it's easy to exhaust superlatives in assessing his accomplishments. His success as a closer has been detailed, but his first full year in the majors, when he set up for John Wetteland, was one of the great middle-relief seasons in the annals of the game. Ditto for Duane Ward, who, over a three-year span, totaled 161 PRAR. Ward, despite that unfortunate and precipitous end to his career, stands as one of the great relievers of the past quarter century.

Dave Smith's 1980 season ranks as the fifth-best middle-relief season on the list, with 49 PRAR. Smith also happened to be a 25-year-old rookie in 1980, when he was the most valuable reliever on the team. In $102\frac{2}{3}$ relief innings, Smith posted a 2.10 R/G, struck out 85, and surrendered only a single homer on the season.

The Astros selected Smith in the eighth round of the 1976 amateur draft out of San Diego State, and it was a sage pick indeed. In terms of career value, Smith still stands as the greatest reliever in franchise history. A little more than two seasons into his career, Smith tried his hand as a member of the rotation in June '82 against the Dodgers. Three balks and two innings later, he'd made his first, last, and only major league start. Back in the bullpen, Smith resumed building a stellar relief career. By 1985 he was named the Houston closer, and he responded by recording 27 saves in 31 chances. The following season he saved 33, a franchise record that would stand until 1992, when Doug Jones tallied 36 saves. The '86 season also brought Houston's second division title of the decade. That year, Smith coughed up a homer to Darryl Strawberry of the Mets on July 19; he wouldn't surrender another one until the ninth inning of game three of the NLCS (also against the Mets, but this time to Lenny Dykstra). Unfortunately for Smith and the Astros, that homer would be a critical one, and it would be emblematic of Smith's failings in the postseason. In two NLCS appearances in '86, Smith blew two ninth-inning save opportunities. The Astros, of course, lost to the Mets in six.

For a more holistic view, let's look at the entire middle relief corps. In scrutinizing the best middle-relief teams, we'll consider only the top four relievers, in terms of PRAR, with the exclusion of the team's closer. The teams will be ranked according to their cumulative middle-relief PRAR. Any pitchers who worked as both a starter and a reliever in a given season will be considered on the basis of their relief work only. The results:

Ranking	Team	Middle-Relief PRAR
1.	2002 Twins	132
2.	1997 Orioles	129
3.	1991 Blue Jays	123
4.	1996 Yankees	113
5.	1999 Rangers	112
6.	1985 Blue Jays	110
6.	1999 Braves	110
6.	1995 Rockies	110
9.	1995 Indians	107
10.	1988 Dodgers	106

The 1995 Rockies were a team that played squarely over its head. Despite outscoring their opponents by only two runs on the season, the Rockies finished 10 games above .500 and claimed the NL wild card for the abbreviated '95 campaign.

Mostly because of their wildly aberrant playing environment, the Rockies, in a vain attempt to gain purchase on success, have beta-tested more prevailing visions and governing philosophies than your garden-variety West African banana republic. Only once, in 1995, did it work. That season, their pitching staff gave up a league-worst 5.44 runs per game (although that's not a thoroughly damning indictment, considering they pitched half their games in Coors Field), and only two Rocky starters had ERAs of less than 4.00.

Of Colorado's 110 middle-relief PRAR that year, Curtis Leskanic and Steve Reed contributed 76 of them. Leskanic, whom the Rockies had plucked from the Twins in the 1992 expansion draft and who would later become closer in Milwaukee, put together a remarkable season in 1995. Six rounds earlier, in the '92 expansion draft, the Rockies robbed the Giants of Reed, who was also one of the league's best relievers for the 1995 season.

What's remarkable about the accomplishments of the Rockies' bullpen, and Leskanic and Reed in particular, is that they pitched their home tilts in the run-inducing crucible that is Coors Field. In '95, Coors Field, because of its lofty altitude and spacious outfield gaps, inflated run scoring by 28 percent, which made it easily the greatest hitting environment in the game. Despite the hostile conditions in Denver, Leskanic worked 98 innings with a 3.49 R/G, 107 strikeouts, 3.24 strikeout-to-walk ratio and seven homers allowed. Reed went 84 innings on the season with even better numbers: 2.57 R/G, 3.76 strikeout-to-walk, 79 whiffs. That the pair posted these numbers while working half their games on Planet Coors is nothing short of amazing. Reed, for instance, posted a park-adjusted ERA 150 percent superior to the league average. Also keep in mind that the 1995 season was abbreviated to 144 games because of extended wrangling over the collective bargaining agreement. Adjusting the innings pitched of Leskanic and Reed to a 162-game schedule, we find that the duo would have worked 109 and 93 innings, respectively, that year. Those are highly uncommon relief loads for the 1990s.

Because of the statistical contortions necessary to view the Rockies in a vacuum, many observers believe they won in 1995 because of a great offense. That couldn't be farther from the truth, and Coors Field is the source of the misconception. The Rockies did lead the NL in runs scored that season, but that's due more to the playing environment rather than a collection of great hitters. The Rox of '95 scored only 293 runs on the road. Prorated to span the entire 1995 season, that total would rank next to last in the National League. On the pitching side, the Rockies ranked last in the league in runs allowed, but prorate the far more neutral road numbers and they'd finish second to the Braves as the most miserly staff in the game. Such is the influence of baseball in Denver.

Only one starting pitcher for Colorado that season, Kevin Ritz, pitched at least 120 innings while maintaining a better-than-average park-adjusted ERA—only one starter on one of the best pitching-and-defense squads in the game. The upshot is that the 1995 Rockies bullpen—anchored by the middle-innings offerings of Leskanic and Reed—were one of the greatest bullpens ever and one of the most overlooked.

It also may come as a surprise to learn that the '02 Twins cobbled together the greatest crop of middle relievers of any playoff team since

1980. Minnesota in 2002 took advantage of lusterless intradivision competition (they were the only AL Central team to finish with a winning record) to top their loop by 13½ games. The Twins were able to win 94 games and the division flag despite finishing ninth in the AL in runs scored and sixth in runs allowed.

Part of the reason why they were able to succeed was their peerless middle relief. J. C. Romero, who contributed the tenth-best middle-relief season for a playoff team since 1980, had a stellar year. Romero had a reasonably impressive minor league career but had struggled in the majors since being called up in 2000. In fact, just the season prior, Romero had hung an unsightly 6.65 R/G in 65 innings and showed a glaring weakness for the long ball. In 2002, however, his stars aligned, and he was easily the best setup man in the game that season. In 81 innings Romero struck out 76, posted a 1.89 R/G, and drastically reduced his homer rate. Despite being a portsider, Romero wasn't pigeonholed by manager Ron Gardenhire into a strict lefty-specialist role. Romero rewarded Gardenhire's expanded usage by holding the opposite side to a .313 on-base percentage and a .337 slugging percentage. The following season, Romero would regress badly, raising concerns that his superlative 2002 season was an outlier in what perhaps would be an otherwise undistinguished career.

Righthander LaTroy Hawkins also had a strong season. Hawkins was once a ballyhooed prospect as a starter, but after he foundered at the highest level for five seasons the Twins made him a reliever. Eventually Hawkins became a closer, and he had a strong first half in his first full season on the job (2001), but he faltered badly as the season wore on. In one 14-game stretch in late August through early September, Hawkins went 0–3 with a 20.76 ERA. Even so, Tom Kelly, then the Twins' manager, stuck with him for the entire season. For the year, Hawkins logged a 5.96 R/G and struck out fewer batters than he walked.

The following spring, the organization tried earnestly to trade Hawkins, but there were no takers because of his $2.75-million salary and spring ankle troubles. Instead, they made him a setup man going into the 2002 season and gave the closer's job to Eddie Guardado. Whether because of the less pressurized nature of middle relief or because of his response to new pitching coach Rick Anderson, Hawkins made praiseworthy strides that season. He pitched a hearty

80⅓ innings, rang up a 4.2 strikeout-to-walk ratio, and cleaved his R/G down to 2.58.

Veteran reliever Mike Jackson was also a critical member of the 2002 Twins' relief corps. Jackson had debuted back in 1986 with the Phillies as a long reliever-cum-emergency starter, but following the 1987 season he was dealt to the Mariners along with Glenn Wilson and minor leaguer Dave Brundage for Phil Bradley and Tim Fortugno. The Mariners made him a setup man, and in 1988 he posted the lowest ERA on the team. Jackson battled arm troubles for much of the early '90s, but reestablished himself in Cincinnati as one of the best right-handed relievers in the game. By 1997 he had landed in Cleveland as the primary setup man to closer Jose Mesa. Midway through the season, Mesa was indisposed while he answered to rape charges, and Jackson, despite reputedly lacking a closer's emotional fortitude, picked up the save opportunities in Mesa's absence. The following season, after Mesa had helped fritter away game seven of the 1997 World Series, the Indians named Jackson as their closer and dealt Mesa to the Giants in late July '98. Jackson rewarded their confidence by notching 40 saves and a park-adjusted ERA 210 percent better than the league average. The Twins signed Jackson after a one-year stint in Houston, which was arguably the worst season of his career. But Jackson rebounded to give the Twins 55 innings, a 3.27 R/G, and outstanding control (only 10 unintentional walks on the season).

Along with Hawkins and Jackson, Tony Fiore gave the Twins a trio of devastating right-handed relievers. Going into the 2002 season, Fiore was a journeyman minor league reliever with fewer than 25 innings at the highest level. Fiore was in his second stint as a Twin, having been signed by Minnesota as a minor league free agent in May 2001. The following season, everything went right for Fiore. In 2002, 80⅓ of his 91 innings on the season came in relief, and he was far more effective when pitching out of the pen (2.79 relief ERA versus 6.10 as a starter). But more than anything else, Fiore was lucky that season. As a reliever in '02, Fiore struck out only 48, walked 36, and coughed up nine home runs in those 80⅓ innings. The low strikeout numbers and high walk rate meant that Fiore allowed more than his share of balls in play and allowed more than his share of base runners. As an extreme fly-ball pitcher that season, Fiore relied on the fleet outfield defense behind him to make outs. And that they did. So in spite of poor command and middling strikeout rates, Fiore was a highly effective reliever that season.

The 2002 Twins marshaled together peerless relief in the middle innings thanks to a lightning-in-a-bottle performance, a failed starter who'd found his niche after years of fits and starts, a veteran with one final great season in him, and an exceedingly lucky nomad with just the right gloves behind him. Such resourcefulness and, well, blind luck are common to all great bullpens. Adding the closers' PRAR to the bullpen calculus, let's look at the greatest overall bullpen performances of playoff teams since 1980:

Ranking	Team	Total Bullpen PRAR
1.	1997 Orioles	186
2.	2002 Twins	177
3.	1995 Indians	168
4.	2001 Yankees	165
5.	1999 Braves	162
5.	1996 Yankees	162
7.	1997 Yankees	160
8.	1999 Rangers	157
9.	1991 Blue Jays	156
10.	1996 Indians	153
10.	1990 Reds	153

The 1997 Baltimore Orioles won 98 games and the AL East and helped provide what would be in retrospect, for many, a much-needed intermezzo to the Yankees' looming run of dominance. That season, the O's finished sixth in runs scored but paced the circuit in fewest runs allowed. While they did have an excellent front of the rotation in Jimmy Key, Mike Mussina, and Scott Erickson, much of Baltimore's run-preventing prowess was concentrated in the bullpen. That bullpen, in fact, was one of the greatest ever assembled.

From the right side, the dominating (yet easily unhinged) Armando Benitez was the primary setup weapon. Benitez would later gain fame as closer for the strong Met teams of the late '90s and early 2000s, but in '97 he was working in middle relief and as apprentice to closer Randy Myers. Benitez, a solidly built product of the Dominican

Republic, regularly pumped his fastball in excess of 100 miles per hour, but he often needled Oriole management by reacting to the scoreboard radar-gun reading rather than leveling his focus on the hitter at hand. Still, Benitez, despite wavering control and an occasional propensity for gopher balls, was dominance unabated in '97.

In $73\frac{1}{3}$ innings Benitez surrendered only 49 hits, struck out 106, and logged a 2.70 R/G for the season. With 43 walks on the year, his control was distressing at times, but he was otherwise so overwhelming that he more than made up for his occasional inability to find the plate. As great as he was in the regular season, he was just as noxious in the playoffs. The Orioles fell in the ALCS to the Indians, and Benitez gave up the game-winning run in three of Baltimore's four losses, including an eleventh-inning blast to Tony Fernandez in the decisive game six. And Benitez continued to fall apart in pressure situations deep into his career.

The O's that season put together the greatest tandem of lefty relievers in recent memory. Half of that tandem was Arthur Rhodes. Like any number of quality relievers, Rhodes was originally a failed starter. Rhodes worked exclusively as a member of the Baltimore rotation for the first four seasons of his major league career, and of those four seasons he could charitably be characterized as suboptimal in three of them. In 1995 Rhodes began the season by posting a 7.15 ERA in his first nine starts of the season. Manager Phil Regan opted to move him to the bullpen, and, save for a pair of spot starts in 1996, he would remain there for the rest of his career.

Although he debatably had a better year as a member of the 2002 Mariners, that wasn't a playoff team. Among playoff teams since 1980, Rhodes's '97 offering stands as the thirteenth-best season of any middle reliever. It's his workload that may have been most impressive: $95\frac{1}{3}$ innings, second only to Bob Wickman of the Indians among AL relievers. In those $95\frac{1}{3}$ innings, Rhodes fanned 102 and posted a 3.92 strikeout-to-walk ratio and a 3.02 R/G.

Jesse Orosco, the post–Hoyt Wilhelm Methuselah (or Strom Thurmond sans revolting backstory) of relievers, would pitch until age 46 and become one of only four players (joining Rickey Henderson, Mike Morgan, and Tim Raines) to play from the 1970s through the turn of the century. Appropriately enough, in 1999 Orosco broke Wilhelm's record for career games pitched. Earlier that same season, Kent Tekulve's record for career relief appearances also fell to Orosco.

Orosco was the consummate specialist. His sidearm curve made him especially baffling to lefties, and his easy delivery and light workloads allowed him to work almost whenever needed. Because of his tightly confined role, Orosco logged more appearances than innings pitched in each of his final 13 seasons. He's also famed for his yeoman's efforts in the 1986 postseason, during which he posted three wins in the NLCS against the Astros and recorded the final out—a strikeout of Marty Barrett—of the Mets' game seven win over the blighted Red Sox.

Orosco debuted with the Mets in 1979 at age 22 after being acquired from the Twins as a player to be named in the deal for Jerry Koosman (oddly enough, the man who was on the mound when the Mets clinched their only other World Series, in 1969). In 1983 he crafted one of the finest relief seasons in history (110 innings, 2.21 R/G, 84 strikeouts, and only three home runs allowed), albeit for a bottom-feeding team. Even so, he managed to finish third in the NL Cy Young voting that year. In his 24-year career, Orosco would suit up for ten different clubs, and he also managed to go the first 19 seasons without ever landing on the disabled list. He came to the Orioles as a free agent just after the start of the 1995 season. Once in Baltimore, Orosco peeled off four straight quality seasons as the Orioles' lefty specialist. He was at his best in '97. That year, he pitched $50^1/3$ innings with a 2.32 R/G (and a park-adjusted ERA 88 percent better than the league mean), struck out 46, and gave up only 29 hits. And in the postseason, Orosco wasn't scored on in four appearances.

Closing games for the 1997 Orioles was lefty Randy Myers. Myers was a hard-throwing lefty raised, like Orosco, in the Mets organization. With a blazing fastball and hard slider, Myers fashioned a reputation as an intimidator, an image he buttressed with clubhouse flourishes such as wearing military fatigues, practicing martial arts, and conspicuously perusing gun magazines. Myers pitched for five playoff teams in his career, including the 1990 Reds and their "Nasty Boys" bullpen (which ranks "only" 10th on the list above despite being the most heralded of any relief corps). Myers also set the NL record for saves in 1983 when he notched 53 for the Cubs. The record would hold until Trevor Hoffman tied it in 1998 and John Smoltz and Eric Gagne broke it 2002 and 2003, respectively.

The 1997 season was Myers' finest: $59^2/3$ innings, 1.81 R/G, 56 strikeouts, two home runs allowed. Adjusting for park effects, Myers'

ERA in '97 was a hefty 191 percent above the league average. His PRAR of 57 that season was also the highest of his career, and his performance as closer that season was the capstone of one of the greatest bullpens ever assembled.

The next truly great bullpen may come when the shrewdness and happy accidents demonstrated and enjoyed by the 1997 Orioles and 2002 Twins intersect with enlightened deployment. Since closers are most often conspicuous additions, that shrewdness and those happy accidents are most often found in the assembling of the middle relief corps. Great teams, whether by accident or design, generally thrive in terms of preventing runs in the middle innings.

CHAPTER 6

The Base Stealer

(or, Uses and Misuses of Speed)

Mainstreamers have never been terribly fond of the andante approach to baserunning. It's lazy, it's unimaginative, it's ill equipped to ferry teams through the inevitable batting slumps. You need a handful of legitimate base-stealing threats if you're going to win.

Fans also love to see a hyperactive running game. There's a palpable tension in the air when an adroit base stealer takes his lead in the late innings of a tight game, and once he finally goes, it's almost always a close play at the bag. I recall the invigorating feeling of hearing Jack Buck growl to his listeners that Vince Coleman, the Cardinals' unchallenged speed merchant of the mid-1980s, had sneaked his lead off first to the point that he had "both feet on the carpet."

On the other side of the aisle, dogmatist statheads would have you believe that stolen bases are all but useless, harmful unless achieved at a high rate of success, and perhaps even a net negative when successful because of the tendency for the hitter to take strikes or swing wildly in an attempt to protect the runner. In this instance, the statheads are mostly—but not completely—correct. The stolen base adds very few runs and most assuredly hurts the cause of the offense unless the outs made on the bases are few and far between. However, there's no evidence that the act of stealing or attempting to steal a base negatively affects the hitter in any way. Additionally, while the stolen base itself is a vastly overvalued tactical option, team speed itself is highly valuable and common among winning teams. And what better way to begin a discussion of the stolen base than with the man who did it best.

The inestimable Rickey Henderson swindled 100 bases in his first full season, set the all-time single-season record at age 23 and eventually became the first player in major league history to steal 1,000 bases. Along the way, Henderson also fashioned a reputation for being something of a savant by constantly peppering his speech with malapropisms and third-person references to himself. One story, since revealed to be brazenly apocryphal, has him making a semifamous remark in 2000 to Seattle teammate John Olerud. Olerud, as recounted earlier, because of a brain aneurysm suffered in college, wore a batting helmet even while playing in the field at first base. "I once played with a dude who wore his helmet all the time," Henderson supposedly said.

"Yeah," Olerud replied. "That was me." The pair had been teammates in New York the previous two seasons and in Toronto seven years earlier.

Then there was one that went something like this: Henderson is on a bus (a plane in some versions), and he humbly follows the queue of players down the aisle and takes his seat in the back of the bus/plane (he's already seated in some versions). Teammate Tony Gwynn (Steve Finley in some versions) yells to him, "Hey, Rickey. You can sit anywhere you want. You've got tenure." To which Henderson replied: "Ten Years? I've got 16, 17 years!" (In some versions it's, "Ten years? Rickey's got 19 years!")

It seems that whenever you run across hoary recollections of Henderson's personality mannerisms, it inevitably becomes a haphazardly racist attempt to paint him as some semiliterate noble savage whose brilliance on the diamond belied his modest intelligence and comical reliance on Pidgin English. In truth, he was nothing of the sort. Henderson was a thoughtful iconoclast who eschewed contemporary modes of training and performance trends to craft an improbably long career that today stands as one of the greatest ever. His occasional ruminations on the value of on-base percentage reveal a more nuanced grasp of the game than that of those who've endeavored to mock him. Much like his intellect was misunderstood, so was his value as a ballplayer.

"The Man of Steal" was born in Chicago but grew up in inner city Oakland as the fourth of seven children. A lavishly gifted and indefatigably hardworking athlete, Henderson was hotly sought as a running back by elite Division I college football programs such as those at Southern Cal and Arizona State. Henderson's mother persuaded him to stick with baseball, mostly because she feared he'd be seriously injured on the gridiron. As a baseball player, he was a bit of an oddity. He threw with his left hand but batted from the right side, which is plainly a rarity in the baseball world. According to Henderson, this foible came about because of peer pressure. "All the other kids playing around me were batting right-handed," he said. "So that's the way I thought you were supposed to do it."

Over the years, Henderson also crafted a highly unorthodox batting stance. He would stand at the plate in a drastic crouch with his weight back and his left foot slid forward toward the plate. His claim was that the deep crouch allowed him to see the bottom of the ball more clearly and hence better recognize and adjust to pitches. Arguing with the results is a fool's errand.

His talents overwhelmed any concerns about hitting mechanics and signability issues, and the A's drafted Henderson in 1976 in the fourth round of the amateur cattle call. Selected ahead of Henderson, an "inner circle" Hall of Famer if ever there were one, were guys such as Pete Redfern, Bill Paschall, Kim Seaman, and Dennis Burtt. Henderson wasted no time in making the A's look like geniuses. He was a fan favorite in Oakland, and denizens of the "Henderson Heights" section of the left-field seats forged an immediate rapport with him. Henderson often earned the scorn of A's brass by waving to his left-field fans, blowing kisses, and even posing for pictures while the game in front of him was ongoing.

Despite being productive by any standard as an Athletic, Henderson was traded to the Yankees following the 1984 season for Stan Javier, Jay Howell, Tim Birtsas, Jose Rijo, and Eric Plunk. Soon after, the Yankees hired Henderson's longtime manager in Oakland, Billy Martin. Henderson had helped make "Billy Ball" the prevailing and adored style in Oakland, and now they'd do it in New York. In 1985, his first season in the Bronx, Henderson was the catalyst for arguably the best nonplayoff team of all time. That season, Henderson scored 146 runs, posted a .419 OBP, and clouted 24 homers. But in spite of his magma-hot start in pinstripes, the fans soured on his extroverted tendencies and seemingly distracted manner of play. After the Yankees fired Martin, Henderson feuded with his new manager, Lou Piniella, who raised Henderson's ire by openly questioning whether his leadoff man's spate of injuries might actually be a case of malingering.

So midway through the '89 season the Yankees traded him back to the A's for relievers Greg Cadaret and Eric Plunk and outfielder Luis Polonia. No one trade really undoes a franchise, but the Henderson deal certainly augured lean times to come for the Yankees, who would go on to record four straight losing seasons for the first and only time in club history. Back in his hometown, Henderson would be a lynchpin for the great Oakland teams of the late '80s and early '90s and would win his only MVP Award, in 1990.

The following season brought further hurrahs for Henderson. On May 1 against the Yankees, Henderson pilfered the 939th base of his career, thus pushing him past Lou Brock into first place on the all-time list. During the midgame ceremony to honor the feat, Henderson, widely known for his braggadocio and with a politely smiling Brock not 10 feet from him, thundered into the microphone, "Today, I am the greatest of all time." Hours later, revered (and overrated) fireballer Nolan Ryan pitched his seventh career no-hitter, thus relegating Henderson's accomplishment to the nation's collective short-term memory. The media seemed frothy with delight to point out that Ryan (the plainspoken Texas white guy) had trumped Henderson's appointment with history. They also seized upon Henderson's apparent aweless treatment of Brock during the midgame festivities. What they failed to report was that Henderson's "greatest" line was homage to his idol Muhammad Ali, and that he had received Brock's permission over dinner the night before to say those very words. Eight years later and back with the A's for a fourth stint, Henderson, at age 39, would become the oldest player ever to lead the majors in steals and walks in the same season.

Over his quarter-century career in the majors, Henderson wore nine different uniforms, scored the most runs in major league history, became one of seven players to reach base at least 5,000 times, tallied more than 3,000 hits, and set the record for leadoff home runs. He also made ten All-Star teams and won a pair of World Series rings. But that's not why most people remember him.

Henderson was most famous for his base-stealing and his indecorous acceptance of the accolades that followed. In terms of base-stealing,

Henderson was demonstrably the greatest. Still, the almost 1,500 career steals weren't what ferried Henderson to the pantheon of the sport. Henderson was indeed baseball's leadoff hitter and speed merchant nonpareil. But as the numbers show, he also showed uncommon power for a top-of-the-order hitter; demonstrated exacting patience at the plate (patience that would eventually and temporarily make him the game's all-time leader in bases on balls); and, of less import, stole bases with ruthless frequency and efficiency. It's the latter skill that we most often associate with Henderson; it's also his least valuable one.

Of the 124 playoff teams examined in this book, Henderson, by virtue of his picaresque meanderings around the league, toiled for eight of them. His greatest season, at least for a team that made the postseason, came with the 1990 Oakland A's. In a season that would garner Henderson AL MVP plaudits, he batted .325, led the AL with a .439 on-base percentage, and finished second in the loop with a .577 slugging percentage—the latter an outstanding number for a leadoff hitter. Additionally, Henderson swiped 65 bases while being caught only 10 times. But for all his derring-do on the basepaths, he contributed less than eight runs via stolen bases to his team's cause that entire season. Less than eight runs.

To throw this into brighter relief, let's look at Henderson's entire career. The following table shows the run values of each offensive event that occurred in Henderson's 25-year stay in the majors:

Positive Offensive Event	Number	Run Value
Singles	2,182	1,003.7
Doubles	510	382.5
Triples	66	68.2
Home runs	297	416.4
Unintentional walks	2,129	645.1
Intentional walks	61	10.7
Hit by pitch	98	32.3
Reached on error	158	75.5
Stolen bases	1,406	271.4
Total		2,905.8

As you can see, on the positive offensive side of the ledger, Henderson contributed, on his own, roughly 3,000 theoretical runs over the course of his career (this isn't accounting for negative events such as outs and sacrifice bunts). His runs from stolen bases amount to 9.3 percent of his positive career total. Of course, those 271.4 runs via the steal aren't counting for his 335 career times caught stealing and the 146.4 runs he lost as a result. That's a net gain of 125 runs over 25 seasons—five runs per year gained by the very avatar of base-stealing. That's a patently underwhelming total.

Consider that he was a plus defender for most seasons and you'll see that even in the case of Henderson, exploits on the basepaths are but a fractional piece of a player's value. And Henderson, of all people, is no exception. In terms of runs contributed to his teams, Henderson's base stealing lags his ability to hit singles, doubles, and home runs and his penchant for drawing walks. That Henderson was a great player is a notion beyond reproach; however, the contents of his greatness are widely misunderstood.

We know the precise value of the stolen base because of research performed, variously, by George Lindsey, Steve Mann, Pete Palmer, and John Thorn (the latter two in one of the seminal works of baseball analysis, *The Hidden Game of Baseball*). These four men all married play-by-play data with germane probability theory to devise run values for everything that happens in a baseball game. Years later, David Smyth would create his BaseRuns system, which would be further massaged by Tangotiger.net to yield updated and adjusted run values. In any event, the most recent research has shown that on average, stolen bases will roughly result in 0.185 run, while a caught stealing will dock a team about 0.45 run. The value for a steal comes from the fact that a runner on first will score about 26 percent of the time, while a runner on second will plate about 43 percent of the time. The difference comes to 0.17, and the possibility of a throwing error on the steal raises the value to 0.185 or thereabouts. As for the 0.45 figure, it reflects not only the harm of losing a base runner, but also the negative value of expending one of the team's 27 outs. These run values also allow us to determine the "break even" point for success rate on stolen bases. Since a caught stealing is roughly $2\frac{1}{2}$ times more damaging than a stolen base is beneficial, a player or team needs to be successful at least 72 percent of the time for the practice to be a net gain.

One common misconception about the steal is that it's far more valuable when leveraged during critical instances in a ball game. Intuitively this sounds fine: a steal attempt in the third inning of an 8–0 game naturally has less import than a steal attempt in the ninth frame of a one-run affair. Not so. The leveraged value of the stolen base varies negligibly from the random value. It may sound implausible, but the numbers bear it out.

In any event, these values fluctuate slightly from year to year, and by using the data from a particular year, you can calculate how many runs a player added to (or took from) his team's total for the season. It's this theoretical underpinning that leads us to observe that Henderson's base-stealing chipped in only about eight runs in 1990. That's less than one win over the course of an entire season.

As mentioned, Henderson's gaudy base-stealing numbers have never been the sine qua non of his staggering statistical bestowals; it's his peerless on-base skills and occasional power that have made him an immortal. His steals are merely a complementary skill: nice to have, but of only marginal value—the prehensile tail of baseball skills.

This knowledge squares with neither instinct nor perception. In almost any pursuit—ranging in consequence from global economics to beery games of foosball—there's a tendency to conflate what is exciting or engaging with what is vitally important. Sometimes this is perfectly appropriate; at other times it's downright misleading. The art, practice, and distraction of base-stealing constitute an object lesson of this idea.

In spite of the visceral appeal of the stolen base, it's just not all that important in generating runs for an offense. Leveraged during situations of critical mass and with a high rate of success, the stolen base can be a vaguely, modestly, and possibly remotely mentionable supporting piece of a team's offense by some standards somewhere. However, build an attack around the stolen base, and you'll likely confine your club to novelty status and vacuous plaudits from those who, by God, think you're at least trying out there.

The 124 teams I've examined, generally speaking, exemplify the dubious value of the stolen base. These teams have combined for 14,224 steals and 6,288 times caught stealing. Using the run values mentioned above, that comes to an aggregate of –173.73 runs. Yes, for all the frenzied baserunning, these teams—the best of the best over the past quarter century or so—have cost themselves about seventeen wins through their exploits on the basepaths.

To demonstrate just how feckless base-stealing is, let's present the other side with an accommodating hypothetical. Let's say instead of −173.73 runs, that total was actually +173.73 runs. There's no remotely defensible reason for doing this, but I have a point here. The 124 teams have combined for a total of 99,082 runs. While there's a bit of a logical schism to be considered when comparing theoretical and actual runs, it's nonetheless noteworthy that 173.73 comes to a measly 0.18 percent of these teams' total runs.

Golly, let's get even stupider in an attempt to muster a case for a crack-fueled running game. Let's say these teams never—not even once—made an out on the basepaths when attempting to steal. That would come to 14,224 steals without being caught, which tallies 2,711.09 runs. Even then, with such ridiculous and counterfactual contortions performed to make base-stealing resemble a simulacrum of a rendering of a semblance of a facsimile of a productive endeavor, it's only 2.74 percent of the offensive attack. In reality, the practice actually runs counter to an offense's stated goal of adding runs to the scoreboard. To put a deadlier point on it, playoff teams since 1980 owe −0.17 percent of their runs scored totals to stealing bases. The upshot is that winning teams in the modern era, whether they fully realize it or not, don't depend upon the running game to score runs.

For instance, the greatest base-stealing team of the modern era is also one that won its division—the 1985 St. Louis Cardinals. Here's the list of the ten most productive base-stealing teams of those I've studied for this book:

Ranking	Team	SB	CS	Net Runs
1.	'85 Cardinals	314	96	17.8
2.	'80 Royals	185	43	15.2
3.	'87 Cardinals	248	72	13.4
4.	'83 White Sox	165	50	9.6
5.	'93 Blue Jays	170	49	9.3
6.	'99 Diamondbacks	137	39	7.8
7.	'92 Blue Jays	129	39	7.5
8.	'89 A's	157	55	6.0
9.	'98 Astros	155	51	5.4
10.	'91 Blue Jays	148	53	5.2

In 1985 the Cards were already known as a freewheeling team whose home digs—Busch Stadium and its outrageously speedy (and billiard-felt green) artificial surface—lent itself to a game of speed. More than one announcer, desperate to gain purchase on a novel metaphor, likened Cardinal games of the 1980s to a track meet. In 1985 the Cardinals were three seasons removed from their ninth world championship. With folksy manager Whitey Herzog at the switch, the Cards had built their intermittent dynasty around speed, defense, and pitching. "Whitey Ball" became an indelible part of base-ball parlance in the 1980s.

Much like Henderson, except on a macro level, the '80s-model Cardinals are known best for their base-stealing prowess; in reality, that's the least of their merits. In 1985 the Cardinals swiped a whop-ping 314 bases (the highest total in the National League since 1912) against 96 caught. Despite the degree to which the Cards luxuriated on the basepaths, they contributed, on balance, only 17.84 runs for the entire season (2.39 percent of the team's total runs scored). On a team level that's not much, and keep in mind this is the best base-stealing team of modern vintage. How the '85 Cards did win was by leading the league in on-base percentage and fewest runs allowed.

It was the aforementioned Vince Coleman, a rookie that season, who was far and away the leading base stealer for the '85 Cardinals. Coleman came to St. Louis in 1985 as an already ballyhooed speedster famous in the minors for often going from first to third on bunts. In six celebrated seasons in St. Louis, Coleman logged 549 steals and appeared to be on an unswerving course for Lou Brock's stolen-base record. But then Coleman signed with the Mets. Coleman's career in New York was little more than a three-year indignity, noteworthy for squabbles with his superiors, a suspension by the team for insubordi-nation, and a felonious-assault conviction for tossing a lit firecracker at a pack of autograph seekers.

In 1985, however, things were rosier for Coleman—in terms of jurisprudence, anyway. By swiping a league-leading 110 bags against only 15 caught, Coleman tallied 9.84 runs on the bases—more than Henderson in his MVP season, but still an unimposing total. In point of fact, Coleman was one of the least productive regulars in the lineup. Coleman, as a poor-fielding, noodle-armed corner outfielder, posted a subpar .320 on-base percentage and hit only a single homer on the season. He was the best base stealer in baseball that season, but that didn't spare him from being a below-average performer. His scampering on the bases contributed, one assumes, masturbatory levels of self-amusement but little in the way of runs.

The 2003 Marlins, who scampered to a stunning World Series win over the Yankees with septuagenarian Jack McKeon at the controls, are often held up as an example of how a team in these modern, slugging times can achieve a competitive advantage by running wild on the bases. The Marlins did indeed lead the NL in steals by a staggering margin. (They tallied 150 swipes, while the second-ranked Expos stole only 100 bases.) Of course, as is so often the case with teams that pace the league in steals, they also topped the loop in times caught stealing, with 74.

As we did with Rickey Henderson above, let's use linear weights to determine just how much of the Marlins' offensive contributions that season resulted from the stolen base:

Positive Offensive Event	Number	Run Value
Singles	966	444.4
Doubles	292	219.0
Triples	44	45.5
Home runs	157	220.1
Unintentional walks	471	142.7
Intentional walks	44	7.7
Hit by pitch	57	18.8
Reached on error	59	28.2
Stolen bases	150	29.0
Total		1,155.4

As with Henderson, this table doesn't account for negative events. However it's framed, the results should snuff out the notion that the Marlins succeeded by way of the stolen base. On the season, their 150 steals amounted to only 29 gross runs—a paltry 2.5 percent of their team total. Of course, the Marlins, by lavishing their opponents with 74 outs on the bases, failed to reach the widely and grossly underestimated break-even point for steals. As a result, they lost 32.3 runs as a result of those times being caught. That's a net negative on the season of –3.3 runs. To hear those who dance around the maypole of the stolen base tell it, the Marlins of '03 were a refreshing and efficacious

throwback to an era when teams realized the value of running; to hear
the facts tell it, their jaunt through the dappled meadows of tradition
only hurt them. In 2003 the Marlins were a worse team because of
their habit of stealing bases.

There are those teams that run, and then there are those that run with
scissors. While the '85 Cards and the '80 Royals (more on them later)
were—to damn them with faint praise—indisputably the best running
teams in recent history, the worst was the 1987 San Francisco Giants.
For maximum schadenfreude, here's the complete list:

Ranking	Team	SB	CS	Net Runs
1.	'87 Giants	126	97	−22.6
2.	'02 Twins	79	62	−14.7
3.	'01 Indians	86	61	−12.9
4.	'82 Angels	55	53	−11.9
4.	'90 Red Sox	53	52	−11.9
6.	'01 Astros	64	49	−11.3
7.	'87 Twins	113	65	−9.6
8.	'00 Mets	66	46	−9.5
9.	'85 Blue Jays	144	77	−9.3
10.	'97 Yankees	99	58	−8.9

The Giants of that year stole 126 bases, which was the third-
lowest total in the NL that season, but they were caught a whopping
97 times, which was the most in all of baseball. Because of that
sherpa's load of outs on the bases, the Giants' stolen-base run value
comes to a grisly figure of more than 20 runs in the red, or −2.88 percent of their total runs scored (both figures easily "top" those of all
other teams studied herein).

Giants first baseman Will Clark was a player of substantial merits—
good power numbers obscured for many years by the run-suppressing
nature of Candlestick Park, plate discipline, an ability to hit for average, excellent defense—but in '87 he was an international incident on
the basepaths. In what was otherwise one of Clark's finest seasons, he
stole five bases against 17 caught that year. As mentioned, a player

needs to be successful on roughly 75 percent of his attempts to make base-stealing a break-even endeavor (in some quarters, you'll hear 66 percent or so as the cutoff for productivity, but the numbers say that's too accommodating). Clark, meanwhile, was successful less than 23 percent of the time that season, meaning he and his team would have been better off if he wore a tracking collar that raised a mighty hue and cry whenever he strayed more than a few steps off the bag.

If the Giants of '87 had resisted scurrying into outs on the base-paths, they would have added almost 23 runs to their season total. That season they finished five games behind the Cardinals for home-field advantage in the NLCS. While 23 runs in theoretical terms aren't enough to make up that gap, they would have at least put them in hailing distance. That year the NLCS was a nip-and-tuck affair, with San Francisco losing in seven games. Shift home-field advantage to the Giants, and who knows?

Had the '97 Yankees exhibited a schoolmarm's restraint on the bases (and by that I mean had they not attempted a steal all season), they probably would have become the first Yankee team since 1950 to score at least 900 runs in a season. Instead they finished nine short of the mark and docked themselves that same number of runs by trying to pilfer bases.

When comparing the clubs within the purview of this study to teams that *didn't* make the postseason, some interesting findings come to light. First, playoff teams are slightly more efficient—or, to be more accurate, slightly less self-immolating—than nonplayoff teams in terms of runs lost to base-stealing. On average, playoff teams since 1980 have averaged −1.40 runs per season on the basepaths, while nonplayoff teams over that same span have averaged −2.29 runs per season. However, that advantage has come not from stealing more often; rather, it's come from minimizing the damage naturally incurred from a gratuitous running game by stealing less often. Playoff teams have averaged 165.4 steal attempts per season, and teams not passing postseason muster have averaged 170.9 steal attempts per season. The difference isn't striking, but it does, to some degree, dispel the notion that a berserk approach on the bases leads to more runs. It doesn't.

Indeed, most of the teams I've studied would have been better off having never attempted a stolen base. In fact, 76 of the 124 (61.3

percent) teams that have made the playoffs since 1980 have posted negative run values in the stolen-base column. In modern times, most teams that win have harmed themselves by stealing bases. Those that haven't subtracted from their run totals, for the most part, have added a negligible number of runs via the purloined base. To approach it from another angle, teams that have led their respective leagues in stolen bases since 1980 have made the playoffs nine times. In contrast, teams that have led their respective leagues in fewest times caught stealing have made the playoffs 16 times. It's yet another piece of evidence that suggests risk aversion is the wisest tack when it comes to the running game.

Since time immemorial the Red Sox have been negatively associated with a highly indolent approach on the bases. There any number of things that elicit much Calvinist boo-hooing within Sox Nation, but this is assuredly one of them. What the Sox have also done since time immemorial is mostly knock the snot out of the ball. While Fenway of earlier years helped make the offense look better (and conversely, the pitching staff worse) than it really was, base stealing for Boston, as it is for most teams, would have been counterproductive.

Historically, the Boston roster has been largely peopled with sluggard Caucasians (this isn't sociocultural hectoring; it's merely an observation), but despite fashionable ante-2004 preoccupations with curses, deus ex machina playoff shortfalls, and other manners of cosmic disfavor, the Red Sox have also been a largely successful franchise. Take the era of present interest, for instance. In the 22 seasons within the scope of this book, the Red Sox have posted 18 winning campaigns and seven playoff appearances. In other words, over that span they've been one of the most prosperous clubs in baseball. Turning an eye toward their base-stealing, over that same span they've finished dead last in thefts 11 times, even in the decidedly nonstealing American League.

To simplify it for former humanities majors like myself, that comes to half of the seasons in question. The Sox finished next to last another five times and never higher than seventh in the 14-team AL. In those years that Boston did make the playoffs, they finished last in the AL in steals in six of the seven seasons. So despite their historic reluctance to steal bases and the usual mélange of complaints regarding such a strategy, Boston has thrived.

Johnny Damon was the rare Red Sock who efficiently stole bases. Boston, under then GM Dan Duquette, signed Damon in December of 2001 to a four-year, $31-million deal. Damon would go on to be a semicritical part of the Red Sox's notable successes over the next handful of seasons. By providing strong defense in center field and passable to solid on-base skills, Damon conferred good value—albeit not on the dollar—to the club. But it was his cachet as a leadoff hitter that earned him misplaced praise. Damon, prior to the 2004 season, garnered something approaching cult status when he showed up in spring training adorned in an unruly beard and shoulder-length hair, looking like the residue of some unholy coupling of a porn star and a neo-Luddite hostage-taker.

Easily the most efficient base stealer in recent Boston history, Damon in 2003 stole 30 bases against only six caught. As effectual as that might sound, he still contributed less than three runs on the season via the stolen base.

On a team level, two of the most successful franchises of recent history, the Braves of the 1990s and beyond and the A's of the aughts, by and large neglected the stolen base. From the time the Braves' NL hegemony began in 1991 through the 2003 season, they made the playoffs 12 times. In six of those seasons, they finished in the bottom half of the league in steals and never once led the league in steals. But even they didn't eschew the steal to the extent the A's have in recent seasons.

Oakland under GM Billy Beane has famously used advanced statistical analysis as the major component of their decision-making calculus; part of that was a determination that stealing bases, save for highly specific circumstances, didn't make sense. From 2000 to 2003, the A's made the playoffs each season. They also finished last in steals in two of those four seasons and next to last in the remaining two seasons.

As the numbers above have shown, the act of stealing bases is at best marginally useful and certainly no way to build a battering offensive attack. Even so, many advocates will point to what they deem to be nonquantifiable benefits of a restive manner on the bases. Stealing will put pressure on the defense, we're told, and distract the pitcher from his essential duty of retiring the hitter before him. The first baseman must hold the runner, and one of the two middle infielders will create a hole by covering the bag at second. The batter will see more fastballs, as the pitcher attempts to hurry the ball to the plate to cut down on the runner's jump. It's these things that don't show up in any statistical analysis of base-stealing. Except they do.

Researcher Mitchel Lichtman, who now works as a senior adviser to the St. Louis Cardinals, tackled this very quandary. In a study spanning four seasons, Lichtman assembled two study populations—prolific and nonprolific base stealers—based on how often a player attempted to steal a base relative to his base-stealing opportunities (defined as man on first with no other runners on base). The prolific group averaged a steal attempt 19 percent of the time, while the nonprolific group didn't attempt a single theft under these conditions.

Previous studies have attempted to isolate what happens to pitcher and batter when a steal occurs during a plate appearance, but what they failed to do—and what Lichtman's study *did* do—was control for the batter-stealer pairing. The problem theretofore was that studies didn't account for the fact that prolific stealers tended to bat in front of middle-of-the-order types while nonprolific stealers usually hit in front of those in the top or bottom of the lineup.

Lichtman tailored his study to correct this flaw by weighting the plate appearances of each batter by whichever occurred less often—a trip to the plate with a stealing threat or stealing nonthreat on the bases. In essence what his research yielded was the average difference of all hitters and their batting stats when there is a threat on first and when there is a nonthreat on first. Here's what he found:

Threats on first:

PA	AVG/OBP/SLG
6,872	.282/.338/.447

Nonthreats on first:

PA	AVG/OBP/SLG
6,872	.279/.336/.446

When there's a base-stealing threat on first, the batter will tend to hit singles more often, walk more often, and strike out less often. However, in terms of overall production (as demonstrated by the key rate stats of AVG/OBP/SLG), the differences are negligible. In other words, it's not helping the batter to have a speedster on first in front of him.

It may be that the batter receives a more accommodating pitch selection, but it may also be that he winds up taking a strike or swinging and missing on purpose to protect the runner and thus tilting the count in the pitcher's favor. Hall of Fame second baseman Joe Morgan, among many others, was wont to complain about runners going when he was at the plate (which is rather importunate coming from a player with 689 career steals), feeling it was too much of a distraction. Whatever the case, Lichtman posits that it's a wash in terms of batter production. These findings also run counter to what's put forth by the other camp. Many analysts, backed by flawed or poorly executed studies, have attempted to make Sabermetric hay by claiming that steals exact a price in terms of negatively affecting the batter at the plate. Lichtman's study dispels that notion as well.

We already know that steals themselves confer very little in terms of run scoring, and now, thanks to Lichtman's work, we know that the previously touted ancillary benefits of the steal are all but vaporous in importance.

As endlessly as I've blistered the proactive running game, I don't mean to conflate the principle of speed with base-stealing, the least valuable of its outgrowths. On the contrary, speed, on both the individual and the team levels, is quite nifty to have. Speed has a direct relationship with fielding range (particularly in the outfield), which, of course, means a better team defense. Speed also helps a player at the plate by cutting down on the number of double plays he hits into. Moreover, a fast runner at the plate can turn doubles into triples, singles into doubles, and infield groundouts into infield singles. On the bases, he can break up double plays more easily and tag up on shallower fly balls.

In terms of individual players, speed also portends of superior career progression, as Nate Silver's research at *Baseball Prospectus* has found. In a study comparing two groups of power hitters—one with good speed indicators and one with poor speed indicators—Silver found that the former group, the one notable for its speed, outproduced the latter group, had longer careers, better maintained performance levels, and produced more Hall of Famers than the latter group. A player who exhibits speed but nothing in the way of baseball skills isn't valuable, but a player who has speed in the presence of a broad base of hitting and fielding skills is indeed a commodity. This may sound painfully obvious, but Silver's research shows that the advantages of a fast player over a slower player with otherwise similar skills are drastic and incontrovertible.

In light of Silver's findings, it's certainly worth our while to consider speed on the team level. One effective way to measure team speed is by using a Bill James concoction called the speed score. The speed score, which was first presented in the *1987 Bill James Baseball Abstract*, assigns its scores based on stolen-base percentage, stolen-base attempts as a percentage of times on first base, triples as a percentage of balls in play, runs scored as a percentage of times on base, grounded into double plays as a percentage of balls in play, and defensive range factor. For our purposes, the defensive range factor component has been left out. Mostly this is because unadjusted range factors without supporting defensive metrics are about as useful as an electric sandwich, which is to say not very useful, and they're even less informative on a team level.

In any event, after speed scores are calculated for each of our 124 teams, we find that playoff teams have better team speed than nonplayoff teams. On average, since 1980, playoff teams have speed scores that are 1.7 percent better than the league average (their advantage over nonplayoff teams would be even greater, since the higher speed scores of playoff teams are used in the calculations, thus driving up the league average scores). Of the 124 teams studied, 59.7 percent posted better-than-league-average speed scores.

Here, then, are the top ten team speed scores expressed as a percentage of the league-average score:

Ranking	Team	Percentage of League-Average Speed Score
1.	'80 Royals	132.4
2.	'85 Cardinals	131.6
3.	'93 Blue Jays	123.2
4.	'83 White Sox	121.8
5.	'87 Cardinals	118.8
6.	'99 Diamondbacks	118.3

7.	'01 Mariners	117.7
8.	'91 Blue Jays	116.8
9.	'02 Angels	114.3
10.	'92 Blue Jays	114.2

As you can see, the '85 Cardinals, the greatest base-stealing team of the modern era (as detailed above), also rank highly in terms of overall speed, coming in at 31.6 percent better than the league average speed score. That's hardly surprising.

The '80 Royals also boast an embarrassment of riches in terms of team speed. Traditionally, the AL has been characterized (most often to pillory the circuit) as the nonrunning league. This is probably two parts the presence of the designated hitter and one part tradition. That the AL has the DH means their reliance on "manufacturing runs," as the pundits like to call it ("disassembling runs" would be more accurate), isn't as great as it is in the senior circuit. They have more true hitters, so they let them hit. And good for them.

Nevertheless, the AL has purveyed some frantic running teams within the aegis of my research. The '80 Kansas City Royals, in terms of runs added via the stolen base, rank as the fastest team I've studied, as you may have noticed above. While they weren't as prolific in the steals department as their Missouri labelmates, they were more efficient. Of all the teams in the annals of the game that attempted at least 100 steals, the '80 Royals, by succeeding in 81.14 percent of their attempts, lag only the '75 Reds and the '62 Dodgers in stolen-base percentage. Among teams that attempted at least 50 steals, the '80 Royals rank fifth all-time in stolen-base percentage. If nothing else, they minimized damage.

Moreover, the 1980 Royals were a team adept at playing the speed game independent of the stolen base. That season, they of course led the AL in steals by an indecent margin while ranking an impressive third in fewest times caught. They also topped the loop in triples and stolen-base percentage, which helped buttress that impressive speed score.

The Royals that year were led, at least on the basepaths, by center fielder Willie Wilson. Wilson, a native of Montgomery, Alabama, was an outstanding athlete who turned down a football scholarship to the University of Maryland in favor of a baseball career. It turned out to be a sage risk. One of the fastest players ever to kick a toe into third base, Wilson set a career high in steals in 1979, under manager Whitey Herzog (whom Wilson was wont to refer to as a "crazy sumbuck"), with 83 (the highest tally in the AL since Ty Cobb swindled 96 bags in 1915) while being caught only 12 times. Wilson in 1980 also legged out a fairly astounding five inside-the-park home runs. Additionally, Wilson ranks second only to Roberto Clemente for career triples after World War II, when they were much harder to come by than in previous eras.

In 1980, George Brett was easily the Royals' best hitter, but Wilson was also a meaningful contributor. That season, the switch-hitting Wilson became only the second player in major league history to record at least 100 hits from both sides of the plate in the same season. He also dazzled as an outfielder in the then spacious Kauffman Stadium.

However, Wilson was most famous for his attainments on the bases. In 1980, Wilson stole 79 bases against only 10 caught. That comes to an 88.8 percent success rate and 10.6 runs added (which is 69.5 percent of the team's total runs derived from base-stealing that year). Still, the gaudy stolen-base numbers weren't Wilson's greatest merits that season. He also batted .327, posted a .357 on-base percentage, smacked almost 50 extra-base knocks, rapped out 230 hits—the third-highest total in the AL since 1928—and provided excellent defense in the outfield. Three years later, Wilson would be one of four Royals indicted on drug charges. He even spent a little time in the pokey for a crime that was patently less harmful to society at large than flinging low-grade explosives at a throng of fans.

Like most successful teams that swipe a lot of bags, the '80 Royals were actually winning ball games by other means. That year they led the AL in batting average and ranked fourth in on-base percentage, fifth in slugging percentage, and fifth in fewest runs allowed. (Oh, and the rest of their division sucked. The A's, who finished second to and 14 games back of the Royals in the West, would have placed a measly sixth in the "rough as burlap nether garments" AL East. Kansas City, incidentally, would have finished third.)

Of course, the Royals also thrived at the less famous elements of the running game that make up the back end of the speed score metric. Brett, Wilson, and shortstop UL Washington (who was variously famous for replacing the overly beloved Freddie Patek, always—

seriously, always—having a toothpick in his mouth, helping fell the Yankees in the '80 ALCS, and being busted for coke along with Wilson et al. in the early 80s) combined for 35 triples, which was as much as or more than the totals of six other teams in the AL that season.

The Blue Jays of the early nineties, as you probably noticed, own three of the top ten speed scores. In two of those three seasons, the Jays paced the AL in steals, and in each season they ranked second in the league in triples. From 1991 to 1993, second baseman Roberto Alomar and center fielder Devon White, the two fastest players on the team, combined for 261 steals and only 53 caught. That comes to a nifty success rate of 83.1 percent, but, as I've already demonstrated, the gain in runs is rather meek (only 24.4 over the three-year span).

As mentioned, Devon White, the greatest major leaguer ever to hail from Jamaica, was a major reason for the Jays' impressive team speed scores. Originally an Angel, White crafted a reputation as a fleet-footed center fielder and effective leadoff man (at least as the term was understood at that time). White once garnered fleeting notoriety by consecutively stealing second, third, and home in an otherwise inconsequential game in September 1989.

Following a extended conflict with California manager Doug Rader, White came to the Jays from the Angels prior to the 1990 season as part of a five-player trade that also involved longtime major leaguers such as Luis Sojo (later to be the Yankees' nearly useless good-luck charm during much of their dynastic run of the late '90s) and Junior Felix. Once in Toronto, White would go on to win a Gold Glove in each of his five seasons as a Blue Jay, and he also proved to be an efficient base thief over that span. White was an indelible and critical part of the championship teams in Toronto and for a while held the record for highest batting average in the League Championship Series.

However, in many ways White embodies some of the limits of the speed score, in terms of putting runs on the board. Part of the speed-scores calculus is that teams or players are rewarded for attempting steals at a high rate relative to their times on base. The upshot is that a sizable number of steals attempts in tandem with a low OBP will boost a player's speed score. That's "Devo" in 1992, when the Jays won the first of their back-to-back World Series. That season, White pilfered 37 bases, which was good for 11th in the AL, but posted a paltry OBP of .303—not what you want from anyone at any position, much less an outfielder. White was astoundingly efficient on the bases (only four caught in 41 attempts), but his speed score is inflated by the fact that he made an out in almost 70 percent of his plate appearances. Moreover, ensconced within that OBP of .303 are 17 homers and seven triples, events in which it is, respectively, impossible and bloody well difficult to follow with a stolen-base attempt. To be fair, '92 was easily White's worst season as a Jay, but it's worth noting that speed scores sometimes reward suboptimal on-base numbers.

Although they don't appear in the top 10, the '93 Phillies somewhat surprisingly rank well in terms of team speed. Their speed score, which is 12.6 percent better than the league average, ranks 13th. The Phils that season won 97 games and the pennant in what was a stunning intermezzo to the Braves' annual appearance in the World Series. Take a gander at the team photo from that season and you'll find that the Phils more closely resembled a stevedores' local than a carefully selected roster of elite professional athletes. Watch them mill about the clubhouse and you'd conclude that body fat, tobacco juice, and poorly executed facial hair would have been more critical to their success than team speed.

Still and yet, the Phils were fast. Leadoff hitter, center fielder, and team philosopher-king Lenny Dykstra paced the team with 37 steals. Dykstra was originally a New York Met. After swiping 105 bases in the Carolina League in 1983, Dykstra was on the organizational fast track and was a major league semiregular by '85. As a hard-charging, dirty-uniformed young outfielder, Dykstra, who formed the "Partners in Grime" tandem with Mets second baseman Wally Backman, endeared himself to Met partisans who relished his intrepid and brash style of play. In 1989 Dykstra, along with relievers Roger McDowell and Tom Edens, came to the Phillies in a wildly unpopular trade (at least from the New York perspective) for outfielder Juan Samuel.

Once in Philly, Dykstra packed on the muscle (long after his retirement, he'd be accused of using steroids during his playing days) and became one of the game's most complete players, but not until he'd endured an array of maladies. In May 1991, a drunk-driving accident landed Dykstra on the disabled list for the first time in his career. In August he plowed into an outfield wall and fractured his shoulder for the second time that season. The following year, a inside fastball from Greg Maddux on Opening Day broke Dykstra's arm and limited him to 85 games.

In 1993, however, he was healthy and wielding all of his substantial skills. Besides showing good speed on the bases and capably manning a key defensive position, Dykstra that year also batted .305, stroked almost 70 extra-base hits, and drew a league-leading 129 walks (for a robust .420 OBP—good for third in the NL). He also scored 141 runs, which was the highest single-season total in the NL since fellow Phillie Chuck Klein tallied 152 in 1932. On another level, Dykstra embodied the hardscrabble (and poorly groomed) ethos that made Philly the team du jour to so many around the country.

Second baseman Mickey Morandini (one of several Phillies who that season sported a lamentable "Kentucky Waterfall" coif) outdid even Dykstra in terms of base-stealing efficiency by swiping 13 bags in 15 tries. The Phils also tallied 51 triples as a team, which ranked second that season only to the Rockies, whose total was inflated by the thin air and commodious outfield of Coors Field.

Now for the other, uglier side of the coin: the following teams played the tortoise to the above litany of hares:

Ranking	Team	Percentage of League-Average Speed Score
1.	'90 Red Sox	74.9
2.	'86 Red Sox	80.5
3.	'96 Braves	82.9
4.	'03 Giants	83.9
5.	'00 Mets	84.1
6.	'95 Braves	84.4
7.	'82 Angels	84.6
8.	'01 Astros	87.1
9.	'83 Orioles	87.3
10.	'96 Padres	87.6

The 2000 Mets, who regaled the nation and the endlessly self-absorbed Gotham media with a subway encounter with the worst Yankee World Series team ever, also rank as one of the slowest playoff teams in recent memory.

No Met that season tallied more than eight steals, and center fielder Jay Payton delighted catchers around the league by stealing only five bases in 16 attempts. The 2000 Mets also ranked next to last in the NL in steals and dead last in triples. In fact, their total of 20 triples is the lowest of any team I studied save for three: the 1999 Mets, who logged a measly 14 triples (the lowest team total in the history of the National League) and the 2002 and 2003 Yankees, who totaled 12 and 14 triples, respectively. Additionally, the Mets' 20 triples in 2000 were matched that season by a single player, Twins shortstop Cristian Guzman. Of course, that's hardly shocking when your first baseman leads the club in three-baggers (Todd Zeile with—prepare yourselves for a numerological juxtaposition that will make your very bones quake—three).

While not exactly a lumbering heap of protohumans, the '82 Angels that season did finish 11th in the 14-team AL in steals (but seventh in times caught stealing), last in stolen-base percentage, last in triples, and sixth in most grounded-into double plays. The Halos also ranked a distant second in runs scored despite placing a distant first in on-base percentage.

California swiped only 55 bases that season, but they were caught 53 times. First baseman Rod Carew that season stole 10 bags, but he made 27 attempts and thus cost his team more than five runs on the season. It's perhaps a damning observation for the Angels of 1982 that their DH, the somewhat corpulent Don Baylor, was their most operative base stealer, with 10 swiped and only four caught (which comes to a foolishly modest net gain of 0.14 run).

The slowest of these, however, were the Boston Red Sox of 1990. As detailed above, the Sox are historically a slow team, and 1990 was a rather naked example of that truth. The list above shows us that the Red Sox's speed score that season was a mere 74.9 percent of the league average, which is the worst such mark of any team I've studied. Additionally, that season the Red Sox attempted 105 steals (the lowest total in baseball that season) and succeeded only 53 times. That comes to a success rate of 51.5 percent, and, since 1972 (the back end of available play-by-play data), no other team attempting at least 100 steals has had such a low rate of success and still made the postseason. Overall, the '90 Red Sox have the 11th-lowest stolen-base percentage of any team since 1972.

The main offender for Boston that year was outfielder Tom Brunansky, who stole only five bases in 15 attempts. As a rule of thumb, no mustachioed corner outfielder of Eastern European heritage should ever be given the green light. Alas, Brunansky was.

"Bruno" was originally selected by the Angels in the first round of the 1978 draft. After contract negotiations dawdled, team owner Gene Autry called in none other than former president Richard Nixon to help. Not long after, Brunansky signed for a then record $125,000, and Nixon basked in the glow of his second-greatest diplomatic hallmark (outdone only by the Sino-Soviet détente of the early 1970s).

Early in the 1981 season, the Angels traded their hometown phenom before he'd even exhausted his rookie status, along with pitcher Mike Walters to the Twins for pitcher Doug Corbett and second baseman Rob Wilfong. Once in Minnesota, Brunansky began an eight-year run that saw him hit at least 20 homers per season. He never hit for high averages, mostly because of his extreme uppercut swing, but he showed good power and boasted a powerful arm in right. He endeared himself to Twins fans by slugging an even 1.000 in the 1987 ALCS, but early the following season he was dealt to St. Louis for second baseman Tommy Herr.

Two years later, the Cardinals shipped him to Boston for closer Lee Smith. Although his numbers for the Red Sox in 1990 weren't terribly impressive, Brunansky did hit five homers in the final week of the season to help the Sox edge the Blue Jays by two games in the AL East. But a base stealer he squarely was not.

Also lowering Boston's speed score is that the team didn't score as many runs as you'd expect given how often they had runners on base. In 1990, Boston paced all of baseball with a .343 on-base percentage; however, they ranked only seventh in the AL in runs scored. While that's not a direct indictment of team speed, the inability to take the extra base, score from second on a hit to the outfield, or advance as expected after a defensive miscue could all be partly to blame for the Red Sox's relative inefficiencies that season.

As I've detailed, winning teams, by and large, do show superior team speed; however, that speed is wielded in more effective ways than by stealing bases. The numbers show that the stolen base is often an instrument of negligible worth, and it's occasionally one of self-destruction. Winning teams don't steal as often as less successful teams, but even when they do, winning teams, on average, tend to squander runs in the process. Speed is good, and winning teams have it, but they'd be better off drastically ramping down their reliance on the stolen base. It might make for a less aesthetically pleasing game, but the verse-chorus-verse approach to scoring runs is so generally unpopular that we'll always have nonbelieving squads around to entertain us.

CHAPTER 7

The Deadline Game

(or, Why It's Hard to Win a Pennant in Two Months)

Each year, Major League Baseball circumscribes—or perhaps hurries along—its clubs with a pair of trade deadlines. The first, which occurs on the afternoon of July 31, marks the end of the period in which teams can trade players without first passing them through revocable waivers. The second, on August 31, marks the deadline for teams to acquire players and still be able to place them on postseason rosters. In that block of calendar from July 1 to August 31, some of the most memorable (or forgettable, depending upon your partisanships) trades have unfolded. It's a frenzied time for fans, execs, and league organ grinders alike. Rumors scamper about like astonished cockroaches, and saturation-level media coverage causes deep-vein thrombosis in many a fan.

If it's not a tacit requirement that a playoff team make an acquisition at the trade deadlines, then it's certainly de rigueur; of the 124 teams I've looked at, 108 (87.1 percent) made a trade at or around those annual deadlines for a player or players who saw action for the team at the major league level that same season. However, for all the deadline activity we've witnessed over the years, these deals, by and large, aren't all that important in terms of winning ball games during the regular season in question.

You'll recall that I previously introduced a *Baseball Prospectus*–created statistic called VORP (Value over Replacement Player or Value over Replacement Pitcher). To reiterate, VORP expresses the number of runs contributed or prevented over what might be expected from a readily available filler-talent type. Using VORP as our operational metric, we can evaluate just how much significance these deadline deals have had for playoff-bound teams. I'll do this by examining what percentage of the total team VORP—both pitching and hitting (VORP does not account for defensive contributions)—has been derived from deadline acquisitions. Obviously, only the VORP that deadliners provided *after* the trade in question will be considered. For our purposes, what these players did prior to the deal is neither here nor there.

Overall, the 108 teams that have made deadline pickups meeting the aforementioned criteria have harvested, on average, only 2.2 percent of their total team VORP from these acquisitions. Suffice it to say, that's not a substantial figure. Although it doesn't cohere with perception, deadline pickups, generally speaking, contribute very little to their new teams, at least in the season in which they're acquired. This is partly because GMs have habits of dealing for overvalued commodities and/or incorrectly assessing their own needs. However, part of it is simply because the July 31 deadline occurs when the season is more than half over. That's often not enough time for the newly acquired players to alter significantly their team's fortunes. On another level, with the remaining sample of games so small in number, players—even very good ones who otherwise constitute wise calculated risks by the acquiring teams—can very easily proffer a bad 150 plate appearances or a stunningly ineffective 75 innings pitched. If that's the case, it still doesn't, from an analytical vista, amount to a sober devastation of the trade in question; rather, it just may mean that there wasn't time for the player's genuine level of performance to rise to the surface.

In all, 252 players were traded to these playoff-bound teams and saw action with that major league club in the same season. More than half the time, teams traded for pitchers. Here's how those acquisitions break down by role (roles are assigned based on where the player spent the majority of his time with the new team):

Role/Position	Number	Percentage of Total
Relief pitcher	78	31.0
Starting pitcher	52	20.6
Third baseman	20	7.9
Designated hitter	18	7.1
Left fielder	16	6.3
Center fielder	14	5.6
Right fielder	12	4.8
First baseman	11	4.4
Second baseman	10	4.0
Catcher	9	3.6
Pinch hitter	6	2.4
Shortstop	6	2.4

Overall, 76 teams acquired at least one pitcher leading up to the trade deadlines. That comes to 61.3 percent of the teams I've studied. In light of this information, it might be tempting to conclude that successful teams become that way, in part, because of their willingness and ability to add arms for the stretch drive. However, most often that's not the case. Given that we've already learned that these teams, broadly speaking, excelled more at run prevention than at run scoring and that deadline trades as a species generally confer little value to the contending club, these teams' penchant for adding arms is perhaps a comfortable vacuity at best.

Of course, there are exceptions to the rule that deadline trades don't mean much. Following is the list of teams that helped themselves the most via the deadline pickup. They're sorted by percentage of total team VORP drawn from all trade acquisitions acquired within the deadline period.

Ranking	Team	Percentage of Total Team VORP
1.	'87 Giants	15.54
2.	'95 Reds	8.49
3.	'03 Cubs	8.17

Ranking	Team	Percentage of Total Team VORP
4.	'98 Astros	7.54
5.	'02 Cardinals	7.10
6.	'00 Cardinals	7.04
7.	'97 Giants	6.70
8.	'95 Yankees	6.66
9.	'99 Mets	6.28
10.	'87 Tigers	6.10

And here are the players those teams acquired, with individual VORPs in parentheses:

Team	Players Acquired at Deadline
'87 Giants	SP Dave Dravecky (26.4), RP Craig Lefferts (10.7), 3B Kevin Mitchell (27.5), SP Rick Reuschel (2.9), RP Don Robinson (12.8)
'95 Reds	SP Dave Burba (16.1), CF Darren Lewis (–6.2), SP Mark Portugal (14.3), SP David Wells (12.1)
'03 Cubs	CF Kenny Lofton (20.5), 3B Aramis Ramirez (14.7), 1B Randall Simon (4.8), 2B Tony Womack (–1.4)
'98 Astros	SP Randy Johnson (41.2), RP Jay Powell (12.1)
'02 Cardinals	RP Jeff Fassero (4.8), SP Chuck Finley (11.2), RP Nerio Rodriguez (–0.4), 3B Scott Rolen (22.6), SP Jamey Wright (1.2)
'00 Cardinals	RP Jason Christensen (0.1), 1B Will Clark (29.4), C Carlos Hernandez (2.7), RP Mike Timlin (9.9)
'97 Giants	SP Wilson Alvarez (5.9), RP Cory Bailey (–3.0), SP Danny Darwin (1.7), RP Roberto Hernandez (11.3), C Brian Johnson (14.0), SP Pat Rapp (–3.2)
'95 Yankees	SP David Cone (27.9), DH Ruben Sierra (5.4)
'99 Mets	CF Shawon Dunston (6.6), CF Darryl Hamilton (17.9), RP Chuck McElroy (4.2), RP Billy Taylor (–2.8), SP Kenny Rogers (17.2)
'87 Tigers	SP Doyle Alexander (44.1), 3B Jim Morrison (–5.4)

As you can see, the '87 Giants stand comfortably alone as the greatest "deadline" playoff-bound team of the modern era. In 1985, the hapless

Giants lost 100 games and finished last in the NL West. With 18 games to go that season, the club fired manager Jim Davenport and replaced him with Roger Craig, a legendary pitching coach credited with teaching the split-finger fastball to Mike Scott and Jack Morris and onetime manager of the Padres. Craig finished the '85 season 6–12, but the next year he guided the Giants to an improbable 83–79 mark and a third-place finish.

Expectations were lofty heading in the 1987 season, and the "Hum Baby" Giants held first in the West for the opening two months of the season. Then the slide began. By the Fourth of July, the Giants had dropped 14 of 20 and fallen 5½ games behind the Reds. It was then that General Manager Al Rosen decided to make a series of bold trades that would change the course of the division.

As a player, "Flip" Rosen held the AL rookie record for home runs for 37 years (until Mark McGwire obliterated it in 1987) and unanimously won the 1953 AL MVP Award. After his untimely retirement following the 1956 season, Rosen went on to a successful postbaseball career as a commodities trader. In 1978, George Steinbrenner hired him to run the Yankees, and Rosen's short tenure was highlighted by a 10-player deal with Texas that landed the Yankees a young minor leaguer named Dave Righetti. After leaving the Yankees in frustration, Rosen worked for several years as a casino exec in Atlantic City.

Rosen's second return to baseball came in 1980, when Astros owner John McMullen hired him to replace Tal Smith as GM. In Houston, Rosen's first team made the playoffs in the strike-truncated 1981 season, but his tenure was otherwise forgettable. In 1985, Giants owner Bob Lurie hired Rosen away from the Astros, and Rosen brought his pitching coach, Roger Craig, along with him.

With the Giants of '87 foundering at the halfway mark, Rosen on July 5 forged a deal with the division-rival Padres that sent Chris Brown, Keith Comstock, Mark Davis, and Mark Grant to San Diego for Kevin Mitchell, Dave Dravecky, and Craig Lefferts. As mentioned earlier, heady fans and analysts often recognize that deadline deals confer only modest value to a team in that same season. As you'll observe, Rosen in '87 made his key acquisitions almost a full month before the deadline. Had Rosen and the Giants idly pared their nails until the end of July and then made the deal, that's 22 additional games (or 13.5 percent of the season) they would have been without

Mitchell, Dravecky, and Lefferts. Credit Rosen and other GMs who take the decisive step as early as possible.

Prior to the trade on July 5, the Giants were 41–40; after the trade they went 49–32 and wound up besting the Reds by six games in the West. As the preceding table shows, the Giants' deadline acquisitions that season accounted for more than 15 percent of the team's total offensive and pitching value in 1987. In other words, had this deal and two other key ones later in the season not occurred, the Giants, in all likelihood, wouldn't have won the division.

Insofar as the 1987 season itself is concerned, almost all of Rosen's trades that summer were masterstrokes to varying degrees, but it was Kevin Mitchell who was the most critical addition. Mitchell, an improbable-looking athlete who was built like a street-corner mailbox, was raised by his grandmother in gangland San Diego. As a youth, he survived three gunshot wounds as a member of the ill-famed Syndos street gang, but his baseball skills rescued him from the projects. As a rookie, he was a key contributor to the Mets' 1986 championship team, playing six different positions afield and hitting a critical two-out single in the now mythic 10th inning of game six of the World Series.

That off-season Mitchell was dealt to the Padres for outfielder Kevin McReynolds, but the lure of San Diego's mean streets proved too much for him and the organization. That's where the Giants and Rosen came in. After only 62 games as a Padre, Mitchell found himself jettisoned to San Francisco and in the throes of a pennant race. In his first game as a Giant, he homered twice in a win over the division-pacing Reds. As the Giants' everyday third baseman that season, he batted .306 with a .376 on-base percentage and a .530 slugging percentage. Additionally, his '87 VORP as a Giant of 27.5 is the highest for any deadline-acquired third baseman I've studied.

Two years later, Mitchell would lead the NL in homers, slugging percentage, and extra-base hits and win the MVP as the Giants edged the Padres for their second division title in three seasons. Eventually, though, Mitchell's choice of friends and penchant for injury would sour the Giants on him. Following the 1991 season, San Francisco dealt him to the Mariners for pitcher Bill Swift. Although exceptionally productive at times, Mitchell would never again be healthy. He was out of the league after the 1998 season, but his years in San Francisco stand as his most memorable and most stable.

Lefty Dave Dravecky also played a critical role in the Giants' success that season. Originally drafted by the Pirates in 1978, Dravecky, after three minor league seasons, was traded to the Padres. There he split his time between the bullpen and the rotation for $5\frac{1}{2}$ years, making the All-Star team in 1983 and thrice finishing with a seasonal ERA of less than 3.00. In '87, of course, he was dealt to the Giants. For San Fran that season, Dravecky tossed $112\frac{1}{3}$ innings and allowed only 3.45 runs per game. In the Giants' failed NLCS against the Cardinals, Dravecky threw a two-hit shutout in game two and tied an LCS record by ringing up 16 consecutive scoreless innings. On the season, Dravecky's VORP of 26.4 ranks fifth among deadline starting pitchers for playoff-bound teams.

Dravecky would get off to another fine start in 1988, but a puzzling arm injury would snuff out most of his season. An arthroscopic surgical procedure revealed a malignancy in his pitching arm, and doctors removed the tumor and half of his deltoid muscle and froze part of the humerus bone to kill any remaining cancer cells. It was a minor miracle that Dravecky, a deeply religious man, was able to pitch again in less than a year. After tossing three complete games during his minor league rehab assignment, he made his return to the majors on August 10, 1989.

In his first major league start since brooking and beating cancer, Dravecky carried a one-hit shutout into the eighth. Craig, his manager, called it the most incredible game he'd ever seen. And Craig happened to witness firsthand Don Larsen's perfect game in the 1956 World Series. More incredible than that, he insisted.

Dravecky's doctor had admonished him that if he felt any pain or unusual sensation in his damaged arm to stop pitching immediately. The freezing process had left his humerus bone weakened and vulnerable. After five shutout innings against the Expos in his next start, Dravecky noticed a numbing sensation in his left arm. He ignored it.

"It sounded as though someone snapped a heavy tree branch," he would later say of the first pitch to the third Montreal batter in the bottom of the sixth. On that pitch, his arm shattered, leaving Dravecky in a tortured, writhing heap on the mound. He would never again throw another pitch.

He rejoined the club later that season, mostly as a symbolic gesture, but he again broke his arm in the clubhouse celebration following the Giants' NLCS victory over the Cubs. Soon after, Dravecky discovered that the cancer had returned. His left arm—the one that had pitched him to 64 major league wins and a sparkling 3.13 career ERA—was amputated above the elbow.

Reliever Craig Lefferts was the third player the Giants acquired in the trade with San Diego that season. Born in Germany and schooled at the University of Arizona, Lefferts was selected by the Cubs in the eighth round of the 1980 draft. After a highly promising rookie season in '83, the Cubs dealt their setup man to the Padres in a three-team deal that also involved Montreal. Once in San Diego, Lefferts became a durable and vital part of the Padre bullpen for the next several seasons. In 1984, Lefferts posted a 2.13 ERA in 105⅔ innings, threw 10 scoreless innings in the postseason, and recorded the final two wins against the Cubs in the NLCS. In the World Series against Detroit, Lefferts notched the save in the Padres' only win. Two seasons later, he led the majors in appearances with 83 and with that same mark broke Rollie Fingers' Padre record.

The following season, of course, Lefferts was dealt to the Giants. Prior to the trade, he had a 4.38 ERA in 51⅓ innings with the Padres. After going to San Fran, he worked 47⅓ innings with a 3.23 ERA. What's curious, however, is that his strikeout-to-walk ratio, which is a vital indicator of pitching effectiveness, was much better prior to the trade. In San Diego it was 39/15, but with the Giants it was only 18/18—the latter hardly being a mark that augured such solid run prevention. In any event, Lefferts posted a VORP of 10.7 after the trade and was a crucial bullpen contributor for the Giants down the stretch.

But Rosen wasn't done buttressing his team. On July 31 he sent catcher Mackey Sasser and $50,000 cash to the Pirates for pitcher Don Robinson, who was in the midst of a midcareer relief intermezzo between stints as a fairly effective starter in the majors.

Robinson, a big-bodied, hard-throwing righthander, came up in the Pirates organization, and as a 21-year-old rookie worked 228⅓ innings with a 3.47 ERA, which garnered the *Sporting News* NL Rookie Pitcher of the Year Award. He was also adroit with the bat, and not just by pitchers' standards. Robinson batted .231 for his career and also logged several pinch-hitting appearances. At one point the presumably desperate Pirates even mulled over moving him to the outfield. However, after that praiseworthy rookie season, Robinson was beset by a litany of arm injuries—perhaps the result of throwing almost 230 frames as a 21-year-old—and never quite realized that early promise. In

1986, recurring knee problems forced him into a relief role, and the following year the Giants acquired him just before the nonwaiver trade deadline. Over the balance of the season, the "Caveman" worked 25 games for the Giants and logged an impressive 2.74 ERA after the trade from Pittsburgh. In the division-clinching win over San Diego on September 28, Robinson homered to break a 4–4 tie.

The trade Al Rosen probably *shouldn't* have made in 1987 was the one he executed on August 21. On that day, Rosen packaged Jeff Robinson, a highly capable reliever, and minor league hurler Scott Medvin to the Pirates for veteran starter Rick Reuschel.

A portly and lumbering sight whose gait these days might call to mind the shuddersome Jar Jar Binks, Reuschel won 214 games over his 19-year career and was one of the most consistent and successful starters of the 1970s (despite toiling for some awful Cubs teams over that span). Armed with great control and one of the most effortless windups ever, he pitched well until age 42. In 1975, Rick and his older brother Paul became the first brothers ever to combine for a shutout. Rick Reuschel would miss the entire 1982 season and most of 1983 with a torn rotator cuff—an injury that threatened to squelch his career entirely. His recovery from major shoulder surgery was arduous and frustrating, and he endured a lackluster 1984 ($92\frac{1}{3}$ innings, 5.17 ERA—the latter easily the worst mark of his career) in an attempt to regain his form. The Cubs released him after that season, but he caught on with the Pirates prior to the '85 season.

That year, Reuschel, circumstances considered, may have cobbled together his finest season. At age 36, with a bum wing and pitching for a team that would finish 57–104, "Big Daddy" (as Mike Krukow nick-named Reuschel in his Cub days) worked 194 innings, went 14–8, and posted a career-best 2.27 ERA. His improbable performance earned him Comeback Player of the Year plaudits and reestablished his reputation as a durable and effective frontline starter. As such, a year and a half later, the Giants traded for him.

Reuschel would throw 50 innings for the Giants and go 5–3 down the stretch; however, his ERA as a Giant, 4.32, was comfortably worse than the 1987 NL ERA of 3.84. Of course, the Giant offense averaged almost six runs per game in Reuschel's nine starts, which shows that his winning mark was mostly a function of run support.

As for Jeff Robinson, the reliever they gave up in the Reuschel trade, the Giants missed his contributions. Prior to the deal, Robinson had worked a whopping 96⅔ relief innings with a 2.79 ERA. After-ward, for the Pirates, he threw 26⅔ innings with a 3.04 ERA. In terms of VORP, Reuschel as a Giant posted a VORP of 2.9, while Robinson in Pittsburgh recorded a VORP of 7.2. That's a difference of less than five runs, but the Giants nevertheless hurt themselves with that one deal. Still, that's an exceedingly minor criticism in light of Rosen's oth-erwise tremendous deadline work that season.

The '95 Reds used the trading season to give the "scorched earth" treatment to the back of their rotation. Cincinnati didn't have many offensive issues that season; they finished second only to the Coors-distorted Rockies in the NL in runs scored. The highly effective lefty tandem of Pete Schourek and John Smiley fronted the rotation, but the back end, for much of the season, was in disarray. Thirteen different Red pitchers made starts that season, including things like Pete Smith, C. J. Nitkowski, John Roper, and the charred remains of Frank Viola.

Two years earlier, Red GM Jim Bowden had risen to power in Cincinnati at the bidding of irascible and firebrand owner Marge Schott and in the process became, at age 31, the youngest general man-ager in major league history. It was a fact seemingly underscored by his "prep school" shock of parted hair and his at times rough-hewn approach to his job.

Cocksure and often willing to play the unpopular angle (he once likened a possible players' strike to the terrorist attacks of 9/11), Bow-den was known for frantically and constantly remolding his team. He made an immediate splash by firing beloved Red luminary Tony Perez only 44 games into his tenure as manager. Scandal of a different sort descended upon Bowden when his ex-wife Amy, from whom Bowden parted ways in a ruinous, two-year public divorce, began openly dat-ing Red minority owner Bill Reik. Reik, to the shock of only the cred-ulous, soon emerged as one of Bowden's more vocal critics within the Reds' ownership group.

Bowden dealt with more than his share of professional challenges as well. For much of his decade-long tenure as GM, Schott was his boss. When someone as unleavened as Bowden ends up supplying political cover for the peccadilloes of his boss (such as a handful of brazenly racist comments and some halting praise for Adolph Hitler), it's an unfortunate arrangement—for everyone but the fourth estate, anyway. Moreover, Bowden, in a very real sense, presided over two distinct organizations. In 1995, the only season the Reds made the postseason on Bowden's watch, they had the second-largest payroll in the league, but over the coming seasons, that payroll would be winnowed down into one of the smallest in baseball. Despite the circumscriptions from ownership and a thoroughly different business model, Bowden's 1999 club won 96 games and lost a one-game playoff to the Mets to determine the NL wild-card winner.

But what should have been Bowden's finest hour—the trade that sent Mike Cameron, Brett Tomko, and two minor leaguers to the Mariners for adored native son Ken Griffey Jr.—wound up being a low-grade disaster for the Reds and came off looking like a prestige project on Bowden's part. Griffey's production declined, and an endless succession of maladies limited him to an average of 92 games per season during his first five years in Cincinnati. Moreover, What looked like a bargain "hometown" contract of Griffey's in early going eventually became an encumbrance in the corrected market for player salaries. After a string of losing seasons and string of soured relationships within the organization, Bowden's time ran out midway through the 2003 season when he, along with manager Bob Boone, were fired. But in '95, Bowden, still in his early 30s, seemed bound for a fruitful career in the front office. It was at the deadline that season that Bowden performed what was in retrospect probably his masterstroke as Red GM.

On July 21 the Reds held a quasi-comfortable $6\frac{1}{2}$-game lead over the Astros in the freshly minted NL Central. While GM Jim Bowden had his weaknesses, complacency wasn't among them. On that day, he packaged minor league lefty Ricky Pickett, whose career in the majors would span less than an inning; novelty outfielder Deion Sanders; outfielder Dave McCarty; and pitchers John Roper and Scott Service to the Giants for outfielder Darren Lewis and starters Mark Portugal and Dave Burba. Ten days later, with the Reds' lead whittled down to four games, Bowden traded Nitkowski, farmhand Dave Tuttle, and infielder Mark Lewis to the Tigers for lefty David Wells. While the acquisition of Darren Lewis would be a net negative for the rest of the '95 season (he would slug only .264 in 180 plate appearances for the Reds), the troika of pitchers Bowden acquired would all be quite effective.

Not only did Mark Portugal play only a single season of high school ball, but he also played it as a catcher/outfielder. Even so, the Twins liked his arm and signed him as a nondrafted free agent in 1980. After making the majors, Portugal suffered through four lousy seasons in Minnesota before he was traded to the Astros for minor leaguer Todd McClure. Once there, Portugal refined his sinker and changeup and in 1993 was one of the best starting pitchers in the National League. In 208 innings that season, Portugal went 18–4 with a 2.77 ERA. Additionally, he paced the loop with an .818 winning percentage and at one point notched 12 straight wins. He did pitch half his games in the Astrodome, which was the best pitcher's park in baseball at that time, but the '93 season saw a substantial increase in run scoring across both leagues. That season, Portugal finished sixth in the NL Cy Young voting.

Fortunately for Portugal, his highest market value happily intersected with his first foray into free agency. Following his excellent '93, he inked a lucrative free-agent deal with the Giants. On balance, Portugal was a league-average hurler for his season and a half in San Francisco—not quite worth the money, but hardly a sinkhole. In any event, Portugal wasn't pleased when word of his trade to the Reds came. "I was misled to believe this organization was committed to winning," Portugal said of the Giants. "That's a blatant lie."

Once in Cincinnati, Portugal turned in a reliable $77^{2}/_{3}$ innings (3.82 ERA) but was torched in his lone playoff start against the Braves in the NLCS (one inning, four earned runs). Perhaps it was that vital failure that led Marge Schott to opine the following season, "Three million dollars, he's not worth a darn."

Portugal's riposte: "Tell her it's four million."

Following the playoff ouster at the hands of Atlanta, the Reds fired Davey Johnson, their outstanding manager, mostly because Schott objected to Johnson's cohabitating with his girlfriend. In fact, Schott stated publicly before the 1995 season that Ray Knight would manage the team the next year. True to her word, Knight was hired. Portugal was among several players who clashed with the disagreeable and dubiously competent Knight. In response, the Reds nontendered Portugal following the 1996 season. He would sign with the Phillies for '97, but his decline phase had begun. In June 1999, while under contract with the Red Sox, Portugal went AWOL because of a searing custody battle with his ex-wife. However, he would return to the Sox within a week to complete this season, his last. The following winter,

Portugal re-signed with the Reds (along with Deion Sanders, for whom he was traded in '95), but failed to make the active roster coming out of spring training and opted for retirement.

Dave Burba arrived in the majors as a Mariner reliever in 1990, but before long was traded to the Giants along with righthander Bill Swift and reliever Mike Jackson for Kevin Mitchell and lefty Mike Remlinger. Despite pitching in run-suppressing Candlestick for half his games, Burba posted below-league-average ERAs in each of his seasons in San Francisco. Despite Burba's underwhelming record of success, the Reds dealt for him and transitioned him into a starter. In '95 Burba made 15 appearances for the Reds, nine of which were starts, and posted a 3.27 ERA. Among those games was a two-hit shutout of the second-place Astros on August 27 that pushed the Reds to a nine-game lead in the Central. Burba would go on to work 4⅔ scoreless relief innings in the postseason that year and pitch two more vaguely effective seasons in Cincinnati.

Burba, an Ohioan who grew up a Reds partisan, was close to fulfilling a life's dream—being the Opening Day starter in front of the home crowd in Cincinnati—when he was traded to the Indians just hours before the first pitch of the 1998 season. Burba would be a rotation stalwart and modestly valuable innings-eater in Cleveland for four seasons and change. By 2003 he had returned to a relief role as his 15-year career in the majors started winding out.

The other key Bowden acquisition that season was David Wells. Wells, a rotund, tattooed lefty with exacting control, for much of his career was conspicuous in his love of motorcycles and his fondness for Bacchanalian excesses. "Boomer," as he was called, went to the same high school—Point Loma in San Diego—as Don Larsen, who threw that perfect game for the Yankees in the 1956 World Series (the one that Roger Craig witnessed), and Wells's mother once dated the leader of the local Hell's Angels chapter. In 1987 Wells came to the majors as a reliever for the Toronto Blue Jays. There he eventually became manager Jimy Williams's favored lefty specialist and played a critical role for the division championship team in '89.

By 1990, the Jays had added lefty reliever Ken Dayley to the fold, and that allowed new manager Cito Gaston, who perhaps wanted to put his own imprimatur upon the club, to move Wells into the rotation. It turned out to be a wise move. Wells hurled 165 innings and posted the seventh-best ERA in the American League that season. He was solid again in 1991, but the following season, a choke point in the rotation—brought about mostly by the signing of Jack Morris and the return from injury of Dave Stieb—forced Wells back to the bullpen. Angered and confused by the decision, Wells put up the worst numbers of his young career. He filed for free agency that winter and said he'd never again pitch for the Blue Jays.

Just two days before Opening Day, he signed with the Detroit Tigers. He won only 11 games his first year in Detroit, but he posted an ERA better than the league average and for the first time as a starter demonstrated the exceptional command that would be his hallmark for years. In 1994 Wells underwent arthroscopic elbow surgery and wound up making only 16 starts in the strike-shortened season. Still, once he was able to pitch, he was highly effective. In '95 he stormed to a 10–3 start (for a team that would finish 60–84), with a 3.04 ERA. With his trade value at peak, the Tigers dealt him to the Reds for three players.

Once in Cincinnati, Wells pitched $72\frac{2}{3}$ innings with a 3.59 ERA and a 3.13 strikeout-to-walk ratio and also logged three complete games. In the NLDS against the Dodgers, Wells tossed $6\frac{1}{3}$ shutout innings in the clinching third game. However, in the NLCS against the Braves, like most everyone else in a Red uniform, he misfired badly. His relationship with Davey Johnson was strained almost from the outset, and in the off-season Bowden traded Wells to Baltimore for outfielder Curtis Goodwin and minor leaguer Trovin Valdez. Wells would later land with the Yankees, where he would trampoline both his reputation as a big-game pitcher and his popularity as a beer-guzzling, gout-afflicted layabout who also happened to be an elite professional athlete.

After signing with the Yanks following the '96 season, Wells promptly agitated for the team to dust off Babe Ruth's No. 3 uniform number and permit him to wear it. Needless to say, baseball's Zeus had long ago had his number retired, and Wells's entreaty was denied. So he opted for No. 33. In 1998 Wells, on "Beanie Baby Day" in Yankee Stadium, pitched the 13th perfect game in major league history and became the first to spin a perfecto in the Bronx since Larsen, his fellow Point Loma H.S. alumnus. That October Wells would record four postseason wins as the Yankees capped off their red-letter year with a World Series sweep of Wells's hometown Padres. After being traded to Toronto and then to the White Sox, Wells returned to the

Yanks for the 2002 and 2003 seasons. After the '03 campaign, Wells's lifetime record as a Yankee stood at 68–28.

And speaking of the Yankees . . .

Coming into the 1995 season, the Yankees hadn't made the postseason in 14 years—the longest such drought for baseball's most dynastic franchise since Babe Ruth was acquired. What made it all the more rankling for Yankee fans is that, in the unfinished 1994 season, they had a comfortable 6½-game lead in the AL East at the time of the players' strike and were on pace for 100 wins.

Needless to say, the run-up to the 1995 campaign brought with it the usual Yankee mishmash of haughty optimism tempered by trickle-down urgency with the organization. It was time for the Yankees to get back to being the Yankees.

In 1994, staff ace Jimmy Key had gone 17–4 with a 3.27 ERA and paced the AL in wins and starts. Obviously, he was critical to Yankee fortunes in '95. However, Key, barely a month into the '95 season, went on the DL with tendinitis after making two straight painful starts. That case of tendinitis turned out to be a torn rotator cuff, and by the All-Star break he had undergone season-ending shoulder surgery. It also didn't help that Scott Kamieniecki, the Yanks' highly capable fifth man from the year before, regressed badly in 1995. A trade that December with the White Sox brought Jack McDowell into the fold, and he was effective, if not of ace quality. (Of course, McDowell's contributions were not without some standard-issue Yankee Sturm und Drang. Following a particularly rough home outing in July that season, "Blackjack" responded to the booing throngs by extending his middle finger to the already profoundly displeased Yankcc Stadium crowd. Not to mention the unblinking eyes of the camera. The following winter, McDowell, a free agent, would opt for the more staid shores of Cleveland.)

At the close of play on July 28, the Yankees were 41–42, in third place in the AL East, and 5½ games behind the division-leading Red Sox. Most assuredly, it was time for action. (In recent seasons, participants in the "Sons of Sam Horn" online Red Sox forum have taken to lampooning the Yankees' countless afterthought personnel additions and manifest weakness for conspicuous consumption by calling those players, as a group, "Raul Whitecock," a derisive amalgam of Raul

Mondesi, Rondell White, and Sterling Hitchcock, three notable and largely fruitless recent acquisitions by the Yanks.)

On that same day, GM Gene Michael pulled the trigger on a pair of deals. First, he sent a troika of utter forgettables (Marty Janzen, Jason Jarvis, and Mike Gordon, who would combine for 27 games in the majors—all courtesy of Janzen) to the Blue Jays for David Cone. Toronto GM Gord Ash originally angled for a deal that would have sent Cone to the Yanks for Bob Wickman, Matt Drews, and a promising minor league hurler named Mariano Rivera. Michael passed and wound up getting Cone for an infinitely lower cost. As Don Mattingly said of the Cone deal, "We got him for nothing. I don't even know the other three guys."

A native of Kansas City, Cone came up with his hometown Royals alongside other talented young hurlers such as Mark Gubicza and Danny Jackson. Rather than let the pitching bottleneck sort itself out (a blissful quandary if ever there were one), the club made what owner Ewing Kauffman would later call "the worst trade in Royals' history." Certainly it was also the worst trade in then-Royals GM John Schuerholz's personal history. That trade in the spring of 1987 sent the 24-year-old Cone and outfielder Chris Jelic to the Mets for catcher Ed Hearn, who would go on to play 13 games for Kansas City; righthander Rick Anderson, who would go on to post a 4.75 ERA in $96^2/3$ career innings; and reliever Mauro Gozzo, who would never appear in a game for the Royals.

Cone, meanwhile, blossomed into an ace in New York. In 1988 he went 20–3 with a 2.22 ERA and finished third in the NL Cy Young balloting. He also became only the fifth pitcher in Mets history to win 20 in a single season, and he tied Preacher Roe's 1951 NL record for fewest losses by a 20-game winner. Cone had worked assiduously to develop command of six pitches and was famous for varying his arm angles and release points as situations warranted. To opposing batters, no matter how many times they'd seen him, it seemed as though Cone pitched with the randomness of lightning. Beginning in 1990, he led the majors in strikeouts for three straight seasons—the first pitcher since Nolan Ryan (1972–1974) to do so—and in '91 even fanned 19 Phillies in a single game (which tied the NL record until Kerry Wood whiffed 20 Astros in 1998).

Over the years, Cone fashioned a reputation as a bit of an eccentric. He would leave game tickets for *Wheel of Fortune* geisha Vanna White (never to be used) and Elvis Presley (also never to be used). He once held the ball and argued with the home plate umpire over a call while a pair of opposing base runners rounded the diamond and scored. However, as the Mets' fortunes began to decline in the early '90s, Cone's reputation took a harrowing turn. Cone faced two rape allegations within five months. The first involved a woman (whose claims were later dismissed by police) allegedly assaulted by Cone the night before his record-tying performance against the Phillies in 1991. The second linked his name to a teamwide scandal involving Darryl Boston, Vince Coleman, and Dwight Gooden. Cone was not charged in either case, but he also endured a sexual harassment lawsuit from three women who claimed he exposed himself to them from the Shea Stadium bullpen in 1989. The suit was eventually dismissed.

Between 1992 and 1995 Cone would pitch for four different teams. In late August of '92 the Mets dispatched him to Toronto for Ryan Thompson and second baseman Jeff Kent. Cone was thrown into the midst of a heated pennant race. Since the Jays acquired him well after the first trade deadline, he had time to compile only 53 innings. However, he made the most of those innings, posting a 2.55 ERA after the deal. Cone went on to throw a gem in the decisive game six of the World Series against the Braves, allowing only one run in six innings of work.

His combined numbers between New York and Toronto in 1992 ($249^{2}/_{3}$ innings, 2.81 ERA, 17 wins) made him one of the winter's most hotly sought-after free agents. Cone wound up signing with his home-town Royals. He would pitch well in '93, but lackluster run support cost him win upon win. In strike-blighted 1994, however, great pitching intersected with good fortune, and Cone wound up winning the AL Cy Young. With Cone's value, perceived and otherwise, at its highest, the Royals that off-season traded him for a second time, in this instance back to Toronto for infielder Chris Stynes and two minor leaguers—David Sinnes and Tony Medrano—who would forever remain two minor leaguers.

Although he pitched well during his second Canadian tour of duty, Cone didn't last even four months before he was traded again, this time to the Yankees. As mentioned, the 1995 season was shortened to 144 games. Even so, as a Yankee, Cone that season put up a VORP of

27.9, which ranks as the third-best postdeadline VORP for any pitcher I've studied. Prorate his VORP to a full season, and it comes to 31.0, which is still good for third among pitchers, but, lumping hitters and hurlers together, makes Cone the fourth-most-valuable deadline acquisition since 1980. In 99 innings as a Yankee in '95, Cone posted a 3.82 ERA, but what endeared him to New York fans and media alike is that he went 9–2 down the stretch (partially a function of good run support) in an AL wild-card race that turned out to be decided by a single game. Without Cone, the Yankees very likely would have failed in their bid to fend off the Angels and thus claim the final AL playoff berth.

The only general manager to have two teams in the deadline top ten is Card boss Walt Jocketty. Among execs for quasi-perennial contenders, none has distinguished himself on the trade market quite like Jocketty. Jocketty, who cut his teeth in the A's and Rockies organizations, was named general manager of the Cards prior to the 1995 season. In only his second season at the helm, St. Louis made the NLCS, although he made no significant trades leading up to the '96 deadline.

Following that season, the Cards would wallow in mediocrity for the next three years. Of course, even a cursory, narrow examination of Jocketty's trading chops would be woefully incomplete without mention of his first blockbuster, in which he purloined Mark McGwire from the A's. It *was* a deadline trade, executed on July 31, 1997, but the Cardinals at the time of the deal were five games below .500 and 7½ games out of first in the NL Central. They'd finish the year at 73–89 and in fourth place.

Even so, the deal was thievery for Jocketty and the Cardinals and an example of squandered resources for Sandy Alderson and the A's. St. Louis nabbed McGwire for pitchers Eric Ludwick, Blake Stein, and T. J. Mathews. None would pitch with distinction in the majors. As you know, McGwire broke Roger Maris's single-season home run record in 1998 and engaged baseball fans like few others ever have. McGwire spent parts of five seasons with St. Louis, and over that time he averaged a home run every 2½ games. Unfortunately for those who pined to see McGwire on the broad stage, the Cardinals wouldn't be consequential until 2000, McGwire's penultimate season in the majors.

On the season, McGwire posted astounding numbers (.305 AVG/.483 OBP/.746 SLG), but a degenerative knee condition allowed him to log only 15 at-bats after July 6 and prevented him from running the bases or playing the field. With the team's best hitter convalescing for much of the season, Jocketty knew he needed another fulcrum in the lineup. On July 31, Jocketty traded Jose Leon, a minor league corner hitter of middling promise, to the Orioles for first baseman Will Clark and cash. The Cards were four games up on the Reds in the NL Central at the time of the deal, and Clark, who was in the midst of his final season, seemed to play with a ferocious sense of purpose down the stretch. His numbers after the trade were mighty (.345 AVG/.426 OBP/.655 SLG), and while that's not quite McGwire's level of production, Clark was certainly a suitable proxy. Clark homered in four of his first five games as a Cardinal and helped the team dust the Reds by 10 games. Clark's Cardinal VORP of 29.4 stands second only to Fred McGriff of the '93 Braves as the highest mark of any deadline-acquired hitter. That season, the lefty-heavy Cardinal lineup would be rendered impotent in the NLCS by the Mets and their slew of portsiders, but the season was nevertheless a memorable one for Clark and the fans of St. Louis.

Two days before nabbing Clark, Jocketty acquired reliever Mike Timlin and cash from the Orioles for outfielder Chris Richard and Mark Nussbeck, who would never play in the majors. Timlin, after the deal, became the Cards' primary right-handed setup man, working 29⅔ innings and allowing 3.34 runs per game. Two years later, Jocketty would use Timlin to make yet another headline-grabbing deal.

On August 2 of the following year, Jocketty pulled off another deal of criminal inequality when he shipped longtime Cardinal outfielder Ray Lankford to the Padres for (one thought) mediocre soft tosser Woody Williams. At first the deal looked like an uninspired "default settings" move by Jocketty to get some pitching—*any* pitching—from whoever would give it to him. It turned out to be something much more than that.

Lankford actually played quite well in his 40 games as a Padre (this is usually and conveniently ignored when discussing the Lankford-Williams swap), but Williams proved to be far more valuable over the final months of the season and in the years ahead. Prior to the trade, Williams had allowed 5.46 runs per game in 23 starts for the Padres; in 11 starts and 75 innings after the trade that season, he allowed 2.64

runs per game, and the Cardinals went 8–3 when he was on the mound. St. Louis would go on to nip the Giants by three games for the NL wild card. In his only postseason start for the series, Williams got the win in game two of the NLDS against the Diamondbacks by striking out nine, walking only one, and giving up a single run in seven innings of work. Williams also doubled and scored a run. Over the next three seasons, Williams would give the Cardinals 513⅔ innings and allow 3.92 runs per game. Lankford, meanwhile, was hampered by a hamstring injury in 2002, which limited him to 81 ineffective games. The Padres bought out his option for the following season, and Lankford sat out the entire season. In 2004 he came back to play a reasonably effective bench role for the NL champion Cardinals.

On July 19, 2002, the Cardinals were 3½ games up on the Reds in the NL Central, but the rotation was impaired by the loss of the aforementioned Woody Williams, who missed almost three months with a strained oblique muscle. On that day, Jocketty packaged minor league first baseman Luis Garcia and minor league outfielder Coco Crisp to the Indians for veteran lefty Chuck Finley. At the time of the deal, Finley was 39 years of age and coming off a season in which he posted a 5.54 ERA and endured two stints on the DL because of a strained neck muscle. He was healthy and improved for the first half of 2002, so Jocketty dealt for him. After the trade, Finley made 14 starts, allowed 4.32 runs per game, and tossed 6⅓ scoreless frames against the Diamondbacks in the NLDS. But he wasn't the most vital of Jocketty's acquisitions that month.

Ten days later, the Cardinals, after lengthy and mulish negotiations, acquired third baseman Scott Rolen from the Phillies for soon-to-be-injured lefty Bud Smith, infielder Placido Polanco, and reliever Mike Timlin. Timlin would give the Phillies 35 league-average innings before landing with the Red Sox that off-season. Polanco would be a valuable player for the next 2½ seasons, but Smith would suffer two torn labrums and, as I write this, is endeavoring to salvage a career.

No such worries for the Cardinals and Rolen. In the 55 games immediately following the trade, Rolen hit .278 AVG/.354 OBP/.561 SLG. That comes to a VORP of 22.6 and places Rolen behind only Kevin Mitchell of the '87 Giants as the best deadline third baseman I've studied. A trauma injury to his shoulder in the first round of the playoffs caused Rolen to miss the NLCS, but Jocketty and his charges realized they had a burgeoning superstar who was finally in the right environment. As he did in a few other notable trades, Jocketty leveraged the positive atmospherics of St. Louis and the player's desire to take the field day in day out in front of the adoring throngs of Cardinal Nation. That was doubly the case for Rolen, an Indiana native whose time in Philadelphia left him mushy for that midwestern sense of decorum. Before the 2002 season was over, Rolen signed an eight-year, $90-million extension that would keep him in St. Louis for the balance of the decade.

In addition, Jocketty used the trade market over the years to acquire such talents as Jim Edmonds, Edgar Renteria, Darryl Kile, Fernando Vina, Dennis Eckersley, Fernando Tatis, Steve Kline, Todd Stottlemyre, and Pat Hentgen. Let's also not forget Jocketty's 2004 deadline pickup of Larry Walker, which falls beyond the scope of this book. Whatever your standard for evaluation, Jocketty is peerless among modern GMs in making impact deals for his organization, deadline or otherwise.

Needless to say, some deadline deals have ranged from ham-fisted in conception to self-destructive in execution. On occasion, the players acquired were awful over the balance of the season. In other instances, the contending team would part with seemingly undistinguished prospects who would later become some of the game's most prominent luminaries.

In terms of harm done in the season in question, here are the 10 worst deadline teams I've studied (you'll find below a number of conspicuous and prominent names—some acquired waist-deep in their decline phases, some prey to untimely cold streaks, all embodiments of the idea that pretending you can project two isolated months of performance is a fool's errand):

Ranking	Team	Percentage of Total Team VORP
1.	'95 Rockies	−6.33
2.	'96 Braves	−1.54
3.	'87 Twins	−1.47
4.	'98 Cubs	−1.26
5.	'80 Yankees	−1.23
6.	'83 Dodgers	−1.10

Ranking	Team	Percentage of Total Team VORP
7.	'96 Yankees	−1.08
8.	'86 Red Sox	−0.95
9.	'99 Indians	−0.85
10.	'01 Braves	−0.60

Let's put some names to those bad ideas, with individual VORPs in parentheses:

Team	Players Acquired at Deadline
'95 Rockies	RP Bryan Hickerson (−13.6), SP Bret Saberhagen (−5.7)
'96 Braves	3B Terry Pendleton (−7.3), SP Denny Neagle (−1.1)
'87 Twins	SP Steve Carlton (−5.7)
'98 Cubs	SP Mike Morgan (−6.7), RP Matt Karchner (−0.6), RP Felix Heredia (2.0)
'80 Yankees	3B Aurelio Rodriguez (−5.0), SP Gaylord Perry (−2.0)
'83 Dodgers	RP Rick Honeycutt (−4.4)
'96 Yankees	RP Graeme Lloyd (−6.6), RP David Weathers (−5.8), RP Ricky Bones (−5.7), 3B Charlie Hayes (1.1), DH Cecil Fielder (10.7)
'86 Red Sox	SS Spike Owen (−2.7), CF Dave Henderson (−2.2)
'99 Indians	3B Carlos Baerga (−3.2), 3B Tyler Houston (−2.0), DH Harold Baines (−0.2)
'01 Braves	SS Rey Sanchez (−6.8), RP Rudy Seanez (3.7)

The '95 Rockies, a team that edged the Astros by a single game for the NL wild card that season, could've made the race much more comfortable for themselves had they not traded for reliever Bryan Hickerson and righthander Bret Saberhagen.

At the close of play on July 31, 1995, the Rockies led the Dodgers for the NL wild card by 3½ games. On that same day, Colorado GM Bob Gebhard sent righthander Juan Acevedo and minor leaguer Arnold Gooch to the Mets for Saberhagen and minor leaguer David Swanson. Gebhard also acquired Hickerson from the Cubs in a conditional deal.

Hickerson was a University of Minnesota product who had been drafted by his hometown Twins in the seventh round of the 1986 draft. A year after signing, the Twins sent him to the Giants in the trade that would net them outfielder Dan Gladden, who would score the winning run in game seven of the '91 World Series. Once in San Francisco, Hickerson put up three solid seasons; however, by the time the Rockies acquired the lefty from the Cubs, he was caught in an onrushing pattern of decline. What's astounding is that the Rockies took steps to deal for a reliever who had a 6.82 ERA at the time of the deal and was coming off a season in which he logged a 5.40 ERA. But there's a reason.

The '95 Rockies, despite cobbling together one of the great bullpens of all time, were in desperate straits in terms of left-handed relief. Bruce Ruffin, their primary lefty setup man, was excellent when healthy (34 innings, 2.12 ERA), but an elbow strain sidelined him from late June until late August. Manager Don Baylor tried Mike Munoz in the role, but he was awful. In light of those circumstances, a play for another lefty reliever was certainly wise, but with quality port-siders such as Dennis Cook, Norm Charlton, and Dave Leiper chang-ing addresses near the deadline, the decision to settle for Hickerson looks even more uninspired. Once the already terrible Hickerson began plying his trade in the thin air of Denver, he became an affliction on the mound. In 16⅔ innings for Colorado, Hickerson walked more men than he struck out, gave up five home runs and 33 hits, and hem-orrhaged runs at a rate of 12.96 per game. In four of his 15 outings, he allowed at least half of the batters he faced to score. His VORP of −13.6 with Colorado is easily the worst of any deadline acquisition studied for this book. When you consider that he inflicted that kind of damage in less than 17 innings on the mound, it stupefies. Hickerson was released shortly after the Rockies' NLDS loss to the Braves. He would never again pitch in the major leagues.

Gebhard's decision to acquire Saberhagen made far more horse sense, even though his performance looks good only according to the charitable standards set by Hickerson. Too clever by half, I suppose.

Saberhagen lasted until the 19th round of the '82 draft, when the Royals nabbed the Chicago native. By the time he was 21, Saberhagen found himself pitching in the World Series. In game three of the '85 Series against Cardinals, Saberhagen, with the Royals having lost the first two games of the Series, pitched a complete game, allowing six hits and only one run. He came back in game seven to shut out the Cards 11–0. He was awarded the World Series MVP Award, and less than a month later he became the youngest pitcher ever to win a Cy Young.

Superficially, his numbers slipped the following season, but that was mostly a function of the shoddy defense behind him and ebbing luck. It somewhat encapsulates what a string of oddities his career was that, at age 23, he won AL Comeback Player of the Year honors in 1987. At an age when most players were still in the minors, "Sabes" had won a Cy Young and a World Series MVP and been singled out for his statistical resiliency. Much was made of the "odd year = good, even year = bad" dynamic that seemed to hold sway throughout much of his career. To be more accurate, it should be called "odd year = great, even year = good." Saberhagen's year-to-year numbers vacillated quite notably, but he never had a full season that could accurately be termed dreadful.

In any event, following a putative decline in '88, Saberhagen rebounded the next year to lead the AL in ERA, innings, and complete games and claim his second Cy Young Award. His 2.16 ERA that season was the best in the junior circuit since Ron Guidry's 1.74 mark in 1978. The next two seasons, Saberhagen would pitch effectively but was often hindered by injuries. So in the winter of '91, the Royals packaged him along with infielder Bill Pecota to the Mets for outfielder Kevin McReynolds, infielder Gregg Jeffries, and utility man Keith Miller.

Injuries limited Saberhagen's play for his first two seasons in New York. In 1994, however, it all came together for him. On the field, that is. What most people remember about Saberhagen's 1994 season is that he was suspended for five games and fined for spraying bleach at a pack of reporters in the clubhouse. That's unfortunate, because Saberhagen's incivilities overshadowed what was one of the great pitching seasons of all time. For the strike-shortened season, Saberhagen logged 177⅓ innings, posted a 2.74 ERA, struck out 143, and walked only 13. Yes, he walked only 13 batters *all season*. His 11.0 strikeout-to-walk ratio, an excellent indicator of a pitcher's command and general level of dominance, was the best single-season mark for any qualifier ever. *Ever*. (The second-best mark, 10.0, belongs to someone called Jim Whitney way back yonder in 1884.) For further perspective, the average NL strikeout-to-walk ratio that season was 1.95.

From May 16 through June 8, Saberhagen went five starts without walking a batter, and he also became the first pitcher since World War

I to record more wins than walks in a season. Prorate his work that year to a full season, and he would have logged 254 innings and gone 20–6 with 2.74 ERA. He would have finished third in innings, third in wins, and second in ERA. That year, he did finish third in the Cy Young balloting, but if writers had grasped the historic nature of his command numbers that season, they would have unanimously given Sabes his third award. Alas and alack, labor strife and the bleach-speckled Members Only jackets of sportswriters have kept us from giving his work in '94 its fitting due.

In 1995 he got off to another strong start with the Mets, but with "the worst team money can buy" heading into a rebuilding mode, Sabes was expendable. Hours before the July 31 deadline, Gebhard and the Rockies acquired him. Again, a sage move on paper, but not in execution. For the Rockies that season, Saberhagen made nine starts spanning 43 innings, but his 6.28 ERA, even on a park-adjusted basis, was still 15 percent below the league average. A strong performance by Saberhagen in the postseason would have been something more than cold comfort; however, in game four of the NLDS, the Braves detonated him for five runs in four innings.

Saberhagen missed the entire 1996 season because of a shoulder injury, but the following year he signed with Boston. He pitched only 26 innings in '97, but the next two seasons he was highly effective when healthy. In '99, his feeble shoulder abided only 119 innings out of him, but he posted a sparkling 2.95 ERA and walked only 11 batters all season. But that was about all his body would allow him. He attempted to pitch again the following season, but his right shoulder was in tatters. He ended his career in the top 50 all-time for park-adjusted career ERA relative to the league. In the 1990s alone, Saberhagen spent almost 1,000 days on the disabled list—989 to be exact. As such, his career numbers, in gross terms, aren't what you need to merit serious deliberation for the Hall of Fame. However, when healthy, he indubitably *was* a great pitcher. We seem to forget that about him.

It may sound trenchant and unceremonious to say so, but the '87 Twins are probably the worst team ever to win the World Series. They join the 1926 Cardinals, the 1945 Tigers, and the 2000 Yankees as the only teams to play a full season and win the World Series despite winning fewer than 90 games. Their 85 wins are the fewest of any team to win the World Series in a season that wasn't truncated by a labor stoppage. Had they played in the AL East in 1987, they would have finished in fifth place. The Twins' .525 winning percentage is easily the worst of any World Series winner, and their run differential of −20 (yes, that's a negative figure) is downright appalling for a World Series–winning club. In fact, three teams in their own division posted better run differentials that year.

The Twins' primary weakness was run prevention. They ranked a paltry 10th in the AL in ERA, and of the 17 pitchers who made appearances for the Twins that season, only two—ace Frank Viola and middle man Juan Berenguer—posted ERAs of less than 4.00. Certainly, it was prudent for the Twins to deal for an arm at the deadline. However, trading for a "starting pitcher emeritus" such as Steve Carlton, who at the time was in his 23rd major league season, is the transactional approximation of running out of bullets and just throwing the darn gun at the guy. Nevertheless, that's what the Twins and GM Andy MacPhail did.

When he was growing up, friends (or, perhaps, enemies) nicknamed Carlton "Ichabod" because of his meager and rangy build. Most of the pro scouts he encountered said he lacked the fastball to make it as a major leaguer. In part, that's why Carlton was unswervingly devoted to strength training throughout his career. He was a dedicated weight lifter, and he also regularly took part in unconventional training methods such as squeezing metal balls and, somewhat famously, jamming his hand into a barrel of uncooked rice over and over again. At the time, weight training, particularly among pitchers, was a verboten practice. Although Nolan Ryan gets most of the credit for changing the way pitchers regarded resistance training, Carlton had much to do with it as well.

The Cardinals originally signed Carlton as an amateur free agent in 1963 (the amateur draft didn't begin until 1965) for $5,000 while he was enrolled at Miami-Dade Junior College. By age 20 Carlton was pitching in St. Louis. By 1967 Carlton was a regular in the Cardinal rotation and even started game five of the World Series. The following year, he worked 231⅔ innings, but his ERA was below league average. That off-season, on a trip to Japan with some of his Cardinal teammates, he began tinkering with a slider. Carlton found he had a penchant for throwing it effectively, and the lefty discovered the pitch was especially baffling for the opposite side. Once he refined it, Carlton's slider became one of the most devastating breaking pitches in the history of the game, and it ferried him to a Hall of Fame career. But that was after scrapping the pitch early in 1971, revisiting it in '72, losing command of it in '73, and then bringing it back for good. Once he did master the slider, Carlton was nearly unhittable when he was on. According to fellow Hall of Famer Willie Stargell, hitting Carlton was like "eating soup with a fork."

Carlton missed spring training in 1970 because of a contract holdout, and after a 20-win season in 1971, he again held out for more money. Team owner August Busch Jr. then ordered GM Bing Devine to trade their 27-year-old three-time All-Star. The dispute came down to $15,000, which, in the here and now, sounds like an uncommonly trifling sum, but in those days it was enough to force Devine to make one of the worst trades in franchise history. So on February 25, 1972, the Cards dealt Carlton to the Phillies for righthander Rick Wise, who himself was embroiled in a contract squabble. (The Cards, having not yet had their fill of vengeful imprudence, traded Jerry Reuss, another disgruntled young lefty, before Opening Day.) Wise would go on to have an 18-year career in the majors (and he would also pick up the win as a Red Sock in the extraordinary game six of the 1975 World Series), but Carlton would become one of the game's pantheon dwellers.

In 1972, Carlton's first in Philadelphia, he won 27 games for a team that tallied only 59 wins for the entire season. He also claimed the ERA title, struck out 310 batters, logged the second-most innings in the NL since 1920, and tossed 30 complete games. Today it still stands as one of the great single-season performances in the annals of the game. His performance declined a bit for the next three seasons, but altered mechanics (and, perhaps, a reunion with Tim McCarver, his former Cardinal batterymate) helped him reclaim greatness.

Over the course of his career, Carlton won 20 games in a season six times, became the first pitcher to win four Cy Young awards, wound up as the second-winningest lefthander of all time (behind Warren Spahn), and is one of four pitchers to log at least 4,000 career strikeouts. At age 38 he would lead the league in strikeouts and innings and notch his 300th career victory.

Carlton suffered an injured rotator cuff in 1985 and spent more than two months on the DL. The Phillies encouraged him to retire, but Carlton, recalcitrant to the end, refused. Stints with the Giants and White Sox followed, and he opened the '87 season with the Indians. As of July 31, Carlton had logged 109 innings with a 5.37 ERA. In spite of those numbers and his age, the Twins on that same day sent minor leaguer Jeff Perry to Cleveland for him. At the time of the trade, the Twins were 2½ games up on the Angels in the AL West, but, as mentioned, they had readily identifiable weaknesses in the rotation. Trading for a starting pitcher was a good idea; trading for the vestiges of Steve Carlton wasn't. Down the stretch, Carlton worked 43 innings for the Twins over seven starts and two relief appearances. Over that span, he allowed 7.33 runs per game and struck out only 20 batters against 23 walks. On a park-adjusted basis, his ERA was 31 percent worse than the league mean, and although he was the Twins' marquee deadline acquisition, he'd be left off the postseason roster.

Carlton would be released by the Twins that December, but they re-signed him a month later. He broke camp with the team, but after four horrible outings, Minnesota cut him loose before the 1988 season was even a month old. Carlton's career was over. After being elected to Cooperstown on the first ballot in 1994, Carlton broke his long-standing policy of silence with the media. From a bunker in Durango, Colorado, Carlton, by then a certifiably paranoid enfant terrible, warned writer Pat Jordan that, variously, "the Russian and U.S. governments fill the air with low-frequency sound waves meant to control us," "twelve Jewish bankers meeting in Switzerland rule the world," and "the revolution is definitely coming." While Carlton may have wound up crazier than anyone who's run for president and lost more than three times, he was still one of the greatest pitchers ever to play the game. However, he wasn't much of a Twin. Even so, I'm quite sure his manifesto is a scorching read.

The great Bill James had an entertaining habit of peppering his books with ad hoc all-star teams tied to whatever issue he was riffing on at the moment. With a nod to Mr. James, let's pull together the "Trade Deadline All-Star Team" since 1980. Selections are determined by highest VORP at each position:

Position	Player	Team	VORP
C	Charles Johnson	'00 White Sox	21.6
1B	Fred McGriff	'93 Braves	33.2
2B	Craig Counsell	'97 Marlins	11.3
3B	Kevin Mitchell	'87 Giants	27.5
SS	Royce Clayton	'98 Rangers	10.7
LF	Shannon Stewart	'03 Twins	19.1
CF	Kenny Lofton	'03 Cubs	20.5
RF	Jermaine Dye	'01 A's	22.7
DH	Glenallen Hill	'00 Yankees	22.6
PH	John Vander Wal	'98 Padres	1.5
SP	Doyle Alexander	'87 Tigers	44.1
SP	Randy Johnson	'98 Astros	41.2
RP	Ugueth Urbina	'03 Marlins	17.9

And now a smattering of observations regarding the above list and other stuff I couldn't seamlessly fit in anywhere else. Bullet points for the busy executive:

- Charles Johnson as a White Sock in 2000: .326 AVG/.411 OBP/.607 SLG. Charles Johnson the rest of his career: .243 AVG/.327 OBP/.428 SLG.

- This wouldn't be much of a sports book if I didn't hopelessly commingle correlation and causation at some point, so here goes: The '93 Braves before the Fred McGriff trade: 53 wins, 40 losses for a .570 winning percentage. The '93 Braves after acquiring McGriff: 51 wins, 18 losses for a .739 winning percentage. Sure, McGriff hit .310 AVG/.392 OBP/.612 SLG after going Bravesward and was the greatest deadline-acquired hitter since 1980, but still, 51–18?

- Doyle Alexander may have the highest VORP (more on him in a moment), but no deadliner comes within hailing distance of Randy Johnson in '98 in terms of dominance. Fathom his line as an Astro: 84.1 innings, 57 hits, 126 strikeouts, 25 unintentional walks, 1.28 runs per game, and a park-adjusted ERA 218 percent better than the league average. Also consider that before the trade from Seattle (in exchange for Freddy Garcia, Carlos Guillen, and John Halama), he was en route to his worst season since his second year in the majors.

- It's mighty difficult to rack up a VORP of 17.9 in only 38⅓ innings pitched. To do that, you'd have to do what Ugueth Urbina did in 2003, when he gave up only six runs as a Marlin.

- Jim Bruske and his various handlers pulled off an exceedingly rare feat in 1998–playing for both World Series teams. On July 23, the future NL champion Padres acquired Bruske from the Dodgers for minor leaguer Widd Workman. Exactly a month later the Padres dealt Bruske and Brad Kaufman to the Yankees, whom they would lose to in the World Series, for Ray Ricken and Shea Morenz. Bruske wouldn't see action in the postseason.

- Random oddity: the Braves in 1997 and 1998 made only one deadline acquisition each season–first baseman Greg Colbrunn, both years. On August 14, 1997, the Braves acquired Colbrunn from the Twins for minor leaguer Mark Lewis. Then the following July, after granting free agency over the winter, they pried Colbrunn from the Rockies for righthander David Cortes and lefty Mike Porzio. The Braves then once again allowed Colbrunn to depart via free agency.

- Outfielder Dave Henderson came to the Red Sox along with shortstop Spike Owen on August 19, 1986. To acquire the duo, Boston sent the Mariners Rey Quinones, Mike Brown, John Christensen, and cash. During the regular season, both Henderson and Owen were worse than a novelty cummerbund, but Henderson, of course, defrayed all costs with his folkloric home run in game five of the ALCS. In the ninth inning, the Sox were down by a pair of runs to the Angels and one strike away from elimination. Henderson sent the game to extra innings with his two-run blast (atoning for allowing an earlier Bobby Grich fly ball to bounce off his glove and into the seats for a homer) and drove in the winning run in the 11th with a sac fly.

- I'd be remiss if I let Felipe Lira pass without snarky ridicule. The '97 Mariners, attempting bullpen triage, acquired Lira from Detroit along with Omar Olivares for Dean Crow, Scott Sanders, and Carlos Villalobos. Lira pitched only 18⅔ innings down the stretch, but those innings were bad enough to raise suspicions that he'd been operating as a double agent the whole time (okay, not really). Over that noxious span he allowed 21 runs, gave up 31 hits, walked more than he struck out, and took the loss in exactly half of his appearances.

Among all the teams I've studied and all the deadline deals they made, junkballing righthander Doyle Alexander had the best posttrade numbers of any deadline acquisition. Alexander was a 44th-round pick of the Dodgers in 1968, and by 1971 he was in the majors for good.

After half a season in L.A., the Dodgers traded Alexander to the Orioles as part of a six-player deal that brought future Hall of Famer Frank Robinson to Chavez Ravine. On balance, Alexander was a subpar pitcher during his three-plus seasons in Baltimore, and the Orioles eventually shipped him to the Yankees in a midseason, ten-player blockbuster that would net the O's such future key contributors as Scott McGregor, Rick Dempsey, Rudy May, and Tippy Martinez. That was 1976, and Alexander won 10 games down the stretch for the Yankees and helped them best the Orioles by 10½ games for the AL East crown. Alexander would fare poorly in his only postseason start that year, which came against the Reds in game one of the World Series, and that winter he signed with the Rangers as a free agent. His first season in Texas, Alexander notched 17 wins and posted a 3.65 ERA in 237 innings. However, he faltered the next two seasons and was dealt to the Braves after the '79 season. He pitched well in Atlanta, who then shipped him to the Giants. The 1981 season was, of course, abbreviated because of the players' strike, but it was also Alexander's best to date. He paced the Giants' staff with 11 wins, and his 2.89 ERA, on a park-adjusted basis, was 18 percent better than the league mean. His performance that year once again caught the eye of George Steinbrenner, and the Yankees traded for him a second time, this time sending Andy McGaffigan and Ted Wilborn to the Giants.

Alexander's second layover in the Bronx was decidedly less auspicious than his first. In '82 he went 1–7 with a grisly 6.08 ERA (especially grisly considering it was 11 years before run scoring levels vaulted in '93) and 14 homers allowed in only 66⅔ innings. The next year, he further raised Yankee hackles by punching a wall in frustration and going on the DL with a broken hand. Steinbrenner intimated that Yankee infielders were scared to play behind Alexander. Third baseman Graig Nettles quipped, "If I was in the bleachers, I'd be scared."

The Yankees defenestrated him early in the '83 season, but the Blue Jays were quick to nab the struggling 32-year-old. That's about the time things changed for Alexander. He finished out 1983 on a modest high note with a sub-4.00 ERA, and the next year he crafted, to that point, the best season of his career. In '84 Alexander worked $261^2/_3$ innings (the third-highest total in the AL), posted a 2.36 strikeout-to-walk ratio (good for sixth in the AL), and logged a 3.13 ERA (good for eighth in the AL). Additionally, he finished 17–6 on the season and spun 11 complete games. The next year he was almost as good and placed sixth in the AL Cy Young voting.

In 1986 Alexander got off to a slower start, and he sounded off in the press on what he saw as management's lack of commitment to winning (and to paying him more). After going on to criticize the enthusiasm of Toronto fans, the Jays finally traded him to Atlanta for reliever Duane Ward. After pitching reasonably well for the balance of the season, Alexander re-signed with Atlanta for $650,000. His solid start to the '87 season was belied by his 5–10 record with the Braves. So Atlanta cut bait on him at the deadline and sent him to Detroit for a struggling young righthander named John Smoltz, who had serious control problems and a 5.68 ERA in the lower rungs of the Tigers' minor league system.

Smoltz, of course, would go on to become one of baseball's best starters for the decade of the '90s, helping pitch the Braves to a World Series win in 1995 and winning the NL Cy Young Award in '96. Later, after clawing his way back from reconstructive elbow surgery, Smoltz refashioned himself as one of the game's elite closers. As of the end of the 2004 season, Smoltz, in sixteen major league seasons, had tallied 163 wins, 154 saves and a park-adjusted ERA 25 percent better than the league average (the 52nd-best mark of all time). Suffice it to say, had Smoltz, a Michigan native and lifelong Tiger fan, met with the same success on Detroit's watch, he would have been one of the most popular players in franchise history.

Often, you'll hear the Alexander-Smoltz trade recast as one of those Faustian bargains in which the acquiring team mortgages forthcoming glory for gratification in the here and now. In hindsight, that's certainly what the Tigers did, at a demonstrably high cost, I might add. Still, the deal they made was eminently defensible at the time, and no amount of due diligence could have foretold what Smoltz was to become. At the time of the trade, Smoltz had two minor league seasons in his professional dossier. In his first, which took place in the A-level Florida State League, he posted a 3.56 ERA, but he struck out only 4.4 batters per nine, which is patently inadequate for a pitcher in the low minors. The following season, as mentioned, he was even worse while still pitching in the low minors. That season he made middling strides with his strikeout rate but walked a whopping 81 batters in 130 innings. In other words, if you're looking for an augury of success in the 20-year-old John Smoltz, you won't find it in his minor league statistical record. That's not even accounting for the tremendously high attrition rate experienced by prep-trained righthanders, of whom Smoltz was one.

But just as Smoltz exceeded expectations after the trade, so did Alexander. The Tigers acquired him on August 12, when they were $1\frac{1}{2}$ games behind the Blue Jays in the AL East. So, the Tigers' status as a playoff team was very much in peril. At the time of the deal, Detroit's fourth and fifth starters, Don Robinson and Dan Petry, had 5.00 and 5.96 ERAs. Obviously, the back of the rotation was the soft underbelly of a team that would go on to win 98 games that season. Alexander supplanted Petry in the rotation, and his performance was such that the Tigers wouldn't have won the division without him.

Alexander had time to make only 11 starts down the stretch, but over those 11 starts he posted a 1.53 ERA in $88\frac{1}{3}$ innings pitched. He never went fewer than six innings in any start, he gave up only three home runs, and the Tigers won every game he started.

At the close of play on September 26, the Tigers were $3\frac{1}{2}$ games behind the Blue Jays. The next day, with the Tigers having lost the first four games of a dire series against those same Blue Jays, Alexander turned in a yeoman's effort that saved the season for Detroit. Against Toronto, he worked into the 11th inning and gave up only two runs. In the 13th, a Kirk Gibson single scored Jim Walewander from second; then Mike Henneman, Mark Thurmond, and Dickie Noles combined to blank the Jays in the bottom frame; and the Tigers won, 3–2. Five days later, Alexander took the mound again opposite the Blue Jays, this time with the Tigers trailing in the East by one game with three to play. Alexander worked seven effective innings in 4–3 Detroit victory. The Tigers would go on to sweep the series from Toronto and win the AL East by a pair of games. In the '87 postseason, the Tigers went down in five to the putatively overmatched Twins, and Alexander, for his part, posted a 10.00 ERA in two ALCS starts. Even so, Alexander added roughly four wins to the Tigers' total that year, and had they not made the trade for him, the Jays would have won the East.

This raises the subject of other later-for-now trades made by playoff-bound teams. The often-cited avatar of such deals is (depending upon your rooting druthers) the infamous or treasured Jeff Bagwell-for-Larry Andersen swap perpetrated by the '90 Red Sox and GM Lou Gorman. Boston that year prevailed by two games over the Blue Jays in a downcycled AL East. To be sure, Andersen was effective; in 22 innings of work after the trade (which occurred on August 30), he allowed only three runs, no home runs, and 21 base runners. Still, that comes to a VORP of 9.5, which is, in rough terms, just shy of one win. The upshot is that the Red Sox, even with a bottom-feeding reliever in Andersen's stead, likely would have won the flag anyway. And they could have kept Jeff Bagwell in the fold. Lest this be dismissed as abject ex post facto criticism, let's observe that my pillorying of the Bagwell trade embodies two key concepts I've already laid out. One, deadline deals—particularly those that are executed in late August—can be only so valuable because so much of the season has already passed. Second, relievers, since they pitch only so many innings, can be only so valuable. The acquisition of Andersen entailed both.

Another such swap was the one the '90 Pirates made for lefty Zane Smith. The Braves drafted Smith in the third round of the 1982 draft out of Indiana State, and by the end of the '84 season he was in the majors to stay. After a solid showing in 1987, when he made the *Sporting News*'s All-Star team, Smith developed elbow and shoulder maladies, which derailed his progress for a handful of seasons.

The Braves, as you may recall, spent much of the 1980s committing long strings of evitable missteps and canoodling with ineptitude. Smith fell victim to just that. Over the first five seasons of his career, he pitched tolerably to decently but nevertheless racked up some appalling win-loss marks. In 1988 the Braves quietly opened the season 0–10 (I say quietly because the Braves that year were playing baseball *in excelsis* compared to the Orioles, who would start the year 0–21), which was the worst start in NL history. However, it was

Smith who earned the complete-game win in game 11 when the Braves topped the Dodgers 3–1. In 1989, his final half season in Atlanta, he began the year a nearly unthinkable 1–12 before being dealt to the Expos for Sergio Valdez, Nate Minchey, and Kevin Dean (advantage Expos).

Following a serviceable 13 months in Montreal, the Expos traded him to the Pirates on August 8, 1990, for lefty reliever Scott Ruskin, minor league infielder Willie Greene, and a rookie outfielder named Moises Alou. Smith would pitch exceptionally well for the Pirates for the remainder of the season. In 76 down-the-stretch innings for the Bucs, Smith struck out 50, walked only nine (!), gave up only four homers, and posted a stellar ERA of 1.30. After his Expo and Pirate numbers for the 1990 season are combined, Smith ranks second in the NL in ERA, fourth in park-adjusted ERA, and eighth in fewest base runners allowed.

For his time in Pittsburgh, Smith logged a VORP of 23.4, which means he contributed just more than two wins to the Pirate cause in 1990. Since the Pirates topped the Mets by four full games in the NL East that season, the Bucs likely could have made the postseason without ever having made the trade in question. That's in sharp contrast to, say, Detroit's pickup of Alexander. Considering that Smith posted a 6.00 ERA in the Pirates' NLCS loss to the Braves, it's difficult to marshal a case that he was essential to the team's accomplishments in '90.

That's especially the case when considering what the Pirates gave up for him. Little more than a year after the Smith deal, the Expos packaged Greene (the cherished prospect at the time of the trade), Ruskin, and outfielder Dave Martinez to the Reds for relievers John Wetteland and Bill Risley. Alou, meanwhile, went on to, as of the end of the 2004 season, play in more than 1,600 major league games with a career batting line of .300 AVG/.367 OBP/.513 SLG and 278 home runs. Alou, after being dealt to Montreal, missed almost the entire 1991 season after injuring his shoulder in the Dominican winter leagues. Once he returned from surgery, however, he established himself as a broadly skilled hitter, and he certainly would have been a better proxy for Barry Bonds, who left Pittsburgh via free agency after the 1992 season, than Orlando Merced was.

Still, from the Pirates' perspective, Greene was the true concession, and Alou, who had a career slugging percentage of .437, didn't figure to become a premier power hitter at the highest level. But that's what he did.

A noteworthy player not quite making the above All-Star team is Cesar Cedeno, who was acquired by the '85 Cardinals and served as their starting first baseman down the stretch. His VORP as a Cardinal that season is 19.1, an excellent total but behind McGriff and Will Clark (2000 Cardinals) among deadline first basemen. Cedeno's personal backstory, however, is something else altogether

Surrounding Cedeno are lore and legend befitting John Henry, Stagger Lee, or Buford Pusser. The Cardinals worked feverishly to sign the Dominican phenom when he was only 16. The team offered $500, $700, and then $1,000 to Cedeno, but he refused. Once those efforts came to grief, the Cardinals' scout then flew back to St. Louis to pressure the organization in person for greater financial latitude. While he was Stateside, Astros scout Pat Gillick (later to be GM of the Blue Jays, Orioles, and Mariners) inked Cedeno for $3,000.

By age 19, Cedeno had arrived in Houston as one of the most ballyhooed rookies in memory. Astro manager Leo Durocher blazoned that Cedeno was "better than Willie Mays at the same age." Met manager Yogi Berra said Cedeno would one day lead the Astros to the World Series. Harry Walker said he was a better young player than Roberto Clemente. Houston assistant GM John McMullen observed that both Cedeno and Hank Aaron were called up at age 19, but that "if I give an edge to one of them, I'd have to give it to Cedeno." And on and on.

Suffice it to say, the pressure on Cedeno to realize these portents of greatness was acute and unrelenting. But he responded. In 1970, Cedeno was the youngest player in the majors (edging Expos lefty Balor Moore by exactly a month), but despite playing in the run-squelching Astrodome, Cedeno batted .310, slugged .451, and stole 17 bases in 90 games. The next year, pitchers adjusted and Cedeno didn't, resulting in what would be the worst numbers of his career. Still, on September 2, Cedeno offered a peek at his sweeping panoply of skills when he smacked an inside-the-park grand slam—one of the most improbable of offensive events—against the Dodgers.

In 1972, Cedeno arrived. He played in 139 games; batted .320; tallied 69 extra-base hits; slugged .537 (a profoundly impressive feat for a 21-year-old toiling in the Astrodome); swiped 55 bags; won a Gold Glove in the outfield; and, perhaps most encouragingly, showed much improved plate discipline by drawing 56 walks (against only 62 strike-outs). He also became the youngest player in major league history to record at least 20 homers and 20 steals in the same season. For his efforts, Cedeno made the All-Star team and finished sixth in the NL MVP voting.

The following season, Cedeno's fourth in Houston, he put up eerily similar numbers (same number of games played, same batting average, same slugging percentage, one more stolen base). Another All-Star appearance and Gold Glove followed. Houston fans took to calling the Astrodome "Cesar's Palace," and Astro brass rewarded Cedeno, and presumably themselves, by signing him to a ten-year, $3.5-million contract, munificent by 1970s standards. Things would hurriedly change for the 22-year-old.

On the evening of December 11, 1973, after a long night of drinking, a gun went off in a room at the Keki Motel in Santo Domingo. Cedeno's 19-year-old girlfriend, Altagracia de la Cruz, was dead. Cedeno later told authorities that his girlfriend wanted to look at his .38 revolver. He allowed her to do so, but when he attempted to get it back, a struggle ensued. The gun went off, and de la Cruz was shot through the head.

When he was younger, Cedeno had been married to a young Puerto Rican woman and had fathered a child with her. However, their marriage deteriorated, and they eventually divorced. Cedeno later remarried an American woman. Even under the oaths of his second marriage, Cedeno apparently never lost his taste for prostitutes. So customary were his visits to prostitutes that he became something of a chronic robbery victim, often losing cash and jewelry in thefts perpetrated by the prostitute or her handlers. Eventually Cedeno, rather than cease his patronage of the working girl, purchased a gun. A .38-caliber Smith & Wesson.

That night, his second wife was back in the Cedenos' lushly appointed winter home in Santo Domingo while Cesar was in the seedier crannies of town with his mistress Altagracia.

After the gun went off, Cedeno panicked. He dashed out of the room and fled the Keki Motel in his car. Eight hours later, he turned himself in to the police. "She asked for my revolver because she found it pretty," Cedeno told investigators. "I answered 'no' because it was loaded and very dangerous. I tried to stand up to drink a glass of beer while she insisted that I let her hold it."

Cedeno averred that the gun went off during the struggle, that de la Cruz's death was an accident, and that she had pulled the trigger. Authorities charged him with voluntary manslaughter (an approximation of a second-degree murder charge in the United States), and he spent the Christmas holidays in jail with four other accused murderers.

After 20 days of incarceration, results came back on a paraffin wax test, which revealed powder burns on de la Cruz's right hand. The test results revealed that de la Cruz had pulled the trigger and thus corroborated Cedeno's story. Charges were reduced to involuntary manslaughter, which, in the Dominican Republic, carried a maximum penalty of three years in prison. Instead, Cedeno was fined 100 pesos, or roughly 10 U.S. dollars.

Although Cedeno would again be productive to varying degrees, his unassailable potential and promise as a ballplayer would go unrealized. Whether it's coincidence that his decline occurred after the tragedy in Santo Domingo is impossible to say; what is clear is that he wasn't the same player after the night of December 11, 1973. Cedeno spent 17 seasons in the big leagues, and he was never again as good as he was at age 22. Never again except for a one fleeting month as a St. Louis Cardinal 12 years later.

It's also apparent that whatever lessons Cedeno gleaned from that night, they faded. In 1981, Cedeno was fined $5,000 by Major League Baseball for attacking a Braves fan during a game. The fan, along with two companions, had been clamorously taunting Cedeno's wife and making ill-considered remarks about the shooting death of de la Cruz eight years earlier. In 1985, while arguing with his girlfriend, he smashed his Mercedes into a tree. Two years later, Cedeno was arrested after smashing a beer glass over the head of a man who bumped into him at a bar. The next year, he attacked his girlfriend and drove away with their four-month-old baby. Cedeno would later return and continue his assault upon her. According to police reports, it took four officers to overpower him.

His playing career in Houston lasted until the winter of 1981, when he was traded to Cincinnati for third baseman Ray Knight. Cedeno gave the Reds 3½ ineffective seasons before he was dealt to the Cardinals on August 29, 1985, for minor leaguer Mark Jackson, who would never reach the majors. (Interesting aside: three days before the deal, the Reds, with Cedeno, Buddy Bell, Pete Rose, Tony Perez, and Dave Concepcion, became the first team to have five play-ers with at least 2,000 career hits each to play in the same game.)

Deadline trades are often "lightning in a bottle" endeavors that defy expectations for good or bad. Sometimes otherwise high-quality talents can catch the wrong end of the statistical pendulum and wind up hurting the team that acquires them for the six-week stretch drive. Or sometimes, as in the case of Cedeno, a player of scant consequence for almost five years can suddenly do his thing like a house afire.

The Cardinals in '85 had a quality first baseman (Cedeno's posi-tion by this juncture of his career), but Jack Clark went down with an injury just as the stretch drive was beginning. In Cedeno's first game after the trade, on August 30, he faced his first team. The Astros won the game, but Cedeno launched a seventh-inning homer to pull the Cards closer. He was just getting started. Over the season's final month-plus, Cedeno batted .434 and slugged .750—incredible num-bers, even for such a brief time.

On September 11, Cedeno launched a 10th-inning homer to push the Cardinals past the Mets in 10 innings and into a first-place tie with those same Mets. On October 5, Cedeno went three-for-three with a homer as St. Louis clinched the division on the next-to-last day of the season. The Cardinals wound up edging the Mets by three games in the NL East race. Cedeno would not play well in the postseason, as the Cardinals bested the Dodgers in the NLCS but fell to the Royals in seven in the World Series. However, his performance down the stretch served as an invigorating echo of the player he could have been and almost became.

A young Cedeno, after being deluged with praise, once said of comparisons to Clemente, "I know Clemente. I might be something like him, but not like him. There is only one Clemente."

He was right. If only his handlers and observers had placed such reasonably modest demands on his future.

Contending teams fervently believe they need to do *something* at the trade deadline, and if the objective is to make glancing tweaks to an already strong team, that's perfectly fine. However, if a team's brass is under the impression they can add a single marquee player with two months to go in the season and then their vanilla team is going to molt into a certifiable contender, it's generally a delusion. Deadline pickups are an indelible part of being a winning team, but alchemy they're not.

CHAPTER 8

The Veteran and the Youngster

(or, What Teams Can Learn from a Bottle of Wine)

It's commonly held that teams most often thrive when their rosters are turgid with seasoned veterans. The reasoning goes that veteran players have the requisite wiles and experience to handle the acute pressures of a pennant race and postseason play. They feel peculiarly at home there—like James Caan in the grotto at the Playboy Mansion. On the other hand, many statistically inclined types typically dismiss this as folly and assert that it's more prudent—and more cost-effective—to give jobs to worthy youngsters and otherwise endeavor to build a roster of players close to the usual prime age of 27. Who's got it right?

It seems that reality is consonant with the idea that winning clubs are also veteran clubs; successful teams, by and large, are older than their competitors. With regard to pitching, 88 of our 124 teams (71.0 percent) have staffs that are older than the league mean. As far as hitting goes, 79 of the 124 clubs (63.7 percent) have position players who are older than the league average for hitters. Those are a pair of fairly pronounced trends. Since 1980 (excluding, of course, the strike-mangled 1981 and 1994 seasons), the average age for pitchers is 28.5, and the average age for hitters is 28.7. Among playoff teams, however, those figures rise to 29.3 for pitchers and the same, 29.3, for hitters.

As we'll see in the next chapter, there's a precise reason for this phenomenon. For now, however, let's peer a bit more closely at the age issue itself.

The Hitters

Following is a list of the oldest teams, in terms of hitters, according to percentage of league-average age for positional players. Also included is the team's R/G scored (or R/G allowed for pitchers) rank to show how they fared in comparison to the other teams in the league during that particular season:

Ranking	Team	Average Age	Percentage of League Average	R/G Rank
1.	'83 Phillies	31.9	111.9	3rd
2.	'82 Angels	32.2	111.8	2nd
3.	'86 Angels	31.7	110.1	6th
4.	'98 Padres	31.2	109.5	8th
5.	'87 Tigers	31.0	109.2	1st
6.	'01 Diamondbacks	31.9	108.9	3rd
7.	'03 Giants	32.1	108.8	6th
8.	'97 Orioles	31.6	108.6	6th
9.	'02 Giants	32.0	108.5	3rd
10.	'01 Mariners	31.3	107.9	1st

Topping this list are the "Wheeze Kids," the '83 Phillies team headlined by a coterie of former Cincinnati house specials—first baseman Pete Rose, age 42; keystoner Joe Morgan, age 39; and Tony Perez, age 41, coming off the bench. Although they're the oldest relative to the rest of the league, the '82 Angels, with embalmed vets such as Bob Boone, Rod Carew, Bobby Grich, Don Baylor, and Reggie Jackson, were older in raw terms. The '86 Angels returned Boone and Jackson, then 38 and 40, respectively, and complemented them with Brian Downing and Doug DeCinces, both 35. In 1998, the Padres had an aging Tony Gwynn in right, a 36-year-old Wally Joyner at first, and Ken Caminiti, age 35, at the hot corner. The '87 Tigers had a 40-year-old Darrell Evans at first, 36-year-old Bill Madlock as the primary DH, and underrated (in most years, anyway) reserve Johnny Grubb playing out his final season at age 38.

The 2001 Diamondbacks had no regular younger than 31, and first baseman Mark Grace was the elder statesman at age 37. The '03 Giants had two 38-year-olds, Barry Bonds and Benito Santiago, in the lineup most every day, and most of the time they deployed 42-year-old Andres Galarraga as the first-option pinch hitter and DH during interleague play. In '97 Cal Ripken Jr., then 36, anchored the Orioles (in spirit, if not productivity), and they occasionally turned to 38-year-old Harold Baines for some key at-bats. The 2002 Giant model had Bonds and Santiago both in key starting roles, a troika of 34-year-olds—J. T. Snow, Jeff Kent, and Reggie Sanders—in the lineup, and a 39-year-old reserve in Shawon Dunston. In 2001 the Mariners emerged as arguably the greatest regular-season club of all time, and, with DH Edgar Martinez, age 38, and a bench brimming with dotards such as Mark McLemore, Stan Javier, Tom Lampkin, and Ed Sprague, they were also one of the oldest clubs in history. Now that the introductions are out of the way, it might be interesting to see what's the oldest starting lineup we can assemble from the above 10 teams. Let's do that, with each player's VORP thrown in to reflect how effective they were at the plate despite their advanced years:

Position	Player	Age	Team	VORP
C	Bob Boone	38	'86 Angels	−1.8
1B	Pete Rose	42	'83 Phillies	−6.6
2B	Joe Morgan	39	'83 Phillies	33.2
3B	Cal Ripken Jr.	36	'97 Orioles	23.9
SS	Mike Bordick	31	'97 Orioles	−2.4
LF	Barry Bonds	38	'03 Giants	112.6
CF	Steve Finley	36	'01 Diamondbacks	21.0
RF	Tony Gwynn	38	'98 Padres	37.3

Boone edges out Benito Santiago ('03 Giants) by months, and Bordick does the same to Tim Foli ('82 Angels), Tony Womack ('01 Diamondbacks), and Rich Aurilia ('03 Giants). In terms of quality, most were quite good (with Bonds—and perhaps his hope chest of syringes and ointments—being ridiculously so), while Boone, Rose, and Bordick really had no business being there. Rose, with his rancid-batting line of .245 AVG/.316 OBP/.286 SLG, which is beyond revolting for a player manning a nonvital defensive position, actually ranked as the worst regular first baseman in all of baseball that season. In fact, Rose's '83 VORP is the one of the worst by any qualifying first baseman since 1972 (second only to Kevin Young's work in 1993). And that appalling .286 SLG of Rose's, among first baseman, is the third-worst league-adjusted mark of the 20th century. There's really no other way to cast Rose as anything other than a searing liability that season. Of course, that probably prepped him for his postretirement career as a professional searing liability.

One of the first things to jump out from this list is the relatively young age of shortstops on these otherwise old teams. However, it's fairly intuitive. One of the first things to go with age is fielding range (just think of how many hitters have remained productive at the plate after being moved to less demanding positions or cosseted away at DH), so it figures that the most demanding position on the diamond would, on successful teams, tend to be manned by players closer to their prime seasons. In keeping with that idea, here's how the average ages for these 10 teams shake out, position by position:

1. SS—28.8
2. CF—31.2
3. RF—31.6
4. 2B—32.2
5. 3B—32.4
6. C—32.6
7. LF—33.0
8. 1B—34.8

Those at the "skill" positions—second base, shortstop, and center field—are generally younger than those at other, less taxing positions. Here are those mean ages, grouped by position type:

Skill positions (2B, SS, CF)—30.7

Other positions—32.9

The teams that have especially venerable offensive units seem, for the most part, to confine those older players to noncritical defensive positions. The oldest team in terms of skill players is the '01 Diamond-backs, who had an average age of 34.0 at second, short, and center. They along with the '03 Giants are the only two teams of the 124 I've studied to be over 30 years of age at all three skill positions. In other words, it's approaching recent historical-imperative status, if you're going to succeed, to have a second baseman, shortstop, and center fielder who are all younger than 31.

And the youngest teams, again in terms of percentage of league-average age for hitters:

Ranking	Team	Average Age	Percentage of League Average	R/G Rank
1.	'02 Twins	26.6	92.3	9th
2.	'00 A's	27.1	93.1	2nd
3.	'01 A's	27.1	93.4	4th
4.	'03 Marlins	27.7	93.9	8th
5.	'00 White Sox	27.5	94.5	1st
6.	'82 Braves	27.0	94.7	1st
7.	'03 Twins	27.3	95.1	6th
8.	'85 Cardinals	27.6	96.2	1st
9.	'95 Dodgers	27.3	96.8	10th
9.	'91 Blue Jays	27.6	96.8	11th

As you can see, the '82 Braves rank among the most apple-cheeked offensive units I've studied. Atlanta that season paced the NL in runs scored despite, one assumes, being the second-youngest offensive unit in the league. They also depended heavily upon those young hitters to win. The Braves in '82 finished 10th in the 12-team NL in runs allowed and below the league average in park-adjusted defensive efficiency. That's to say, the offensive attack was about all they had going for them. The Braves that year were young at every position save first base, where 33-year-old Chris Chambliss roamed. The rest of the infield—second baseman Glen Hubbard, shortstop Rafael Ramirez, and hard-hitting third baseman Bob Horner—were all 24 years of age. Catcher Bruce Benedict and center fielder Dale Murphy were both 26, and occasional starting outfielder Brett Butler was 25.

"Piggy" Horner, growing up in Glendale, Arizona, laid waste to all manner of batting records while playing for Apollo High School. The A's drafted him in the 15th round of the 1975 draft, but he opted instead for a baseball scholarship to Pac-10 juggernaut Arizona State. As a sophomore Horner was named MVP of the College World Series and voted as the first-team All-American second baseman. His junior year saw him tally an NCAA-record 25 homers, and the *Sporting News* named him the College Player of the Year.

The Braves, amply impressed by Horner's collegiate bestowals, made him the first overall pick of the 1978 draft (a draft class that included other prominent performers such as Ryne Sandberg, Kent Hrbek, Kirk Gibson, Mike Morgan, Howard Johnson, and Lloyd Moseby) and signed him for the then remarkable sum of $175,000. The organization originally intended to dispatch Horner to Savannah of the Southern League, but Horner and his agent, the wondrously named Bucky Hoy, beseeched them to take a more aggressive approach with the young slugger, which was not an uncommon entreaty from college-trained players in the years following the institution of free agency and salary arbitration.

After his first visit to Atlanta–Fulton County Stadium, Horner saw his future peer group demystified before his very eyes. "When you see guys like Johnny Bench or George Foster on *Monday Night Baseball*, they look like supermen," Horner mused. "Down there I saw for myself how they look and what they do. They look just like me."

The Braves apparently agreed. Horner became one of those rare players to go directly from the amateur ranks to a major league starting lineup. In his first at-bat in the majors, Horner homered off should-be Hall of Famer Bert Blyleven (more on him in a moment). Coming out of that rookie season, Horner's promise was astounding. At age 20, without having played a day in the minors, Horner, in little more than half a season, mashed 23 homers and bested future Hall of Famer Ozzie Smith for the '78 NL Rookie of the Year Award. Horner went deep once every 14 at-bats that first season, the best such mark ever recorded by a Rookie of the Year (at least until Mark McGwire came along nine years later). Longtime manager Dick Williams called Horner "another Harmon Killebrew."

Going into the next season, Horner was at loggerheads with owner Ted Turner over, of course, his salary. Horner and Hoy won a substantial raise when they successfully argued that Horner's '78 salary should include his signing bonus, which meant, according to the collective bargaining agreement, that Turner couldn't cut his salary by more than 20 percent of his previous year's salary plus signing bonus. The payday for Horner was a big one by late 1970s standards, but it established an acrimonious relationship with Turner that would color the first half of Horner's career. So bitter was Turner over his defeat at the negotiating table that he insinuated to the press that Horner's bear-ish negotiating tactics had led to the untimely death of team vice president Bill Lucas.

Horner broke an ankle on Opening Day, 1979, but he came back to hit 33 home runs and rank fifth in the NL in SLG. On the strength of that performance, the Braves signed him to a three-year, $1-million contract. But the bliss was short-lived. The following year, Horner opened the season two for his first 38. Turner, notionally hoping to stem the young player's struggles but most likely just sniffing out his pound of flesh, tried to send him down to the minors. However, Horner refused the assignment, and as a result, the team suspended him for three weeks. Horner returned in mid-May and wound up with a career-best 35 homers on the season and placed second behind Mike Schmidt in SLG.

In '82, Horner hit 32 out and made his first and only All-Star appearance, and the team won the NL West by a single game over the hated Dodgers. However, in the NLCS sweep at the hands of the Cardinals, Horner foundered badly, putting up a horrifically symmetrical batting line of .091 AVG/.091 OBP/.091 SLG. The following January, the Braves inked Horner to a new contract, one that would pay him $6 million over four years. Because of Horner's tendency to pack on the pounds, the team included $400,000 worth of incentives tied to his weight.

More than halfway through the 1983 season, Horner was batting .303 with a .383 OBP (both career highs) and on pace for 60 extra-base hits when he broke his wrist sliding into second base. He missed the remainder of the season. The following May, only 48 games into the season and with the Braves a game and a half off the division pace, Horner again broke the very same wrist. He wouldn't play again that year.

For the 1985 season, the Braves, probably motivated by Horner's declining range and increasing fragility, began gradually transitioning him to first base. Whether by dint of better luck or more cautious play,

Horner logged career bests with 130 games played in '85 and 141 in '86. In 1986 he also emerged as one of the best defensive first basemen in the NL, pacing the league in putouts, assists, and double plays. On the offensive end, he ranked fifth in the NL with 27 home runs. Horner's season was also punctuated by his performance on July 6, when he became the 11th player in major league history to hit four homers in a single game, a losing effort against the Expos. (I remember this game well because it was relegated to a tape-delay broadcast on WTBS by the much-dreaded, glasnost-inspired Goodwill Games.)

Turner and the Braves, however, had less regard for Horner's broad efforts that season and offered him a two-year, $3-million contract, which constituted a $300,000 cut in his annual salary. Horner opted to test the market, but no better offers were forthcoming. Frustrated and perhaps a bit desperate, Horner stunned the baseball world by signing a one-year, $2.4-million pact with the Yakult Swallows of the Japanese Central League. The team was frothy with anticipation, and Swallows brass even boasted to the press that Horner, helped by the cozier parks in Japan, would hit 50 home runs in 1987. Horner began the year in grand fashion, going yard in six of his first seven hits and hitting three homers in a single game. However, he failed to meet the forecasts of ownership, although he was still excellent for the Swallows. In 99 games Horner batted .327 and hit 31 out. However, he felt displaced and isolated and longed to return to the States. After the season, Horner said plaintively, "Life last year was not amusing."

The Swallows offered Horner a three-year, $10-million contract, but the pull of the Occident was too strong. The Cardinals, after Jack Clark emigrated from St. Louis to the Bronx, needed a power source, and Horner peddled himself to them. Manager Whitey Herzog initially said he had no use for Horner, but the Cardinals eventually inked him to a one-year contract potentially worth $1.45 million. However, Horner's reintroduction to the U.S. major leagues was a flop. At the conclusion on play on June 18, Horner was slugging .354 with only three homers in 206 at-bats. Thwarted and overmatched, he retired at age 31. He'd spent ten years in the majors but, accounting for injuries, a suspension, and his Japanese tour of duty, Horner logged roughly the equivalent of only six full seasons in the major leagues. Still, he walked away from the game with 218 career home runs, a top-100 ranking for career SLG, and a better HR/at-bat ratio than luminaries such as Reggie Jackson, Ernie Banks, and Mel Ott.

While Horner never hunted down his early promise, he still managed to put together an enviable career.

The Pitchers

As demonstrated above, winning teams tend to be older on the pitching side of the ledger. To explore this trend a bit farther, let's look at the teams that, in terms of pitching age, reside at the extremes.

First, here's a list of the oldest pitching teams within the sample group, sorted by percentage of league-average pitching age:

Ranking	Team	Average Age	Percentage of League Average	R/G Rank
1.	'03 Yankees	33.6	117.1	3rd
2.	'02 Yankees	33.0	115.0	4th
3.	'99 Mets	32.6	114.8	5th
4.	'80 Yankees	31.4	113.4	2nd
5.	'82 Angels	31.9	113.1	2nd
6.	'90 A's	31.7	111.6	1st
7.	'92 A's	32.0	110.7	4th
7.	'00 Yankees	32.0	110.7	6th
9.	'87 Twins	31.4	110.2	10th
10.	'89 Giants	31.6	110.1	3rd

The recent Yankee teams, mostly as a function of their propensity for signing free agents and acquiring high-salary veterans from the less well heeled, have put together some rather creaky pitching staffs. But there's little arguing with their success. Also making a couple of appearances are the A's of the early '90s, when manager Tony La Russa and pitching coach/rumble-seater Dave Duncan were proving to have a deft touch with reclamation projects such as Dave Stewart, Bob Welch, Mike Moore, and Ron Darling.

The '87 Twins are also among the "cat food crowd," but they weren't a particularly arresting example, ranking a measly 10th in runs allowed that season. Still, you'd be hard pressed to find a more interesting assemblage of pitchers.

Only two Minnesota pitchers that season, ace Frank Viola and middle reliever Juan Berenguer, managed an ERA of less than 4.00. That's probably why GM Andy MacPhail tried things such as disinterring Joe Niekro and Steve Carlton (previously profiled as one of the worst deadline acquisitions in recent memory) for a total of 25 hellish starts and granting a prominent role to Les Straker (a nom de private investigator if I've ever heard one). The team's second-best pitcher was 36-year-old Bert Blyleven, who paced the Twins in innings with 267 and posted a 4.01 ERA for the season, which isn't bad considering he made 22 of his 37 starts in the hitterphilic Metrodome during a season in which the AL ERA was 4.46. Throw the 1986 season into the mix, and Blyleven surrendered 96 home runs over two seasons, including a major league record 50 in '86. These days, it seems Blyleven is mostly remembered for his vaunted gopheritis (in actuality, he posted average to good home run rates in every season of his 22-year career save for that pair with the Twins). That's a disservice to his accomplishments. It's akin to dismissing the oeuvre of John Lennon because he had poor hygiene and dubious tastes in the fairer sex. Blyleven is one of the all-time greats, and his absence from the Hall of Fame is a joke—and not the funny kind.

The greatest player ever from the Netherlands (Honus Wagner, "The Flying Dutchman," was actually from Mansfield, Pennsylvania) and master of one of the greatest curveballs ever (a pitch Dave Winfield once called a "bowel-locking" curve), Blyleven has been woefully neglected on recent Hall of Fame ballots. If there's any horse sense to the process, he'll be ushered into Cooperstown long before his case reaches the nepotistic—and, based on some of their recent selections, seemingly venal—country club better known as the veterans' committee. Come with me, won't you, as we take a guided tour of Blyleven's unassailable Hall of Fame credentials:

- fifth all-time with 3,701 career strikeouts;
- ninth all-time with 685 career starts;
- ninth all-time with 60 shutouts;
- 13th all-time with 4,970 innings pitched;
- 25th all-time with 287 wins;
- 91st all-time with 242 complete games.

That's not all. Blyleven also made a pair of All-Star teams and four times finished in the top 10 for the Cy Young Award (if Cy voters were even vaguely competent at isolating genuine performance, Blyleven would have notched 10 top 10 appearances). In terms of single-season benchmarks, Blyleven's career is festooned with any number of top 10 finishes in his league: ERA—10 top 10s; innings—11 top 10s, led league twice; wins—six top 10s; strikeouts—15 top 10s, led league once; shutouts—10 top 10s, led league thrice; lowest hits/nine innings—seven top 10s; lowest walks/nine innings—eight top 10s; lowest walks-plus-hits/nine innings—11 top 10s, led league once.

What costs Blyleven some Cooperstown traction is that he lost 250 games in his career (10th most all-time) and had what seems at first blush to be a somewhat unspectacular career winning percentage. Need I point out that wins and losses are not meaningful ways to evaluate pitching performances? A hurler's win-loss record has as much to do with run support and quality of opposition as it does with the pitcher's ability. It's fashionable to say that wins and losses, especially over a long career, balance out over time, but that's not always the case. Blyleven's teams over the years managed a winning percentage of .502—only five games over .500 in the aggregate. Blyleven, meanwhile, posted a winning percentage of .534 for his career. That figure becomes much more impressive once you consider the mediocre nature of his teams.

Let us also not forget that Blyleven, for the vast majority of his career, toiled in home parks that favored the hitter. He spent only three seasons in parks that helped the pitcher, three seasons in parks that played essentially neutral, and 16 (!) seasons in parks that boosted offense. That has a lot to do with why you won't find his career ERA of 3.31 among the top 100 of all time. However, once we adjust his career ERA for the effects of park and league, we find that Blyleven's lifetime mark is better than that of Nolan Ryan, Steve Carlton, Don Sutton, Fergie Jenkins, and Gaylord Perry—Hall of Famers all. In fact, Blyleven has the exact same career adjusted ERA as Warren Spahn, who's most assuredly an "inner circle" Hall of Famer.

So if you're seeking a tidy approximation in terms of career value, Blyleven was roughly Warren Spahn minus about 275 innings. How, exactly, is that not a Hall of Famer?

Now we'll look at teams that have defied convention by trotting out those relatively youthful pitching staffs. Here's a list of the youngest pitching teams in terms of percentage of league-average pitching age:

Ranking	Team	Average Age	Percentage of League Average	R/G Rank
1.	'86 Mets	25.8	91.2	2nd
2.	'03 Marlins	26.3	91.3	6th
2.	'00 White Sox	26.4	91.3	4th
4.	'85 Royals	26.1	91.9	2nd
5.	'93 White Sox	26.6	92.7	1st
6.	'88 Mets	26.6	93.3	1st
7.	'84 Royals	26.9	94.7	7th
8.	'89 Cubs	27.2	94.8	5th
9.	'93 Braves	26.8	95.0	1st
10.	'83 Dodgers	27.1	95.1	1st

It's perhaps surprising that the '86 Mets, who are among the greatest teams of the modern era, ran so starkly counter to expectations by having one of the youngest pitching staffs on record. That season, the Mets stormed to 108 wins (in National League history, only the 1909 Pirates and 1906 Cubs managed to win more games in a season), won the division by 21½ games over the second-place Phillies, and prevailed over the Red Sox in a white-knuckled World Series.

As for the pitching staff, they paced the NL in ERA and, as shown above, ranked second in runs allowed per game. All that seemingly despite a rotation populated by 21-year-old Dwight Gooden; 25-year-old Ron Darling; 23-year-old Sid Fernandez; 24-year-old Rick Aguilera; and elder statesman Bob Ojeda, age 28. Additionally, 25-year-old Roger McDowell paced the team in saves. Heck, even Jesse Orosco, whom we think of as being somehow perpetually ossified, wasn't even 30.

It's a task to impart just how brilliant Gooden was early in his career and the level of enthusiasm he engendered among fans of the game. Whatever his human failings and however disappointing the sum total of his career in light of his early promise, he was, for a fugitive time, the greatest pitcher anyone had ever seen. Like Hercules strangling the serpents at his crib, Gooden, even from an improbably young age, seemed on an unswerving course for greatness.

Less than two years before his major league debut, Gooden was pitching for Hillsborough High School in East Tampa. During his senior season, Gooden began drawing the attention of scouts with his blazing fastball and tremendous hammer curve (a pitch that would later be called "Lord Charles," a more distinguished variant of "Uncle Charley," the common baseball colloquialism for the curveball). The Mets were duly impressed and made Gooden the fifth overall pick of the 1982 draft.

Going into the 1984 season, accomplished minor league manager Davey Johnson, who was up for the Mets job and had been Gooden's skipper the previous year in Double-A, joked that in the upcoming season he'd be managing wherever Gooden was pitching. The message, couched in humor, was that Johnson wanted Gooden at his disposal were he to manage the Metropolitans. It was hard to blame him. Gooden, in his first full minor league season, led his league in ERA and struck out an unthinkable total of 300 in 191 innings. As much as those numbers might lead you to believe that Gooden's "prospect meat thermometer" was poking out, GM Frank Cashen favored a more conservative tack for his 19-year-old phenom. Fresh in Cashen's mind were memories of Tim Leary, a then recent Mets pitching über-prospect who, less than three years prior, blew out his arm pitching on a frigid, inclement day in Chicago while concealing an arm injury. Cashen, aware of Gooden's redoubtable promise yet wary of the fragile nature of young pitchers, envisioned a more neighborly debut for his prize prospect. As for Johnson, he learned all this only after accepting the Mets' job. Still, he didn't have to wait long.

Cashen and Johnson agreed that Gooden would make his major league debut on April 7, 1984, against Houston in the Astrodome. Johnson liked the date on the calendar; Cashen liked the atmospherics. Not only would Gooden be spared from unfriendly weather while pitching in the domed ballpark, but he'd also be working in a prominent pitcher's environment and in front of what figured to be a modest crowd—both in terms of numbers and conviction. "Dr. K," as he was called in the minors, delivered. In five innings, Gooden allowed one run, whiffed five, and walked three.

Later that season, after he cut an untrammeled swath through the

Cub lineup for an entire afternoon, a reporter asked Cub manager Jim Frey what he thought of Gooden's poise. "The guy has a 93-mile-per-hour fastball and one of the best curves in baseball and you ask me about his poise?" Frey sniffed. "What the hell does he need poise for?"

To say Gooden's rookie campaign went swimmingly is to indulge in criminal levels of understatement. It didn't take long for the Dr. K nickname to catch on and begin an upper-deck trend that's still very much with us. Fans in the far reaches of Shea Stadium, after every Gooden strikeout, would hang a red "K" placard over the railing. In '84, Gooden gave those fans plenty to keep track of. He set a major league record for rookies with 276 strikeouts in 218 innings (in the process becoming the first teenager in history to lead the majors in whiffs). On consecutive starts on September 12 and 17, he broke Sandy Koufax's NL record by striking out 32 batters in back-to-back outings. Throw in Gooden's September 7 start (a one-hitter against the division champion Cubs), and his 43 Ks broke Herb Score's record for strikeouts over a three-start span. Gooden also became the youngest player ever to play in an All-Star game (in that game, he and Fernando Valenzuela combined to break Carl Hubbell's record by fanning six straight hitters) and the youngest player ever to be named Rookie of the Year. Believe it or not, he was even better the following season.

In 1985, the Mets would win 98 games—at that time the second-most in franchise history, behind only the '69 club—but they'd finish second to the Cardinals in the NL East. Gooden, however, was second to no one. That season he led the majors in innings (276.2), wins (24), and ERA (1.53), thus making him the youngest hurler ever to win the "pitcher's Triple Crown," the first to do so since Steve Carlton in 1972, and the first New York pitcher to turn the trick since the Yankees' Lefty Gomez in 1937. Gooden's ERA in 1985 was the lowest since Bob Gibson's 1.12 mark in 1968, and Gooden also paced the league in complete games, with 16. As the Mets tried in vain to run down the Cardinals in the season's final weeks, Gooden was at his best; in five September starts totaling 44 innings, he surrendered not a single earned run. As such, Gooden became just the ninth pitcher ever to win the Cy Young Award by a unanimous vote and finished fourth in the balloting for NL MVP. When the season ended, he was still only 20 years old.

It's too tidily cinematic to say that after reaching such breathtaking heights, Gooden declined overnight, but he was never again quite the same. It could have been the imprudent workload foisted upon such a young arm. It could have been that the Mets, in an effort to improve Gooden's ability to hold runners, had pitching coach Mel Stottlemyre reconstruct his mechanics over the winter. It could have been that hitters were finally learning to abstain from Gooden's high fastball, which often popped in the mitt well out of the strike zone. Or it could have been the young man's baneful lifestyle exacting an early price. Whatever the reasons, Gooden would again be good in a handful of seasons, but he'd never again be great.

In '86, he gave up a home run to the first batter he faced that season, the Pirates' R. J. Reynolds. It was an augury of things to come. Gooden still had a strong season, but he declined in almost every regard compared to his work the previous two years. In particular, his strikeout rate plummeted from 9.9 in 1984–1985 to 7.2 in 1986. Even so, Gooden managed to become the first pitcher in major league history to strike out at least 200 batters in each of his first three seasons. His '86 ERA of 2.84 looks sparkling by today's standards, but consider that the NL ERA that season was only 3.54 and that Gooden was pitching half his games in Shea, one of the league's better parks for pitchers. In fact, away from Shea in '86 Gooden's ERA was 3.47, or just a hair better than the league mean. Gooden managed to make the All-Star team in '86 (mostly by virtue of his 9–3 record in the first half), but he took the loss in the midsummer classic, giving up a two-run bomb to Detroit's Lou Whitaker.

In the postseason, Gooden dazzled in the NLCS, although he wasn't credited with a win in either of his two starts. He suffered a nail-biting loss in game one against Mike Scott, the Astros' briefly untouchable ace, by the score of 1–0, with the lone run coming on a Glenn Davis home run. The Mets won Gooden's game five start, but it took them 12 innings to do so. Gooden squared off against Nolan Ryan and allowed only one run in 10 innings of work. It was the first time Davey Johnson had allowed Gooden to pitch beyond the ninth inning. In the process he set the NLCS records for strikeouts (20) and walks (eight) in a seven-game series. In the World Series, he was much less effective. Pitching on short rest, Gooden logged an 8.00 ERA in two starts.

Following the '86 season, Gooden's off-field troubles began in earnest. He and his nephew, future All-Star Gary Sheffield, were assaulted by police in Tampa over the winter, and the organization sent Gooden to a drug rehabilitation program after he tested positive for cocaine just before the 1987 season began. He didn't pitch until

June 5, but performed well upon his return. Still, the Mets lost the division to the Cardinals that season by three games, and some within the organization blamed Gooden's absence for the first two months of the season.

Going into the '88 season, Gooden declared that he was a different pitcher than he had been in the past. As such, he requested that he be called "Doc" instead of "Dr. K." That year, Gooden pitched a full season and won 18 games; however, his 3.19 ERA was just a tick better than the league average. In the postseason, Gooden set a record by fanning 20 batters in three NLCS appearances, but the 100-win Mets suffered a stunning defeat at the hands of the manifestly inferior Dodgers (whom the Mets that year had beaten in 10 of 11 regular-season contests). In 1989 Gooden missed more than two months with a shoulder injury, but his 9–4 record on the season ferried him into the record books once again. He became the first pitcher in 90 years to post a winning record in each of his first six seasons, and Gooden also became the third-youngest pitcher in the modern era to reach 100 career wins. Additionally, he reached the 100-win mark with the second-best winning percentage ever, only points behind legendary Yankee lefthander Whitey Ford. Even so, Gooden was able to return for only a pair of relief outings in September, and the Mets finished six games behind the division-winning Cubs.

In 1990 Gooden struck out 200 batters for the first time in four seasons, but his ERA was worse than the league mean. Still, as he racked up a 16–2 record after June 2, it seemed that the Gooden of yore had returned. That year would be his last healthy one as a Met. The first half of the decade would be a particularly cruel one for him. In the '90s, Gooden would spend 264 days on the DL with an array of shoulder maladies, a toe injury, and a hernia, and off the field he burnished his reputation as a troubled soul. Just three starts into the 1994 season, he hit the DL with a case of turf toe. He returned in June, but it wasn't long before an illness of another sort took hold. Gooden battled addictions to alcohol and cocaine throughout the latter stages of his career, and in September of '94, after he once again violated baseball's substance abuse policy, Commissioner Bud Selig suspended him for the balance of the '94 season and all of 1995. The day after news of his punishment came down, Gooden sat on the edge of his bed with a loaded 9 mm pistol jammed against his head. But he didn't pull the trigger. Following the '94 season, the Mets allowed him to become a free agent.

In February of 1996, the defrocked superstar got his second chance. Yankee owner George Steinbrenner signed him, and Gooden was determined to seize the opportunity. Going into his May 14 start in the Bronx against the Mariners, Gooden was lugging around a 5.67 ERA and was in danger of losing his job as the Yanks' fifth starter for a second time in the young season. Twenty-seven outs later, he had pitched around six walks and a wild pitch to no-hit the best offensive team in the majors. In fact, he was only the fifth AL pitcher in history to spin a no-hitter against a league-leading offense (joining Dave Stewart against the '90 Blue Jays, Hoyt Wilhelm against the '58 Yankees, and Ernie Koob and Bob Groom on back-to-back days versus the 1917 White Sox). It was a stunning flash of brilliance from a pitcher who seemed to be drawing his final breaths as a ballplayer. Incidentally, Gooden's no-no was the 11th by a former New York Met. The count is currently 13 (more than half of which belong to Nolan Ryan), which is notable since the Mets have yet to record a no-hitter in their 40-plus years as a franchise.

Gooden, suddenly beloved and revered again, was granted the key to the city by Mayor Giuliani. One great day aside, Gooden wasn't particularly effective that season, in spite of his 11–7 record. The Yankees even opted to leave him off their postseason roster, thus depriving him of the chance to be a part of the first Gotham World Series winner since his Mets a decade earlier.

He returned to the Yankees in '97, pitched marginally better for the season (although a misdiagnosed hernia cost him a good chunk of the season), and this time pitched on the October stage for the first time since 1988. In game four of the ALDS, he limited the powerful Indians to one run over $5\frac{2}{3}$ innings of work, but Cleveland touched the Yankee bullpen and won it 3–2 with runs in the eighth and ninth.

The next season, Gooden caught on with those same Indians and worked 134 innings with a park-adjusted ERA 27 percent better than the league average, his best such mark since his mind-blowing season in '85. The year, however, did not end happily for Doc, who was ejected for arguing balls and strikes in the first inning of his ALDS start against the Red Sox. He was also roughed up in his lone start against the Yankees in the '98 ALCS. He returned to the Indians the following season, but his decline resumed. In 115 innings he posted a 6.26 ERA and was deservedly left off the Tribe's playoff roster.

The Astros signed Gooden that winter, but he made only one start for Houston before they sold him to his hometown Tampa Bay Devil Rays. He struggled terribly with the Rays in 36⅔ innings before they released him. Once again, however, the Yankees took a flier on him. Working primarily in relief, Gooden gave the Yanks 64⅓ innings and a 3.36 ERA in the second half and a strong relief outing in the ALCS win over the Mariners. The 2000 season would be his final one, but his troubles weren't over. During the course of Gooden's divorce from his wife, Monica, the extent of his financial difficulties came to light. According to court documents, the Goodens regularly burned through $40,000 a month in expenses, and Mrs. Gooden managed to pile up an additional $50,000 in credit card debt. Monica Gooden even testified that she would habitually write personal checks until the account was overdrawn; then and only then would she call one of the couple's financial counselors to clean up the mess. In fact, despite making roughly $35 million over the course of his 17-year career in the majors, Gooden met with financial destitution in the years following his retirement. It's impossible to remember Gooden without an eye toward the flotsam of his life outside of baseball.

Still, in those early days, when he was young, when his future—and even his present—seemed honeycombed with possibilities, he was really something, wasn't he?

The winners tend to be older, that's true. But age shouldn't be pursued for its own sake. The stalwart veterans on these clubs probably do confer substantial leadership qualities and impart hard-won wisdom to their younger labelmates, but more vitally, they're elite ballplayers who defy the aging curve. And how do you get those players? You raid the coffers for them.

CHAPTER 9

The Money Player

(or, Why This Is No Place for the Faint of Wallet)

Thanks mostly to the framing efforts of owners, it's impossible to have a discussion about winning baseball without also addressing team finances. The perception at large is that the competitive structure in baseball is as sickeningly plutocratic as a Southampton tennis club, leavened only once in a great while by the skinflint successes of teams such as the A's and the Twins. Certainly, success isn't foreordained merely because a team has deep coffers, but it does confer a competitive advantage. Time and again, teams such as the Yankees have treated bad contracts as sunk costs and merely taken on other high-dollar players to replace them. Needless to say, most other teams aren't willing or able to manage their rosters in such a fashion.

The question at hand is this: how have these economic inequalities manifested themselves in the standings? Thanks to the efforts of researchers such as Maury Brown, Gary Gillette, and the late, great Doug Pappas, we have the necessary payroll data at our disposal. Since 1980, playoff teams, on average, have exceeded the league-average payroll by a fairly hefty 19 percent. Additionally, of the 124 teams studied for this book, 89 (71.8 percent) have surpassed the league-average payroll. That's a strong trend, and there's an overarching relationship here: winners tend to be older, which means they tend to be more expensive.

To hear ownership/management tell it, this bent toward the well heeled has become more pronounced in recent seasons. Let's see whether the data bear this out. Using the same two measures, we'll break it down by five-year periods, save for the final four-year epoch from 2000 through 2003:

Time Frame	Percentage of League-Average Payroll	Percentage of Teams > League Average
1980–1984	122.5	56.3
1985–1989	109.8	75.0
1990–1994	113.5	62.5
1995–1999	127.6	85.0
2000–2003	115.2	65.6

It's fairly clear that the "dark age" for competitive balance, to the extent that it applies to teams making the postseason, was from 1995 to 1999. During this five-year period, playoff teams exceeded the league mean payroll by an average of 27.6 percent, and exactly 85 percent of all teams making the postseason eclipsed the league's average payroll in their respective seasons. However, it's also an overarching trend that holds, albeit by varying degrees, throughout all of recent history: teams that win generally spend more money than those that don't.

In recent years, MLB has seized upon this competitive-balance problem and wielded it as a potent weapon against the Players' Association. Too often, however, concerns over the unequal sharing of revenues and structural advantages afforded to teams with larger revenue streams are conflated with owners' spurious claims of financial ruin. This unfortunate phenomenon allows MLB to drum up public support for an industrywide salary cap, similar to the one the NFL has. The "salary cap as promoter of competitive balance" is one of the great canards in sports today. Salary caps do nothing but suppress player salaries and increase owner profits. Baseball has always suffered from comparisons to the NFL, but because of stark and undeniable foundational differences in the ways the two sports operate, those comparisons are odious. Consider: if baseball had its clubs play only a 16-game slate, for years jimmied schedules so that the better teams faced a tougher docket of opponents, gave teams a week between games to scout and prepare for the opposition, offered no guaranteed player contracts, increased the number of playoff spots from eight to twelve, and went to a single-elimination postseason format, then suddenly MLB would be a paragon of egalitarianism. It's not the blessed salary cap that results in the NFL's supposedly superior competitive balance; it's the distinct nature of the sport when compared to baseball.

To be sure, the NFL's superior revenue-sharing structure helps. Late NFL commissioner Pete Rozelle in the 1960s, when the league was facing a critical juncture in its history, persuaded owners to agree to a revolutionary—in the sporting world, at least—business model. Rozelle recognized that to thrive a sports league must necessarily have a "command economy" of sorts. As such, he brought his power to bear on NFL owners and wisely coerced them to establish the NFL Trust, a common pool of revenues from broadcasting rights and merchandise sales. In recent years the trust has been assailed by gilded team owners such as Jerry Jones of the Dallas Cowboys and Dan Snyder of the Washington Redskins. Too often the desirable effects of this vital element of the NFL's financial structure are confused with those of the hard salary cap, which is something pro sports owners of all stripes pursue with catechistic devotion.

In contrast, Major League Baseball does not share its revenues so evenly. In the most recent collective bargaining agreement (2002), the League and the Players' Association agreed to share 34 percent of local revenues and distribute ever-increasing portions of the central fund from upper-class to lower-class clubs. The problem with revenue sharing is that there are no mechanisms in place to ensure that team owners actually reinvest in the club rather than swelling their personal estates. Still, increased revenue sharing is a necessary and overdue step for baseball. However, owners' continued bleating for salary caps (or de facto caps in the form of luxury taxes) are best ignored—they have nothing to do with competitive balance and will accomplish zilch to that end.

Baseball owners and Commissioner Bud Selig are particularly skilled at conflating, in the mind of the public, the need for more revenue sharing in the game and the entirely perfidious notion that the sport will totter and fall if labor costs aren't reined in. Selig isn't the first captain of industry to lie about his financial straits to extract concessions from labor and consumers—the gambit has been around since powdered wigs were staples of men's fashion—but few have wielded it so effectively.

For the 2001 fiscal year, MLB claimed operating losses of $232 million. However, *Forbes* magazine—hardly the Cesar Chavez of biz rags—failed to concur and, in fact, estimated that MLB's teams turned an aggregate profit of $76 million. For the most part, *Forbes* declined to take baseball at its word on reported expenses. There are countless ways for baseball owners to massage their P&L statements until they get a desirable outcome. There are related-party transactions, conferring outside business losses onto the team's books, drastically underpaying for media rights when a broadcast outlet falls under the same corporate umbrella, "salaries" granted to owners, etc. Or, as longtime MBL exec Paul Beeston once put it, "Anyone who quotes profits of a baseball club is missing the point. Under generally accepted accounting principles, I can turn a $4 million profit into a $2 million loss, and I can get every national accounting firm to agree with me." Years after that moment of ill-considered candor, Beeston would be named MLB's chief operating officer. At least he knew the drill.

In any event, Selig and his spear-carriers attacked the *Forbes* piece as "dishonest" and "a very sad day for journalism in America." Never mind that MLB would make an awfully odd random and fellow-traveling target for the virulently promanagement *Forbes*. Of course, you need not be a financial journalist or a forensic accountant to figure out that baseball is not to be trusted in matters of financial disclosure. For one, they're not a publicly traded entity, which means they have no legal obligation to tell unvarnished truths about their financials. Two, if baseball teams really were such lousy investments, they wouldn't appreciate like mad before passing from one owner to the next. It takes a peculiar kind of naïf to believe anything Selig says about the league's fiscal health.

So why all the deception, all the talking points, all the solemn frowns before congressional committees by Selig and his retinue? It's a profitable business, pretending to be flat broke when you have a product that people seek out with bated breath. Besides currying favor with the public when it comes to taking on the players every five years or so in collective bargaining negotiations, the Oliver Twist act also helps MLB raid the public trough. Most often, this comes in the form of the publicly funded stadium, a semirecent phenomenon for which baseball has a voracious appetite. MLB, under Selig's leadership, has fronted a trend that's seen U.S. taxpayers spend more than $2 billion per annum on sports facilities. If those dollars aren't coming

directly out of municipal budgets, then they represent a serious opportunity cost with regard to the revenue bases of cities.

Cities are so eager to cough up the public monies because having
a major league baseball team carries with it an ineffable prestige. Once
expansion or relocation is announced, city leaders work feverishly to
sell the public on the costs of a new ballpark. Most often, this is done
by making thoroughly spurious claims about the economic development that will follow. However, what new ballparks do is create a
handful of seasonal, part-time, low-wage jobs and redirect discre-
tionary income away from local businesses. If the economic windfall
isn't negligible, it certainly doesn't begin to justify the $500 million or
so that it cost to build the stadium.

What many teams are learning is that the shine comes off a new
ballpark rather quickly unless coupled with a team actually worth
watching. There's only so much that dot races and nifty architecture
can do if the hometown team is lousy. But I digress. . . .

These 124 playoff teams have an average ranking of 9.2 among
their peers in terms of payroll. Of course, a high payroll is no guaran-
tee of success. In fact, in the 22 seasons I've studied, the league leader
in payroll made the postseason only 54.5 percent of the time. Some
other numbers: 45.2 percent of the 124 playoff teams had a payroll
that ranked in the top quartile of their respective season, and 78.2 percent of teams had a payroll that ranked in the top half. In other words,
it's not vital to have a payroll in the top quartile, but by and large it is
necessary to have one in the top half.

Now let's look at the profligate spenders in our midst. The table below
shows the teams with the highest payroll relative to the league average.

Ranking	Team	Percentage of League-Average Payroll
1.	'03 Yankees	212.5
2.	'80 Yankees	188.9
3.	'82 Angels	188.5
4.	'02 Yankees	186.7
5.	'99 Yankees	179.5
6.	'80 Phillies	169.6

Ranking	Team	Percentage of League-Average Payroll
7.	'00 Yankees	166.2
8.	'01 Yankees	165.2
9.	'96 Yankees	162.4
10.	'99 Rangers	158.0

The New York Yankees are baseball's landed gentry, and they're often held up as the exemplar of imprudent spending and corporatist defilement. As such, it's probably not a shock to see that the Yankees occupy seven of the 10 spots on the highest-payroll list. The presence of the 1980 Yankees, mixed in with some of the more recent models, drives home the point that the baronial excesses of the Bronx Bombers are in no way a recent phenomenon. In point of fact, they've been leveraging their financial ascendancy for decades upon decades. The most conspicuous example, of course, is when, in 1920, they shelled out $125,000 and floated a $300,000 loan to Red Sox owner Harry Frazee for Babe Ruth. The sale price was more than twice the previous record for a player, none of which went to Ruth himself. However, the season before, they also bought off another of the Red Sox's most successful players.

Midway through the 1919 season, Boston submariner Carl Mays walked off the mound during the second inning of a road game against the White Sox. He wasn't injured; he was disgruntled over what he viewed as a lack of support and earnest effort from his teammates. Mays took a train back to Boston and then demanded a trade. American League president Ban Johnson, who wasn't one to countenance dissent, ruled that Mays could play for no other team until he reported back to the Red Sox. However, Frazee, who was already in precarious financial straits, was hard at work attempting to pawn off his latest malcontent. The Yankees, under owners Colonel Jacob Everett and Captain Tillinghast L'Hommedieu Huston (surely one of the most pretentious names in the history of recorded time), who had purchased the team in 1915, were seeking to make a splash and offered Frazee $40,000 cash and a pair of undistinguished hurlers, which the Sox's owner eagerly accepted. However, Johnson adhered to his original mandate and nullified the trade, reiterating that Mays must return to the Red Sox before any deal was to occur.

In an attempt to enjoin Johnson's ruling and rescue the trade, Everett, Huston, and the Yankees went to court. Luckily for the Yanks, a deferential New York City court ruled in favor of the club on the grounds that Johnson had acted beyond the bounds of his authority. Carl Mays was a Yankee. Down the stretch that season, Mays worked 120 innings after the trade with a 1.65 ERA. Over the next four seasons he'd be one of the best starters in the AL (today, however, he's mostly remembered for slaying Indians' shortstop Ray Chapman with a fastball to the head in 1920). What the Mays trade did was provide the first glimpse at the Yankees' organizational prowess and begin the inexorable decay of the Red Sox. The Ruth trade was merely the capstone. In 1923, when the Yankees won their first of 26 World Series, the club had a decidedly Bostonian strain to it. Exactly half the starting lineup—catcher Wally Schang, shortstop Everett Scott, third baseman Joe Dugan, and right fielder Ruth—four of the team's five starting pitchers—Joe Bush, Waite Hoyt, Sam Jones, and Herb Pennock—and the team's best bench player—Elmer Smith—had been acquired from the impoverished Red Sox between 1920 and 1922. That's not counting Mays, who worked $81\frac{1}{3}$ innings for the Yankees in 1923. Suffice it to say, if not for the confluence of financial latitude of the Yankees and apparent penury of Boston, it likely would have been the Red Sox who won the '23 World Series. It wasn't the last time the Yankees lorded over another organization to such a degree.

In the 1950s, the Kansas City Athletics, in an unsavory arrangement, occasionally operated as an ersatz farm system for the Bombers and also provided New York with, in essence, additional roster space. Like all things Yankee, there's a backstory. In 1953, Del Webb and Dan Topping, who in 1945 had purchased the Yankees from the estate of Colonel Ruppert, perpetrated some transactional chicanery by selling Yankee Stadium, its parking lots, and Blues Stadium (home of the flagship Yankee farm team, the Kansas City Blues) to themselves as individuals without a single dollar changing hands. In December of that same year, Webb and Topping, again acting as individuals and not as the team, sold all their new real-estate holdings, along with the Blues, to a Chicago businessman by the name of Arnold Johnson for $3.6 million.

Johnson promptly rented the stadium back to the Yankees for a $2.9-million mortgage and long-term lease agreement (both of which were agreed upon before the original sale took place). Topping and Webb had initially paid $2 million for the team (and Yankee Stadium and four farm clubs) and then bought out Larry MacPhail's remaining shares for $2.8 million. So in less than a decade, Topping and Webb had sold the stadium alone for not much less than they'd paid for the stadium, team, *and* farm system. To boot, after the sale of the ballpark to Johnson, Topping and Webb could then write off lease payments against their taxes. Johnson subsequently sold the land he had acquired—not the buildings and structures, just the land—to the Knights of Columbus, who then leased it back to Johnson, who then leased it back to the Yankees. Convoluted, tortuous, and cagey, but for the team's owners, highly profitable. Interestingly, Topping was on the board of directors of Johnson's company. That wouldn't be the last instance of collaborative dirty pool between the two sides.

Back in 1940, Connie Mack, the languid patriarch who managed the Philadelphia A's for an even and amazing 50 seasons, became majority owner of the team. However, over the next decade the A's foundered both on the diamond and at the turnstiles. Following the 1950 season, Mack stepped down as manager and gradually began a transfer of power to his sons Earle and Roy. By '54, the A's were on the cusp of bankruptcy, and the Mack sons mortgaged the team to the Connecticut Life Insurance Company so they could have complete ownership of the club. At the same time, the American League began entertaining cursory offers for the beleaguered franchise. That's when Johnson entered the picture.

Johnson was among the prospective buyers of the Athletics, and he wanted to move the franchise to Kansas City, where the Yankee farm club he'd purchased was located. To grant a berth to such a move, the Yankees sold the Kansas City territorial rights to Johnson and moved their top farm club to Denver. The Mack family pled with the league to keep the team in Philadelphia, but there was a curious groundswell of support for Johnson's bid, despite the widespread notion that better offers were on the table. That's because Dan Topping canvassed his fellow owners and persuaded them to approve Johnson's offer. The relationship that would eventually develop between the two clubs gave Topping's efforts the whiff of malice aforethought.

After Johnson contracted Del Webb's construction firm to remodel Blues Stadium (later renamed Municipal Stadium) and retrofit it for major league play, the A's were ready to play ball. The team made Kansas City its home from 1955 to 1967. Over that span they never placed better than sixth in the AL and finished in last place in six of 13 seasons. They played some lousy baseball, but the A's did send a number of talented players to the Yankees in a flurry of curiously one-sided deals. Over the years, George Weiss, the Yankees' ball-busting misan-thrope of a general manager, pilfered from KC such talents as Roger Maris, Ralph Terry, Ryne Duren, Clete Boyer, Hector Lopez, Bobby Shantz, and Art Ditmar. One notable example of these deals—a 13-player whopper—went down in February of '57, when the Yankees sent a passel of largely depleted veterans to the A's for Shantz and Ditmar, two effective pitchers, and the 20-year-old Boyer, who would go on to be the Yankees' starting third baseman for seven seasons and change and establish himself as one of the greatest defenders ever at his posi-tion. This isn't to say that the A's got no useful players in return (Norm Siebern and Bob Cerv stand out as pleasing outliers), but that was mostly because the Yankees either misread the player's talents, Casey Stengel thought the guy was a considerable jackass, or the player had otherwise exceeded his peccadillo quota.

Of course, if the Yankees did prematurely cut bait on a player and send him to the gulag in Kansas City, they could always get him back later if the notion took them. This is precisely what they did with Enos Slaughter in '56, Ralph Terry in '59, and Cerv in '60. This parasitism by the Yankees went beyond merely stripping down the Athletic jalopy for parts. As mentioned, they also used Kansas City as a stowaway roster of sorts. Heck, MacPhail even said so himself after sending Slaughter to the Athletics with every intention of getting him back when they had the room for him: "We've got too many big leaguers and had to cut down. And we were not going to let them go for the $10,000 waiver price."

Fans in Kansas City feverishly resented being under Yankee "colo-nial rule," and after Johnson's untimely death, new owner Charlie Fin-ley made a point of promising he'd conduct no further deals with New York. Finley would eventually uproot the team and move them to Oakland, but he did, at the very least, torpedo the abusive relationship the club had developed with the Yankees.

To see the Yankees as an evil contemporaneous with the free agency era or with baseball in the post-1994 era requires the revision-ist vigor of a Texas schoolbook committee. As researcher Michael A. Rice has discovered, the Yankee payroll, in terms of standard devia-tions from the league mean, was almost exactly the same in 1977 and in 2003. Baseball has survived such financial disparity, and it will continue to do so. However, that doesn't mean the substantial revenue advantages of the Yankees, Red Sox, Dodgers, and other teams of their ilk shouldn't be abated. The Yankees have done a fine job of penetrating their market and branding themselves; however, the lion's share of their revenue advantage comes from the fact that they split a market of 20 million people with only one other team (and they're working with a 59-year head start on their Gotham labelmates in Queens). That's not quite fair. History tells us it's always been this way with the Yankees—and that's a common argument from those advocating the status quo—but that really boils down to a plea not to sunder the present model because it hasn't killed us yet. The Clash sang cautionary songs about these people.

It may surprise some to find the '82 Angels among the biggest spenders. But there they are, topping the league-average payroll by almost 90 percent. A glance at the team's roster reveals why they were a pricey lot: they were old, and they were famous—particularly in the lineup. As is the case in most industries, the more tenured an employee is, the more expensive an employee is. We've already learned that the '82 Angels were one of the oldest playoff teams of the modern era, and with names such as Reggie Jackson, Rod Carew, Bob Boone, and Fred Lynn peppering the roster, they were also the residue of conspicuous consumption by team owner Gene Autry. Here's their regular lineup:

C—Bob Boone

1B—Rod Carew

2B—Bobby Grich

3B—Doug DeCinces

SS—Tim Foli

OF—Brian Downing

OF—Fred Lynn

OF—Reggie Jackson

DH—Don Baylor

Looking over the remainder of the core contributors, we find that only one player, righthander Mike Witt, was a product of the Angels' system. Taking this cue, let's see how these most expensive teams break down in terms of the three most common sources of talent: free agency, trades, and homegrown. In doing this, I'll consider the eight position players, DH when relevant, regular members of the rotation, and closer:

Team	Percentage by Trade	Percentage by Free Agency	Percentage Homegrown
'80 Yankees	57.1	35.7	7.1
'03 Yankees	26.7	26.7	46.7
'82 Angels	46.2	46.2	7.7
'02 Yankees	20.0	33.3	46.7
'99 Yankees	40.0	26.7	33.3
'80 Phillies	42.9	7.1	50.0
'00 Yankees	46.7	13.3	40.0
'01 Yankees	46.7	13.3	40.0
'96 Yankees	33.3	40.0	26.7
'99 Rangers	40.0	40.0	20.0

It may run counter to expectations to learn that such teams rely more on internal solutions than they do players bought on the market. Although trades are the most common means of talent procurement, the homegrown route is still a vital one for wealthy teams. Although that sounds like something lifted from the small-market battle plans, there's a key difference. These guys are older. All of the above 10 teams are older than the league average for both hitting and pitching units, and half of them rank among the 10 oldest since 1980 for either pitchers or hitters. As the relatively advanced ages of these teams imply, they have the wherewithal (or the willingness) to retain their own players beyond the arbitration and free agency thresholds. Although the recent Yankee teams get much attention for this approach, the '80 Phillies were the only team to have at least half of its core contributors come from within. In all, seven of their key players— catcher Bob Boone, third baseman Mike Schmidt, shortstop Larry Bowa, outfielder Greg Luzinski, and pitchers Bob Walk, Randy Lerch, and Larry Christenson—were products of the Philly system. Only one regular, Pete Rose, was acquired via free agency.

Lock your doors and roll up your windows; it's time to tour the unde-sirable neighborhoods of MLB. Here are the lowest payrolls, as a per-centage of the league average, of playoff teams since 1980:

Ranking	Team	Percentage of League-Average Payroll
1.	'01 A's	50.9
2.	'00 White Sox	55.9
3.	'00 A's	57.4
4.	'02 A's	58.8
5.	'02 Twins	59.6
6.	'80 Royals	62.5
7.	'03 Marlins	68.7
8.	'03 A's	71.5
9.	'91 Braves	78.1
10.	'03 Twins	78.9

The relationship between age and payroll holds at this end of the continuum as well. As previously shown, a number of these teams rank among the youngest in recent history. More specifically, of these 10 teams, six place among the 10 youngest I've studied in terms of average age of hitters or pitchers. Additionally, these teams are all younger than the league-average age save for the pitching units of the '00 A's, '02 Twins, '80 Royals, and '03 Twins. As far as hitters—who, of course, constitute the bulk of the roster—all 10 clubs are younger than the league mean. The upshot is that these teams are cheaply assembled. The fact that these cut-rate teams also tend to be quite young is a direct function of baseball's economic structure. That system—the one that's in place today—embodies hard-won changes almost a century in the making.

For decades upon decades, baseball operated under what was known as the "reserve clause." In essence, the reserve clause bound a player to the team that signed him until that team traded or released him or the mountains crumbled into the sea. The foundations of the reserve clause extend all the way back to 1879, when an undisclosed arrangement among teams prevented a club from pursuing a player under the employ of any other club. Prior to the formation of the National League in 1876, players moved freely among teams in search of higher salaries, sometimes even jumping ship in the middle of the season. NL owners initially banded together to bar players from switching teams in midseason, but player movement after annual contracts expired continued to be a problem for management. As a result of these market conditions, player salaries constituted almost two-thirds of a team's budget. If owners were to turn a more comely profit, they'd need to drive down labor costs. The mechanism by which they'd accomplish this, first put forth by Boston's Arthur Soden, was the reserve system. This allowed teams to "reserve" up to five players—or roughly half the roster—by keeping them as long as they wished. No other club was allowed to sign these players even after their individual contracts had expired. When a rival major league, the American Association, materialized in the 1880s, the agreement was extended to allow teams in all three leagues (the National League, the American Association, and the Union Association) to secure, in this manner, up to 11 players, effectively each team's entire roster. Soon enough, the arrangement, one sub rosa in nature throughout the early seasons of its existence, became officially codified in the 1883 Tripartite Agreement. Players were then the inviolable property of the team that first signed them. Furthermore, it behooved teams to pay their players just enough to keep them from saying the hell with it and selling shoes for a living (which many of them did in the off-season to make ends meet).

Over the years, players would form slapdash unions and loose associations representing their labor interests. From time to time they'd mount offenses against the reserve system but with little success. In 1953, players banded together to form the fledgling Major League Baseball Players' Association. Whatever leverage they might have had, however, was undermined by some early decisions. In selecting Robert C. Cannon, a management-sympathizing toady whose retainer was paid by the owners, as chief counsel and permitting owners to handpick the player reps, the association allowed itself to be defanged at the outset.

In 1965, a contract dispute with Cannon led the players to hire as their new point man one Marvin Miller, an economist for the United Steelworkers of America and a deeply accomplished labor advocate, but only after an arduous and occasionally unpleasant ratification process. When Miller was finally named executive director of the Players' Association, they had but $5,400 in their bank account. Soon enough, Miller gained the players' trust and made inroads with ownership. However, the quixotic goal of dismantling the reserve clause—the bête noire of Miller and the players—would be an incremental exercise years in the making.

The basis of the reserve clause lay in Major League Rules 10A and 3C. Rule 10A stated, "If prior to March 1 . . . the Player and the Club have not agreed upon the terms of such contract, then on or before 10 days after said March 1, the club shall have the right . . . to renew this contract for the period of one year."

Rule 3C, meanwhile, forbade a player to suit up for a team until after he'd signed a contract. Wielded together, these two decrees allowed teams to sign players to a contract, banish that player if he refused to sign a successive contract, and otherwise exercise a contract option that, according to their reading of the rules, they could extend in perpetuity. Needless to say, Miller interpreted things a bit differently. According to his reading of the clause, if a player played out the option year without a contract, that ended his obligation to the team and he'd thus become a free agent. Miller also believed that an impartial outsider would agree with the union's parsing of the reserve clause. But Miller and the players needed just the right case to mount a challenge.

Talented righthander Andy Messersmith, a seven-year vet who had established himself as one of the most consistent starting pitchers in the game, was at odds with the Dodgers over his contract. Messersmith reported to spring training unsigned and began more intensive contract talks with GM Al Campanis. The exact nature of this conversation is to this day unknown, but as some point during their discussions Campanis stung his pitcher with a withering personal insult. Infuriated, Messersmith broke off talks, refused to resume discussions with anyone other than team president Peter O'Malley, and demanded that he be granted a no-trade clause as part of his next contract. O'Malley declined even to discuss a no-trade provision, and Messersmith refused to sign.

Perhaps it was his indignation toward Campanis, O'Malley, and the Dodgers that buttressed his already imposing skills, but whatever the case, 1975 was the best season of Messersmith's career. That season he led the league in innings and ranked second in ERA, second in park-adjusted ERA, third in strikeouts, first in complete games, and first in shutouts. He also made the All-Star team and won a Gold Glove.

The 1975 season opened with six players playing without contracts—and thus, for the players, six potential challenges to the reserve clause—but by August only Messersmith remained. As the season deepened and it became increasingly clear that Messersmith was unlikely to sign under any circumstances, players around the league, realizing they might finally have their coveted test case against the reserve system, rallied around him. In a late-season meeting with Miller, Messersmith confirmed that if he completed the year unsigned, he'd file a grievance seeking free agency.

By the final month of the season, the Dodgers, impressed with Messersmith's performance but perhaps more fearful of an assault on the reserve system, offered him a three-year contract that would pay him a total of $540,000; however, the club would not include a no-trade clause, something no team had ever granted a player. The money was overwhelming to Messersmith, but he wanted protection from an unwanted trade, and he also found himself in driven accord with Miller and the union—the reserve system must be razed.

Coincidentally, the collective bargaining agreement was also set to be renegotiated that winter. As the season drew to an end, the owners closed ranks to prepare. Despite glancing support for negotiating changes to the reserve system so that an outside arbitrator didn't mandate from on high more drastic measures later on, most owners—the vocal ones, anyway—wanted to go to battle for the status quo. And so they did.

Meanwhile, Miller, fearing a late-hour capitulation from Messersmith, brought semiretired pitcher Dave McNally into the grievance fold. McNally was unsigned for the season, inactive after pitching the first two months of the season, and still harboring some bitterness toward his former team, the Montreal Expos. So he agreed to join Messersmith in his fight. It was a brilliant gambit by Miller. With McNally now headed for his own hearing, the Dodgers backed off their efforts to sign Messersmith—after all, what was the point if there would be a challenge case regardless of how l'affaire Messersmith played out? Early in the month of October, the Players' Association filed grievances on behalf of both players.

Before the cases went forward, the owners, already embroiled in other internecine squabbles, began arguing whether Peter Seitz, the arbitrator who had famously granted free agency to Catfish Hunter the previous year, would be amenable to their interests. Eventually, however, the owners' Player Relations Committee (PRC) voted to approve Seitz. After the case went before Seitz, the owners rolled out a scorched-earth approach that entailed using documents stolen from the Players' Association and risible doom-saying that predicted, if the reserve system were overturned, not only the end of expansion and the minor leagues, but also the death of either the AL or the NL itself. After lengthy and feverish arguments from both sides, Seitz adjourned the hearing and began deliberation.

According to John Helyar's excellent book *Lords of the Realm*, before Seitz reached a decision, he summoned Miller and the owners' lead negotiator, John Gaherin, to his New York apartment in December. There, he asked whether both sides would be willing to negotiate a settlement before subjecting themselves to his binding ruling. Yes, said Miller. One hopes, but let me get back to you, said Gaherin. Gaherin, long an advocate of negotiating revisions to the reserve system, pressed the PRC to take the decision out of Seitz's hands by making the matter part of the forthcoming collective bargaining talks. However, the PRC couldn't decide and put the issue before a symposium of all the owners. They roundly rejected the idea of opening the reserve system to negotiation.

Gaherin notified Miller and Seitz that negotiations would not be possible, and within two weeks Seitz reached a decision: Messersmith and McNally were free agents. The owners promptly fired Seitz as an MLB arbitrator and locked the players out of spring training, but the damage was done: the reserve system was in tatters. As such, the thrust of the collective bargaining negotiations became how to sort out the mess. Players were now entitled to free agency, but under what conditions and with what restrictions? Owners were justly entitled to have some control over a player's career (after all, these days it costs, on average, in excess of $2 million in development costs to bring a player from amateur status to the major leagues).

More important to Miller's cause, however, was that unfettered free agency—every player a free agent every year—would corrupt the balance of supply and demand. Under such an arrangement, supply (the players) would far outweigh demand (the teams), and thus wages would be depressed. It's just such a system that Charlie Finley advocated during negotiations. But Miller, a seasoned economist, knew better. Finley's entire raison d' être, it seemed, was to bring players to heel when it came to negotiating salaries. A few years prior, during contract negotiations with Vida Blue following his masterly rookie season in '71, Finley told him, "Well, I know you won 24 games. I know you led the league in earned run average. I know you had 300 strikeouts. I know you made the All-Star team. I know you were the youngest to win the Cy Young Award and the MVP. I know all that. And if I was you, I would ask for the same thing. And you *deserve* it. But I ain't gonna give it to you."

As Helyar points out, Miller fretted that the other owners would listen to Finley's recommendation, but in the end Finley's reputation as an unhinged, egomaniacal fringe dweller (in the past Finley had committed such oddities as putting a petting zoo in the outfield, giving players bonuses for growing facial hair, proposing MLB use orange baseballs, loaning one of his World Series trophies to a Chicago dive bar, and hiring 11-year-old Stanley Burrell—who later became rap star MC Hammer—as a team vice president and assistant general manager) usually belied whatever horse sense he happened to make at any given time.

In the process of discussions with several players, Miller came to believe that a free-agency threshold of six years was most prudent in terms of maximizing earnings. This rankled some within the union, but Miller made a persuasive case to the rank and file. At that level, not only would supply be helpfully restricted, but also the forces of attrition would have had time to weed out the lesser players, thus allowing only the best ballplayers to set the salary bars. It was another example of improbable prescience on Miller's part. By forcing the owners to think in terms of recouping development costs—six years of reserve system was better than anything less than that—and by feigning the players' widespread insistence on no service-time requirements, Miller was able to force his vision upon them. In the end, it was the *owners* who after some fits and starts proposed a threshold of six years. The players, since it was what they wanted all along, heartily agreed.

For the most part, that's the system we have today. As mentioned, players are eligible for free agency after six years of major league service, and they're eligible for salary arbitration after three—or in rare cases, two-plus—years of service. After players reach that free-agency threshold, the system becomes one that squarely benefits the high-revenue teams. However, that doesn't occur until a player is six years into his major league career. In a substantial number of cases, that means the best years of his career are behind him. By no means is this always the case, but many players have in fact seen their best days by the time they hit the open market. For small-market clubs this means parting ways with most players following their sixth year of service, unless there's sufficient organizational appeal to sign them to "hometown discount" contracts below the market value.

The arbitration system creates distinct pressures on the poorer clubs. In the case of their most talented players, the presence of arbitration often forces them to "buy out" a player's arbitration years by signing him to a long-term contract. This is a stratagem popularized by John Hart when he was GM of a lushly gifted crop of young players in Cleveland in the early and mid-'90s. In the case of players who are of limited potential or have yet to prove themselves, small-market teams often wind up trading or nontendering them once they become eligible for arbitration.

As a result, we'd expect to see among the most successful low-payroll teams a preponderance of homegrown talents and players acquired by trade. We'd also expect to see a dearth of premium free agents on the roster. Let's see whether that's the case. Like last time, I'll use a pool consisting of the eight position players, DH when applicable, regular members of the rotation, and closer to come up with the percentages:

Team	Percentage by Trade	Percentage by Free Agency	Percentage Homegrown
'01 A's	40.0	6.7	53.3
'00 White Sox	35.7	0.0	64.3
'00 A's	26.7	26.7	46.7
'02 A's	46.7	6.7	46.7
'02 Twins	33.3	6.7	60.0
'80 Royals	33.3	0.0	66.7
'03 Marlins	64.3	7.1	28.6
'03 A's	33.3	13.3	53.3
'91 Braves	14.3	42.9	42.9
'03 Twins	26.7	13.3	60.0

Let's also look at how the cumulative percentages of these low-payroll teams compare to those of their high-payroll counterparts:

Group	Percentage by Trade	Percentage by Free Agency	Percentage Homegrown
Low-payroll	35.4	12.2	52.4
High-payroll	39.0	28.1	32.9

Roughly speaking, the two groups depend on trades to a comparable degree, but the low-payroll group is far more dependent on internal talent and, ergo, far less reliant on free agents. The free-agent gap is even wider than these percentages would indicate. Of the 18 free agents signed by the top 10 low-payroll clubs, eight of them are of the lower-tier, waiver-claim variety. Put another way, almost half of the low-payroll free agents aren't the premium, hotly pursued kind that come to mind when you hear the words "free agent." That manner of mercenary is largely beyond the grasp of the frugal club.

As for the group as a whole, it's certainly not surprising to see the likes of the A's, Twins, and Royals on the list, but one that's bound to jump out is the '91 Braves, who, of course, went from worst to first and began the club's unfathomable run of success that's still with us as I write this.

Ted Turner's decision to purchase the Atlanta Braves in early 1976 was actually a bit of an afterthought. The irrepressible Turner was many things—high school debating champion, student of the classics and naval history, voracious reader, college dropout, inveterate womanizer, heavy drinker, risk-taker—but predictable wasn't one of them. His actions, his manner, and his character all defied the simple taxonomy we use to describe the overbearing figures of history. Ted Turner was Ted Turner and everything that went along with it.

Turner's father, Ed, was an austere, self-made millionaire who made his fortune in the billboard business and seemed forever disapproving of his brilliant yet capricious son. During Ted's childhood, his father would beat him with coat hangers and force him to read a book every two days. He sent young Ted to military school, and after Ted was suspended from Brown for drunkenness, he wrote to his son, "I think you are rapidly becoming a jackass."

Turner was eventually kicked out of Brown for having a coed in his dorm room, and he then went home to Georgia to learn the family business. Not long after, however, his father committed suicide by shooting himself in the head. After the shock and grief subsided, the younger Turner realized he had a business to run. Against the resolute advice of his advisers, Turner, eager to put his own imprimatur on his father's business empire, purchased a failing UHF channel and branded it with the call letters WTCG—Watch This Channel Grow. At the time of the purchase, Channel 17 was the lowest-rated of Atlanta's five stations and was hemorrhaging cash at a rate of about $600,000 per year. But once Turner had an idea that excited him, no amount of gloomy fiscal projections could dissuade him. With WTCG, Turner, who served as his own advertising salesman and programming director, came up with a concept called "counterprogramming," in which he'd show what he considered to be the diametrical opposite of what competing networks were televising during a given time slot. Opposite the news, he'd show *Rifleman* reruns. Against Sunday worship service broadcasts, he'd show *Academy Award Theater*, which, naturally, Turner himself hosted. Against prime time lineups, he decided he'd televise sports. And that led him to the Atlanta Braves.

Now relishing his new role as cable television wildcatter, Turner purchased the team's broadcasting rights in 1972 for $3 million. However, by '75 the Braves were backsliding on the field and at the turnstiles. For much of the early part of the decade, the only reason to go see a Braves game was to catch a glimpse of Hank Aaron's advance on history. But once he broke Babe Ruth's career home run record in 1974, the Braves shortly thereafter sold him to the Milwaukee Brewers. In Aaron's absence, the Braves posted their worst record in more than 30 years and barely drew half a million fans for the entire 1975 season. That's about the time the team's owners began entertaining offers for the club, and rumors flourished that the Braves were bound for Denver or Toronto. This put Turner in a panic. Braves telecasts constituted the sum total of his original programming and were his most reliable prime time offerings. If his haphazard cable channel were to make inroads, he'd need the Braves to stick around. So, without ever having much intention of owning a baseball team, Turner made an offer to purchase the Braves and thus keep them in Atlanta and on his beloved cable station. In January of '76 his offer was accepted by the outgoing owners and approved by MLB.

Now that he owned the club and was thus responsible for its fiscal health, Turner promptly resorted to the last refuge of those who own crappy teams: stupid promotions. In Turner's early years as Braves owner, he tried such gimmicks as motorized bathtub races, ostrich races, promotions that allowed contest participants to search for the keys to a new car inside a giant bowl of salad (seriously), wet-T-shirt contests, mattress stacking competitions, and—my personal favorite— "Wedlock and Headlock Night," which entailed a mass wedding on the diamond followed by a wrestling match. In any event, he was on to something. Although the Braves continued to struggle on the field, the team under Turner gained a cult movielike novelty appeal, and people began showing up.

But Turner, like most "sporting gentleman" owners, wanted to win. This led him to attempt briefly to manage the club himself, but eventually, prior to the 1978 season, he brought in as his new manager one of Billy Martin's coaches for the world champion Yankees. His name was Bobby Cox. Cox was originally signed as a $40,000 "bonus baby" by the Dodgers in 1959, but as a player he failed to live up to the press clippings. Cox did make the majors with the Yankees in 1968, but he would spend only two undistinguished seasons in the bigs. As a manager, Cox's fortunes would be quite different. However, his career in the dugout was not without fits and starts. During Cox's first Atlanta tenure, the Braves made strides but never finished better than fourth over four seasons and change. To hear Turner tell it later, he was pleased with the team's progress under Cox, but his television executives wanted a skipper who was more affable and more at ease with the media. So Turner, in what he'd later call the biggest mistake of his career, fired Cox in favor of former Met manager Joe Torre. The decision paid immediate dividends, as the Braves won the NL West title in '82, but by then Turner had turned over the reins of the team to his baseball people so he could focus his efforts on CNN, his incipient and revolutionary all-news cable network. Those baseball people gradually grew disaffected with Torre and fired him following an 80–82 season in 1984.

Over the next six seasons the Braves would finish in last place every year but one and lose 188 more games than they won. However, beneath the carnage they were quietly assembling the rudiments of a dynasty. The Braves in '86 brought back Cox, as general manager. It was under his watch as GM that they traded for John Smoltz and drafted, among others, Chipper Jones, Kent Mercker, and Mike Stanton. However, before Cox returned to the organization, farm director Paul Snyder was drafting future core contributors such as Ron Gant, Mark Lemke, Tom Glavine, Jeff Blauser, and David Justice. After running through managers such as Eddie Haas, Chuck Tanner, and Russ Nixon, Cox decided to return to the dugout in June of 1990. By October of that same year he had determined that the dual role was too taxing, and he stepped down as GM after five seasons on the job.

As Cox's replacement in the front office, the Braves hired Royals GM John Schuerholz, who over the previous decade had guided

Kansas City to four division titles and a World Series victory in 1985. Schuerholz promptly made it clear that he had a different way of doing things. Whereas Cox, when he was GM, had signed only one marquee free agent (the disastrous signing of Nick Esasky, who would play only nine games as a Brave before being forced into retirement by a case of vertigo), Schuerholz had no reservations about dipping into the free-agent market to fill holes. Going into the '91 season, he signed a total of four prominent free agents: first baseman Sid Bream, third baseman Terry Pendleton, shortstop Rafael Belliard, and closer Juan Berenguer. All three position players were of modest offensive potential, but all three had exceptional gloves. The emphasis was on defense. The rotation consisted of Charlie Leibrandt, Smoltz, Steve Avery, Glavine, and occasional spot starts from Pete Smith, Armando Reynoso, and Mercker.

In 1990 the Braves had finished with the worst record in the NL and had placed last in their division in four of the five previous seasons, so aspirations heading into '91 were indeed modest. Bream and Pendleton, two of Schuerholz's free-agent signings, sensed early on in spring training that the struggles in recent seasons had enervated the team to the point of prevailing hopelessness, so they called a closed-door team meeting. In that meeting, Bream and Pendleton, two respected veterans on a team of distinct youth, commanded their new teammates to believe that they could win and to carry themselves accordingly. According to Pendleton, the team's attitude changed almost immediately.

Atlanta played better than expected in the first half of the season, but at the break they were in third place in the West and a hefty $9\frac{1}{2}$ games behind the division-leading Dodgers. And then the Braves took off. From August 1 onward, the Braves went 41–22 and pulled within two games of the Dodgers on September 26, drew even on October 2, and pulled ahead for good on the next-to-last day of the season. Atlanta had won its final eight games of the season to take the division, which was an essential flourish by the Braves, since the Dodgers were a robust 20–8 in September. What followed was a gripping win over the Pirates in the NLCS and a loss to the Twins in one of the greatest World Series ever.

On the performance side, Glavine led the rotation with the second-highest innings total in the NL and a park-adjusted ERA 53 percent better than the league average. Stanton and Berenguer had excellent seasons out of the bullpen, and Pendleton batted .319, tallied 64 extra-base hits, and won the NL MVP Award (although you can make a compelling case that Barry Bonds, Will Clark, Ryne Sandberg, and Barry Larkin were all more deserving). What's strange about the '91 Braves is their lack of power at certain spots in the lineup. Gant led the team with 32 homers; Pendleton and Justice each broke the 20-homer mark; and Blauser, Lonnie Smith, and Brian Hunter combined for 30 homers in part-time duty. However, two regulars, Belliard and Otis Nixon, failed to hit a single home run on the season. Add catcher Greg Olson's six homers and Mark Lemke's two, and that's half the lineup with a combined eight home runs on the season. Since no Braves pitcher homered in '81, that's five of nine lineup spots with a cumulative total of fewer than 10 bombs.

What's surprising about the '91 Braves is that they increased their win total by 29 games over the previous season and that they did it all despite having the second-lowest payroll in the National League. That was possible because they were young at several key positions. Smoltz, Avery, Glavine, and Mercker combined for 886 innings (or 61.0 percent of the team's season total) and averaged less than two years of service time. Additionally, only one of those pitchers, Glavine, entered the season eligible for salary arbitration. The numbers say it's difficult to win when you're young, and when you're inexpensive. The Braves of '91 are one of the rare teams that pulled it off.

So what kind of payroll do you need to win? One in the top half. If you don't and still aim to win, what should your team look like if you're to be successful? It should be young and mostly peopled with in-house ballplayers and those acquired in trades. For the most part, however, winning teams are expensive and, as a result, older than unsuccessful teams.

C H A P T E R   1 0

A Matter of Luck?

(or, How Teams Create Their Own Luck)

All of this may sound like a fairly exhaustive profile of the winning team, but there's still another matter to explore. A shopworn and dearly held baseball homily is one uttered by Branch Rickey: "Luck is the residue of design." Luck, or randomness, is very much a part of any endeavor. As much as we control for variables and arduously work to master the required skills, the unexpected and the uncontrollable will play roles of some sort. When this happens in baseball (on a macro level, that is), many statistically inclined analysts believe that a signpost of luck is found when a team notably exceeds or falls short of the record projected by its run differential. We can predict with some degree of accuracy a team's record based on its runs scored and runs allowed. When there's a substantial divide between a team's projected and actual records, luck is often pointed to as a cause.

Although the concept of records being related to run differentials is fairly intuitive (i.e., teams that score and allow the roughly the same number of runs should have a record of about .500, while teams that score significantly more runs than they allow should have strong win-loss records that reflect that fact), Bill James was the first to do something useful with it. In his *1980 Baseball Abstract*, while ruminating on that year's Baltimore Orioles squad, James lays out what would eventually be called the "Pythagorean Method." James and the handful of other serious analysts of his day had long sought some linkages among runs scored, runs allowed, wins, and losses. As a teenager, James conjured a formula that attempted to do just this. It went:

$$\frac{\text{Runs} - 1.5 \; (\# \text{ of Team Games})}{\text{Runs} + \text{Opposition Runs} - 3.0 \; (\# \text{ of Team Games})}$$

It was somewhat rudimentary (although not by adolescent standards), but it did establish a relationship among the component parts. The formula posited that a team's win-loss percentage will roughly come to the percentage of all runs in excess of 1.5 per team per game. The fact that the Earl Weaver–led Orioles had exceeded projections by wholly 50 games over a three-season span troubled James. So his unconscious mind began to whittle away at the problem. He came up with this:

$$\text{Runs}^2/(\text{Runs}^2 + \text{Opponents' Runs}^2) = \text{Winning Percentage}$$

The newer method revealed itself to be significantly more accurate than James's previous effort. Because of the formula's superficial similarities to the Pythagorean theorem for right triangles in geometry, this approach has come to be known as the Pythagorean formula. Most iterations these days use 1.83 as the exponent rather than squaring the run totals, but the underpinnings of James's discovery are still very much with us.

As the formula demonstrates, runs scored and runs allowed are crucial to determining what a team's record *should* be. So when a team deviates this by, say, winning lots of games despite a modest run differential or posting a mediocre record despite an excellent differential, we look for reasons to explain the disconnect. For a long time, the rather indolent and uninspired explanation was that the team in question was merely lucky or unlucky. Now, however, we know that there are most often palpable reasons why teams over- or underperform their Pythagorean projections. To wit, bullpen usage and quality, effective and timely use of in-game strategies such as base stealing and bunting, an inordinate number of blowout wins or losses, and extreme home-road variance in scoring.

The bullpen issue, insofar as it relates to exceeding Pythagorean expectations, has a dual thrust. First, there's the quality of the bullpen. Research by Rany Jazayerli and Keith Woolner of *Baseball Prospectus* has shown that there's a strong relationship between bullpen quality and performance relative to run differentials. Jazayerli and Woolner studied a total of 204 bullpens spanning 19 seasons, which they then classified as either good or bad based on certain statistical profiles. They found that one-third of teams with quality bullpens strongly overachieved their Pythagorean records, while barely 10 percent of those teams strongly underachieved. As for the teams with poor bullpens, they showed an opposite trend: a little more than one-third strongly underachieved, and less than 10 percent strongly over-achieved. This is really a matter of leverage. A run spared in the eighth inning of a close game means more than one saved in the second inning. Throughout recent history, the difference between the best and the worst bullpens in a given season comes to about 125 runs prevented. Considering the perilous nature of bullpen innings when compared to earlier frames, that comes to about 15 wins per season. Under standard circumstances, 125 runs would roughly approximate 12 wins. That difference of three wins points to the vital nature of the late innings, and it also explains how a dominant relief corps can ferry a team beyond expectations.

On another level, the bullpen can hold sway over Pythagoras is in terms of deployment. If there's wide-ranging quality within a team's bullpen—that is, pitchers of wildly disparate abilities—and the good pitchers are used most often in high-leverage, critical situations, that can help a team surpass expectations. This is posited mostly because a poor reliever used under circumstances in which the game is a fait accompli can surrender runs without affecting the outcome. Thus the team's run differential is affected in a way that causes the Pythagorean formula to undershoot its target.

Additionally, there's the matter of "small ball" strategies. It's generally unwise for a manager to lose himself in a thicket of tactical maneuvers, but properly and judiciously used, these strategies can be helpful. As we've already learned, base-stealing in tandem with a high rate of success can be modestly beneficial to a team. The same is true for the sacrifice bunt. For a very long time in the analytical community, bunting was believed to be squarely anathema to the goal of scoring runs, whereas in traditional-minded quarters, such strategy was ful-somely praised. The truth, unsurprisingly, lies somewhere in the mid-dle.

James Click of *Baseball Prospectus* wrote a series of articles examin-ing the efficacy of the sacrifice bunt. What he found was that, by and large, it's a bad idea; however, when the bunt is utilized under highly specific conditions, it's a net gain if successful.

Click found that it's a good idea to order a sacrifice bunt when a team needs only one run, has a runner on second, and there are no outs in the inning. The only exception to this is if an MVP-caliber hit-ter is at the plate (specifically, if the batter at the plate has rate stats bet-ter than .351 AVG/.436 OBP/.619 SLG—basically Manny Ramirez in his prime—then he should hit away rather than bunt). In other words, it's almost always prudent to bunt under those exact circumstances. Teams also should bunt if they need only one run, have a runner on first with no outs, and have an improbably awful hitter at the plate (specifically, one with rate stats of .236 AVG/.287 OBP/.332 SLG or worse—of course, there's little excuse for letting someone like that hit in a situation of critical mass). Otherwise, bunting lowers run expectancy and should be avoided. For instance, bunting makes sense only when the team needs but a single run (i.e., in the late innings of a tie or one-run game).

Yet another factor that can mangle projected records is a team's effectiveness when playing at home. This is so because teams who are wildly successful at home tend to have significantly fewer opportuni-ties to bat in the ninth inning than teams who don't win as often in their own digs (and thus have more scoring opportunities). As a result, teams rack up wins despite having only eight frames for their hitters in many home wins. This, of course, can skew any projected record for-mula that uses runs scored, since teams with outstanding home records wind up with fewer total runs than they would have had oth-erwise. This certainly appears to be a factor for our 124 teams. As a group they've posted 680 more wins at home than on the road, which comes to an average of almost 5.5 wins per team per season.

Whatever the reasons, playoff teams since 1980 show a pro-nounced tendency toward exceeding their Pythagorean records. These 124 teams have combined to exceed their projected records by a combined 309 games, which comes to almost 2.5 games per team.

Additionally, 95 of 124 teams (76.6 percent) bettered their Pythagorean records. So, in light of this firm trend, it's safe to assume that winning teams in the modern era make wise use of small-ball strategies (although this is likely the least important reason for beating projected records), have strong bullpens and properly leveraged relievers, win at home often to an inordinate degree, and enjoy a bit of good fortune along the way.

Epilogue

Your team is a winner. On offense, they have a number of potent power hitters in the lineup. Mike Cameron, for instance, often puts up a modest batting average, which, in tandem with his strikeout totals, causes some to dismiss his performance, but his raw power is very much there. Sometimes it's buried underneath the tendencies of his home park, but it's there. And it's critical to your team's success.

Your team doesn't depend overmuch on the microstrategies that are fashionable among some clubs. Your team doesn't rely on "manufacturing runs" save for those scant occasions that call for it. They'll make judicious use of the bunt—just last night, down 4–3 in the ninth, after a leadoff double by Edgar Renteria, Placido Polanco bunted a 1–0 breaking ball down the third-base line. Polanco had deadened it just enough to foil the wheel play put on by the opposition. According to plan, the third man up in the inning, right fielder Vladimir Guerrero, lofted a fly ball to center, which allowed Renteria to tag up and scamper home with the tying run. They won it in the 11th on a Russ Branyan pinch-hit blast.

Your team's been known to bring fly-catcher Dave Roberts off the bench in certain situations for a cameo stolen base. But Roberts knows to go only when the jump is right and only when the situation demands it. They don't steal bases with wild abandon, but they're nevertheless fleet of foot. The outfielders hawk down flies and liners with aplomb. They run the bases with speed and intelligence, and they're quick out of the box. Your team's front office has sought out just this kind of player so that, as history has shown, he'll age well and cling to his skills deep into his 30s.

Still, this team—with hitters such as Cameron, Guerrero, Jorge Posada behind the plate, Richie Sexson at first, and Branyan with frequent platoon duty at third—is graced with beaucoup power; that's how they score their runs. While other clubs while away the innings fretting over OBPs or small-ball tactics, yours beats the ball around the yard, and crooked number upon crooked number follow.

If you pore over the numbers your team puts up, you'd find that, by a thin margin, they hew more closely toward pitching and defense rather than run-scoring. Despite being an older team, they play fairly adroit defense. This probably has much to do with the fact that Cameron, Renteria, and Polanco, the up-the-middle defenders, are all skilled glovemen and generally younger than the rest of the club. They make the routine plays, but their athleticism and heady positioning before the pitch afford them brilliant range. Cameron's defensive chops in center are particularly critical, since a few members of the team's staff have pronounced fly-ball tendencies.

And speaking of that staff, the rotation—Ben Sheets, David Wells, Adam Eaton, Jon Lieber, and fifth man John Thomson—thrive by peppering the zone with strikes. That's how they do it, by pitching within the confines of the strike zone, making hitters miss with movement, deep repertoires, and constant changes in speed. They'll give up the occasional homer, but, undimmed, they continue to adhere to the approach: strikes, and lots of them. For your team's pitchers, command is vital. Strike batters out, keep the ball out of play, don't give up walks. Failing that, the defense will probably bail them out. Sheets is a board-certified ace, and the rotation behind him, while lacking a genuine star, is deep and possessed of consistent and similar skills, spots one through five.

Your team's closer, Keith Foulke, is a tremendous pitcher with the makeup to handle the acute pressures of the late innings. Among closers, he typically logs a few more frames, sees more seventh- and eighth-inning appearances, and he's not often used with three-run leads in the ninth. Buttressing Foulke is a setup corps that's among the league's best, although they remain largely fungible from year to year and therefore eminently affordable. Damaso Marte and Steve Kline from the left side, Francisco Rodriguez and Kiko Calero throwing starboard. Mopping up and spot starting when needed is swing man Ryan Madson. The front office favors relievers who post high strikeout rates, which helps them strand inherited runners, and mostly keep the ball on the ground. As with the rotation, command is the operative. Your team makes liberal use of the middle relievers—they're critical to the team's success; however, manager Larry Dierker is careful to use his best relievers in situations of higher leverage.

In seasons when the division race figures to be corset tight, the front office will take steps to improve the team at the deadline. More often than not, that means peripheral improvements, such as adding a reliever or innings-eater to the back of the rotation. They recognize that late July isn't the time to conjure up sweeping panaceas or barter away a king's ransom in young talent for what figures to be an abortive run at the flag. For instance, last season, with a two-game lead on July 30, the club added Ricky Ledee as a fourth outfielder and Tom Gordon to shore up the bullpen. Both performed well down the stretch, but they were clearly not the primary reasons for the team's success. They didn't need to be.

There's no skating around the fact that your team spends money to win. The payroll is consistently among the 10 highest in the league. That's mostly because your team is, in most winters, feverishly active on the free-agent market. But when they go after players, they go after the right ones. They don't look for players who "find ways to win" or otherwise indulge in expensive myth-making. So no pitchers with good records and poor peripherals. Nobody whose skills consist, part and parcel, of a single, isolated .300 season with the bat and who gains eminence for "making things happen." Most of all, they never chase someone just because they topped the loop in some overrated, overvalued metric.

By taking such an approach in recent seasons, they've procured talents such as Cameron, Guerrero, Posada, Wells, and Foulke, for instance. The club also spent the money it must to lock down distinguished young players such as Sheets, Renteria, and Eaton. Spending money is part of being a winner, and, thankfully, your team's ownership and front office haven't cowed from that fact. The reliance on free agents and otherwise expensive players means your team is older than most. However, team executives have done a fine job of identifying those players who figure to age well and, ergo, hold up as good investments. They recognize that pitchers and hitters age differently. Pitchers who strike out lots of hitters tend to age better. Those with impressive command numbers, such as Wells and Lieber, tend to retain their skills from year to year. Hitters with power and speed abide the aging process much better than others. The organization doesn't waver from these closely held beliefs.

And that's why your team is a winner.

In the winter following their 2004 championship season, Theo Epstein and the Boston Red Sox wielded many of these winning principles. Already in place were accomplished sluggers such as Manny Ramirez, David Ortiz, Jason Varitek, Kevin Millar, and Trot Nixon. They had an ace in Curt Schilling, an effective closer in Keith Foulke, a versatile innings-eater in Tim Wakefield, and a capable back-of-the-rotation type in Bronson Arroyo. That's a prominent core, but it was nevertheless a season of upheaval in Boston. They entered the off-season with more than 15 pending free agents, and the club eventually parted ways with names such as Pedro Martinez, Derek Lowe, and Orlando Cabrera.

To fill those holes, Epstein and Sox brought in Edgar Renteria, who provided excellent defense at shortstop and some gap power; David Wells, whose outstanding command bode well for continued success; and Matt Clement, whose lofty strikeout rates would serve him well for seasons to come. They also fleshed out the bullpen and rotation by bringing in arms such as Wade Miller, John Halama, Matt Mantei, and Blaine Neal.

Like so many other winning teams from recent history, Boston had assembled a team with a preponderance of veterans, an offense fueled by power, a defense with capable fielders up the middle, a rotation with one genuine ace and four solid complementary hurlers, and a staff on the whole notable for its command. Recent history suggested they'd seek out opportunities to improve reliever leverage, caulk holes at the trade deadline, and employ a discriminating running game. That's generally how things get done at Fenway.

Boston's happily enlightened approach, which has been in place since John Henry bought the team, is as close to ideal as any I've seen. Of course, there's no such thing as a single perfect approach to building a winning team—weaknesses in some areas can be overcome by peculiar strengths in others. That it's this way is a good thing indeed. A great many things about baseball are manifestly unique. The game isn't governed by a clock, the defense controls the ball, fans get to keep game balls hit to them, the manager—in what's one of the great oddities of human history—wears a uniform. . . . I could go on. However, what's not unique about baseball is that there are a number of forking paths to success.

In college basketball, Syracuse wins a national championship while relying on the 2–3 zone. Rick Pitino builds a litany of programs around man-to-man defenses and frequent use of the full-court press. In football, some teams run with impunity, while others throw the ball on almost every down. In baseball, there are different organizational paradigms that have proved successful. There are also disparate approaches to the game on the field that have yielded success—pitching-and-defense teams versus those who bludgeon the opposition to death. Happily, there's more than one way to get it done on the diamond and in the front office.

What I've laid out here are the results—of the various and distinct endeavors, philosophies, decisions, and serendipities of the best teams of the past quarter century. This has been, in effect, a guided tour of how they've done it. How they've *chosen* to do it is another matter altogether. That there are so many blessedly different means to the same end is why we watch the games. It's why winning baseball will always enrapture us to no end.

Acknowledgments

This book may have my name emblazoned on the front cover, but it's very much a collaborative effort involving scores of talented and gracious folks. So before the orchestra drowns me out, let me get started on doling out my gratitude.

First, I'd like to thank my agent, Sydelle Kramer. The word "agent" doesn't begin to do justice to her role in making this thing happen. Without her efforts, wisdom, and patience, none of this would have been possible. As agents go, she's straight from heaven.

My editor at Wiley, Eric Nelson, first conceived of this project and trusted me with it. Without his guidance, patience (you'll notice that patience is a recurring trait among people who deal regularly with me), knack for making sense of my ramblings, and ceaseless encouragement, I'd never have pulled this off. I've even forgiven him for being a Met fan.

Throughout this project, I was blessed to have research assistants whose dedication to this book was beyond my hopes. Jason Karegeannes crunched a lifetime's worth of numbers for me with improbable speed and accuracy. Jason hails from Greenfield, Wisconsin, played college baseball for a time, and graduated from the University of Wisconsin with a degree in history. He's presently working toward his masters in sports management at the University of Texas and has worked for *Baseball Prospectus* as an intern and author since 2004. Jason also toils as an associate scout for the Atlanta Braves (who, last I checked, knew a thing or two about hiring good scouts), and he aspires to work his way up in a major league front office (tip: hire him). Jason wishes to thank his parents for their unwavering support of him in all his endeavors.

Ben Murphy, my other research assistant, ran countless database queries for me despite doing Web design, database management, and writing for *Baseball Prospectus* and working toward a five-year bachelor's and master's in mathematical decision sciences at the University of North Carolina. Ben was a four-year baseball letterman in high school and has played club baseball at Duke and UNC. Over the years, Ben has called San Diego; San Jose; Rockville, Maryland; and Raleigh home. Like Jason, Ben's goal is to work in a major league front office (tip: hire him). Ben would like to thank his fiancée, Kristen Kirby; parents; sister Emily; and best friend, Jared Weiss.

Jason, Ben—you'll never pay for dinner again on my watch.

All the guys and girls at *Baseball Prospectus* have served as constant sources of inspiration for me. Their work challenges and educates me and reminds me that there's always more to learn about this perfect game we call baseball. Specifically, I'd like to thank Steve Goldman, Chris Kahrl, Dave Pease, Jonah Keri, Joe Sheehan, Gary Huckabay, James Click, Keith Woolner, Will Carroll, Jay Jaffe, Dave Kirsch, Nate Silver, Michael Wolverton, Derek Zumsteg, Jason Grady, Jim Baker, Rany Jazayerli, Mark McClusky, and Clay Davenport. I'm fortunate to call all of them friends and colleagues.

I'd also like to recognize all my editors and superiors, past and present, at FoxSports.com, gracious purveyors of the greatest day job in the history of history. Richard Schwartz, Kerouac Smith, Jim Reineking, Jim McCurdie, Tom Seeley, Ed Bunnell, Todd Behrendt, and all the others, thanks for everything.

Although there's an exhaustive bibliography contained herein, I'd like to emphasize a handful of sources that were of repeated use to me. These are the *Baseball Prospectus* statistical pages and databases, Baseball-Reference.com, Retrosheet.org, BaseballLibrary.com, and *Baseball: The Biographical Encyclopedia.*

I've made many friends and acquaintances over my handful of years in this business, and they've all had at least a little something to do with this. Brian Dunn (who was brave and charitable enough to give me my first sports writing job), John Brattain, John Perrotto, Susan Slusser, Alex Belth, Alex Ciepley, Richard Lederer, Seth Trachtman, Matthew Leach, Adam Katz, Thomas Harding, Rob Neyer, Tango, Mitchel Lichtman, Terry Brown, Chad Ford, Joe Dimino, Kevin Towers, and others.

Over the years, I've been lucky to have many great friends in my life outside of the environs of sports journalism. Steve Walker, Shawn Welsh, Chip Mabry, Johnny Greer, Joe Nettles, Adam Kilgore, Elsa Decker, and Casey Keil all merit my earnest gratitude. Then there's my family. The Bloomfields—Jim, Cathy, Ashlynn, Ann-Carter and Hunter—and the Perrys—Steve, Marie, Kimberly, Reid, and Neil—what can I say other than that they remain ineffable reminders to me about what's genuinely wonderful about life? My dog Sandy celebrated her 10th birthday during the writing of this book. She lay under my desk each day and night as I pecked away on my laptop, and she endured more than her share of foul moods on my part, but encouraged me by dint of her mere presence. So thanks, pup. Last but most assuredly not least are my parents. My dad cultivated in me a love of baseball, and my mom a love of the written word. Whatever good I've done, it's because of their abiding love and indefatigable support. It takes a unique kind of patience to raise a son who wants to write for a living, and they have it in spades. Ya'll are the best, and I love all of you.

Oh, and if you're reading this, I'd like to thank you, too.

Bibliography

Abrams, Roger I. *The Money Pitch*. Philadelphia: Temple University Press, 2000.

Armour, Mark L., and Daniel R. Levitt. *Paths to Glory*. Dulles, Va.: Brassey's, 2003.

Associated Press. "Clemens Returns for 22nd Season." www.espn.com, January 24, 2005.

———. "Four-Time All-Star Guerrero Acquitted of Drug Charges." www.cnnsi.com, June 7, 2000.

"Baseball Prospectus Statistical Reports." *Baseball Prospectus.*

Brown, Maury, and Gary Gillette. "Databases and Spreadsheets." www.businessofbaseball.com, 2005.

Carminati, Mike. "Kansas City Blues." *Mike's Baseball Rants*, March 7, 2005.

Chadwin, Dean. *Those Damn Yankees*. New York: Verso, 1999.

Chass, Murray. "14 Years Ago, Something Changed in Atlanta." *New York Times*, April 8, 2005.

Cohen, Gary. www.thebaseballcube.com.

Cristodero, Damian. "Players Not Immune to Cash Woes." *St. Petersburg Times*, August 22, 2004.

"Double Play." *Time*, December 28, 1953.

Fisher, Eric. "NFL to Re-examine Successful Revenue-Sharing Plan." *Washington Times*, February 22, 2004.

Forman, Sean. www.baseball-reference.com, 2000–2005.

Fox, Nathan. "Prospectus Q&A: Theo Epstein, Part II." *Baseball Prospectus*, February 10, 2004.

Helyar, John. *Lords of the Realm*. New York: Ballantine, 1994.

Holmes, Dan, and Kirk Robinson. www.thebaseballpage.com.

James, Bill. *The New Bill James Historical Baseball Abstract*. New York: Free Press, 2001.

James, Bill, and Baseball Info Solutions. *The Bill James Handbook*. Chicago: ACTA Sports, 2004.

James, Bill, and Jim Henzler. *Win Shares*. Morton Grove, Ill.: STATS Publishing, 2002.

James, Bill, and Rob Neyer. *The Neyer/James Guide to Pitchers*. New York: Simon & Schuster, Fireside, 2004.

"Jockbeat." *Village Voice*, December 5–11, 2001.

Lewis, Michael. *Moneyball*. New York: W. W. Norton, 2003.

McCracken, Voros. "Pitching and Defense." *Baseball Prospectus*, January 23, 2001.

McGrath, Patrick. "A Brief History of the A's." www.athomeplate.com, April 30, 2004.

Nemec, David. *The Rules of Baseball*. New York: Lyons Press, 1994.

Pappas, Doug. "Doug Pappas's Business of Baseball Pages." www.roadsidephotos.com.

———. "The Numbers: MLB vs. *Forbes*." *Baseball Prospectus*, April 3, 2002.

———. "Summary of the [2002] Collective Bargaining Agreement." *Outside the Lines*, Summer 2002.

Perry, Dayn. "Pedro in the Pantheon." *Baseball Research Journal*, 2001.

———. "What If . . . ?" *Baseball Prospectus*, September 15, 2004.

Pietrusza, David, Matthew Silverman, and Michael Gershman, eds. *Baseball: The Biographical Encyclopedia*. Kingston, N.Y.: Total Sports, 2000.

Rice, Michael A. "Has the New York Yankees Payroll Really Changed Much since 1977?" www.businessofbaseball.com, 2004.

Robinson, James G., ed. www.baseballlibrary.com.

Schwarz, Alan. *The Numbers Game*. New York: St. Martin's Press, Thomas Dunne Books, 2004.

Sharp, Drew. "At Reunion of '84 Champs, Lemon Feels Most Blessed." *Detroit Free Press*, June 28, 2004.

Silver, Nate. "BABIP, Again." *Baseball Prospectus*, April 20, 2005.

"Simpson Says 911 Call Was Misunderstanding." *Jet*, November 1, 1999.

Smith, David. www.retrosheet.org.

Studenmund, Dave. "All about Arbitration." *Hardball Times*, January 31, 2005.

———. "The Best and Worst Teams of the Trade: Revisited." *Hardball Times*, February 14, 2005.

Thorn, John, and Pete Palmer. *The Hidden Game of Baseball: A Revolutionary Approach to Baseball and Its Statistics*. Garden City, N.Y.: Doubleday, 1984.

Thorn, John, Pete Palmer, and Michael Gershman, eds. *Total Baseball*, 7th ed. Kingston, N.Y.: Total Sports, 2001.

Ulman, Howard. "Pedro Settles for Second." Associated Press, 1999.

Weaver, Earl, and Terry Pluto. *Weaver on Strategy*. New York: Macmillan, Collier Books, 1984.

Wolverton, Michael. "Not Earning Its Keep." *Baseball Prospectus*, April 8, 2004.

www.tangotiger.net.

Index